MASTER OF NONE

thol - Hu - Brog.

Master of None

HOW A HONG KONG HIGH-FLYER OVERCAME THE DEVASTATING EXPERIENCE OF IMPRISONMENT

John Hung

Master of None

ISBN 978-988-19002-7-2

Published by Blacksmith Books
5th Floor, 24 Hollywood Road, Central, Hong Kong
Tel: (+852) 2877 7899
www.blacksmithbooks.com

CONTENTS

To Gail
For sharing my triumphs
and for seeing me through my troubles

Acknowledgements

First and foremost, I must thank Bryan Smith who gave me invaluable advice on how the book could be improved which resulted in a much better read. I appreciate the efforts of Beth Kennedy who spent many hours reading the manuscript and gave me useful pointers on additional issues to include, landmines to avoid and the preferred way to publication. Nick Atkinson, Sarah Monks, Desmond Sun and Kieran Hale offered their useful comments. I was lucky to have my daughter Samantha to lean on. She showed almost as much enthusiasm as I did in covering the various aspects of my story, the accuracies therein and the omissions that needed to be plugged. I thank Toby Heale for the encouragement he gave me through correspondence during the actual period of my writing in Stanley, and VG Kulkarni for editing and useful suggestions thereafter. Most significantly, the sponsorship support from Sam Chan has given me a massive leg-up.

Foreword

When I helped mother to pack for her trip to England in 1969, she handed me a few sheets of sepia paper. That was the beginning of a manuscript of a book, handwritten in superb English. It was a pity that my father Walter did not live to complete this work.

I pledged then that I would continue his effort by authoring a book of my own. This attempt had started a few times, but the call of corporate demands always got in the way.

It has taken all this while for me to focus on this book. Although this may not measure up to the quality hinted at by dad's short script, at least I have fulfilled the promise and hope this book has to some extent closed the chapter of what dad had started some 75 years ago.

This book is a reflection of the many events that have affected my life, the success accomplished in a wide array of activities and the accolades bestowed on me. Ironically however, I never managed to reach the pinnacle of any of these pursuits with my true potential fully exploited.

I am thus in essence a jack of all trades, and a...

Master of None

JTH—2011

"I tend to forget the things I wish to remember, and remember those that I wish to forget"

I

STANLEY

I glanced absent-mindedly at my cell in Stanley Prison late on 26th June 2009. My mind was still in shock and I could not accept that I had just been convicted. Harsh reality hit me then. Very quickly I had to resign myself to having to spend the next 16 months in confinement... in that small hole.

The cell was about six feet by nine feet. It had a bolted-down fibreglass bed not quite long enough for me, a tiny corner table, a plastic stool, a polished metal wall-mounted mirror, and a toilet with an attached wash basin both made of stainless steel. This was to be my home for what seemed a long sentence – a grim prospect indeed.

How on earth did I end up here?

The lead article on the front page of the *South China Morning Post* the next morning made a song and dance on how I had fallen from grace – from the highest rung in society to the lowest. My photograph was boldly displayed. The Chinese-language media covered the case in similar vein.

Frustratingly, media observations all seemed reasonable commentaries superficially. The knee-jerk led me to think that I must conduct a conscious reflection of my life to discover where I did things right and where I might have gone wrong.

I was 70 years old and widely regarded in society as a high achiever. There had been a long and sustained successful career in a leading public-listed corporation. I was appointed to various statutory civic bodies; was the chairman of two charities; an accomplished international sportsman; a Fellow of the Hong Kong Management Association; awarded the Silver Bauhinia Star (an award given by the Hong Kong Special Administrative Region after the handover of sovereignty from Britain to China in 1997) and appointed a Justice of the Peace. I was without question at the top tier.

I had now been incarcerated to be away from my wife Gail and from my children for what seemed an eternity. In my mind, I was certain that my family would have to face the social stigma I had brought on them in an unforgiving society. I could already see the sniggering bigotry. I was extremely concerned about the effect this would have on my family. How would they face their relatives, friends and associates? Would this make them uncomfortable with people in general? Would some actually make unkind remarks to them? I was also embarrassed by the stigma this would throw on my close friends, my close associates and even my in-laws. I was consumed by these apprehensions.

The conviction was not anticipated as we all felt that the case went well. I had not prepared for the worst. After the conviction, I was summarily led away without even a few minutes with my family. This left my wife Gail in the terrible position of having to take care of the affairs of the family. She would not have too much knowledge of my banking arrangements nor my detailed financial position. There was no doubt that this was my principal worry and concern, to such an extent that I often broke out in a cold sweat in the middle of the night during the first few weeks.

This meant that I had to contact my bankers urgently. This was exceptionally awkward as we had no access to regular use of the telephone or email. I had no alternative but to resort to old-fashioned letter writing. This process took an inordinate amount of time. As all outgoing and incoming letters were checked by the prison security, it often took two weeks before I would receive a reply, even for local mail, if I was lucky.

Advice to Gail depended on her visits but these were restricted to two 30-minute slots per month. On special application, I could normally secure a further two visits. The visiting rooms were cubicles and we had to talk via telephone across a glass partition. We could not touch each other. I distinctly felt distant from my visitors, especially when I saw Gail or the children. Emotions were unbearable initially. It often brought us to tears.

Anger then came upon me. I simply had to fight on to clear my reputation. I had to appeal.

There had been a period of almost three years when I was "under investigation" before I was charged. To be under surveillance was uncomfortable to say the least because there was always the thought that I was being watched. I had to answer bail every six weeks or thereabouts and this continued on and on. It seemed there would be no end to the tunnel. I could hardly focus on my work. It was torture!

When they eventually decided to charge me, it almost felt like a relief. At least there was a definition of sorts. This emotive reaction was however rapidly dimmed by what ensued thereafter. My name was splashed across the media. Banks called and I had to resign from my directorships on listed boards and the more high-profile private companies. I was no longer permitted to be an accredited Type 4 Asset Manager by the Securities and Futures Commission. My world was shattered. Legal fees continued to mount. Even before the trial, the case had already ruined the lives of my family and I. How did I plunge this far down?

I could not help but feel that government bodies like the Independent Commission against Corruption (ICAC) had been accorded powers that were far too wide. They hardly had any regard for the "subjects" under investigation. We were, just as I said, "subjects". Their only concern was to nail these subjects, oblivious to the hardships caused and at a time when they had not even made up their minds to prosecute or otherwise. So what if they made us wait? That was no skin off their noses!

I slowly got accustomed to prison life. I was bundled together with foreign prisoners, better known as "Other Nationals" or "ONs". This group had their own dining hall as they were on either Western or Indian diet. I found a few friends in that group. We were posted to different workshops and I was allocated to Printing & Finishing, principally involved in book-binding and sundry work. Work was simple and it kept us active for only about four hours per day. People were friendly and the days passed painlessly but with little purpose.

Breakfast, lunch and early dinner before 5pm were all served in the ON dining hall. There was always a break of some 90 minutes for daily exercise, football, volleyball or basketball. We could walk, jog, do Tai Chi or aerobics. This choice was ours. We were trooped back to our cells by 6.30pm daily which meant we were effectively locked in the cell for 12 hours every day.

We had no access to Internet or email, and no effective use of telephones. There were only a couple of hours of television (mainly coinciding with children's programmes) and the *South China Morning Post* was normally available by late afternoon. I relied largely on the radio for news, mainly through the ever-reliable BBC World Service or RTHK Radio 3.

Communication with the outside world was only by means of letters, other than the limited visits by family and friends a few times each month.

I gradually conditioned myself to block out negative thoughts, put bitterness aside and consciously directed my mind to prepare for the days ahead. There was no future in history. Looking forward was my only option. The launch of an appeal against conviction became my top priority.

It seemed logical for me to look back on how things really started. I had a niggling suspicion that it might have been the events after my retirement from corporate life that indirectly gave rise to the troubles leading to my ordeal. It seemed important to understand how my life had been charted. Through the writing of this book, I hoped that I might succeed in throwing some light on this enigma.

Not an easy task, I thought. At my age of 70, I tended to forget the things I wished to remember and remember those that I wished to forget.

"To us, the only pure blood is mixed blood"

2

Heritage

Life is the aggregate of a series of accidents. Not many can foretell from a tender age how their lives would pan out during the later years of their existence on earth. It is impossible to predict one's destiny from an early age, and we often start out with a carefully planned vocation, but end up with quite another.

Opportunities and challenges confront us unexpectedly. Preconceived ideas fall away. External forces change our course, be these economic, geographic, climatic, political or even inter-personal. Advances in global communications have rendered these changes all the more frequent.

My paternal lineage came from the Scottish surname of "Hunt". My grandfather however saw fit to change it to the Chinese name of "Hung" for commercial reasons – it was more acceptable with the Chinese in his China coastal shipping line business if he bore a Chinese surname rather than a Scottish one. My father Walter was born as a Hunt, but also adopted the Hung surname when he joined my grandfather in the business.

My Auntie Doris suggested to me in 1968 that I should change my surname back to Hunt. She believed my career in essentially a Scottish company under the Jardines umbrella would progress faster with a Scottish name rather than a Chinese one. I thought better of it and declined to change on my strong belief that either people liked me or they did not. It had nothing to do with a name.

In 1981, my company Wharf Holdings was acquired by Chinese interests headed by Sir YK Pao. My Chinese surname then stood me in good stead. I climbed the corporate ladder much faster, eventually reaching Managing Director of the parent company of the group, Wheelock & Company Limited. Ironically, with due deference to the well-meaning advice of Auntie Doris, the retention of my Chinese surname had turned out to be a masterful decision – an accident perhaps?

My paternal roots are from Scotland. My great-grandfather arrived in Hong Kong probably in the 1850s. Family history in the 19th century was somewhat murky. My guess is that old Mr. Hunt was probably an adventurer, a merchant or a seafarer who left the shores of Scotland in search of fortune and a broader horizon in the romantic Far East.

My father, Walter Alexander Hunt, was the third generation of Scottish/Chinese mix. Racial inter-marriages were not officially condoned in those days. Hong Kong was British-dominated and discrimination was undoubtedly rife. Locals were second-class citizens. This state of affairs survived even after the Second World War. To be "Eurasian" then was a distinct disadvantage as they were neither accepted by the British nor the Chinese as their own. I grew up in that environment in my early days.

My father Walter died from tuberculosis aged 33, just before the outbreak of war. I was not yet two. My elder sister Wendy could perhaps remember him but I had no similar memory.

Walter's maternal roots were also Scottish, as Grandma was Irene Rivington before marriage. My mother Phoebe was the second daughter of Sir Robert and Lady Kotewall. Lady Edith was a Lowcock, again of Scottish roots. In other words, my parents were both Scottish and Chinese although Sir Robert had passed to us a tinge of Parsee blood. The Parsees are the Zoroastrians (the sect that worshipped fire) from Persia who settled in Bombay (now Mumbai) centuries ago.

Sir Robert was a prominent figure in the Hong Kong community. His untiring efforts in promoting education and community affairs are well remembered. He was a well-read man and had built up a valuable collection of English and Chinese books with wide and varied subject coverage, many of which are now virtually unobtainable. These include thread-sewn books on Chinese classics and books in English on Chinese history and literature. This collection of over 16,300 volumes was bequeathed to the Hong Kong Government in 1957 and was housed in the City Hall Public Library for public use from 1962. A special fund was also established by the Kotewall family to maintain and further strengthen the collection.

Sir Robert was one of the first local residents in Hong Kong to have been knighted and there is a road in Hong Kong named after him. "Kotewall Road" was close to his residence at that time. He was a mixture of Parsee and Chinese. At that time, mixed marriage in the Parsee community was taboo. As his father had defied that rule and married a Chinese woman, young Robert was not openly welcomed in the Parsee community. I am given to understand that it was this reason that caused him to Anglicize his name to "Kotewall".

All my ancestors had taken up residence in Hong Kong as long ago as the 1850s, only a decade or so after Hong Kong was ceded as a colony to Great Britain. Inter-marriages took place from the time of my great-grandparents. We are therefore the product of an exotic cocktail, shaken and stirred. Three of my children have in addition a further ingredient: Maori blood from my wife Gail's New Zealand heritage. I am often asked by curious new acquaintances whether my mother or father was Oriental, and which was Caucasian? A detailed explanation of this mixture of bloodline in a general conversation was complicated. I therefore often answered with a smile and tongue-in-cheek: "To us, the only pure blood is mixed blood!"

By all accounts, Sir Robert's eldest daughter, Auntie Esther, married before Lady Edith passed away. My mother Phoebe was therefore left as the eldest remaining daughter in the Kotewall household. In those days, in the absence of the mother, it was normal practice for the eldest to take charge of managing the home as well as the care of the younger siblings. In Phoebe's case, she had six younger sisters and a younger brother. In the circumstances, Phoebe left school at the age of 14 to assume the duty at home. By her own words, Phoebe did not complain at all and simply took it all in her stride. It was in her nature to be domestic, a trait that remained with her throughout her entire life.

As she grew older, Phoebe assumed the additional role of acting as Sir Robert's hostess when grandfather entertained, which I believe was fairly frequently. The guests were high-level dignitaries, leading businessmen, professionals, civil servants, and academics. The dinners were normally of formal decorum which meant that Phoebe had to take full charge of all preparations including table settings, flower arrangements and the polite greeting of guests on arrival. It was then that she began learning the art of small talk.

The frequency of these functions gave Phoebe a depth of experience and exposure from an early age. By the time she married my father, she had had enough of formal entertaining. We observed that she consciously shunned formal entertaining in later life although she remained a gracious and generous hostess in numerous casual gatherings within the family or with close friends.

With such a privileged upbringing, one would have thought that mother had been wrapped in kid gloves and would expect to be waited upon by servants to which she was accustomed. However, her life was to change dramatically. Father died and the war came. Hong Kong was occupied territory under the Japanese. Wendy and I had been born. Wendy was only three and I was not even two. With two small children, a dead husband and an enormous amount of pride, Phoebe was to use her own resourcefulness and survive the war as best she could. It was Phoebe and her two kids against the world!

The outset of the war with the Japanese presence in Hong Kong swayed Phoebe to escape to Macau as the Portuguese enclave was unaffected by the war. The journey was a ferry ride first and then by boat for the trip to Macau. Anyone who looked remotely Western would be taken by the occupying forces as POWs – many of my uncles had already been held as such. With our mixed heritage, our appearances, in particular mine with a freckled face, would be a dead giveaway! We were conspicuous in a population dominated by dark-haired Chinese. Even though I was very young, I can still recall that it was the height of summer with searing heat. I had to be wrapped in layers of clothes and my exposed limbs and face were toned artificially with darkish yellow tint when we travelled. That journey turned our status to wartime refugees in Macau from 1941 to 1945.

The escape party was composed of Mother, Grandma, Wendy and I, accompanied by Ah Po. Ah Po left her village home to join the Kotewall family as a young servant when she was only 13. That was the common practice at that time. Such a servant girl would be treated as a part of the family and she would be given all the appropriate tutoring and training. The expectation was that she would remain with the family. This was somewhat akin to the practice of young girls entering service in England in the old days. When mother married, Ah Po was, as it were, "permanently seconded" to the Hunt household of my father Walter. Ah Po was thus effectively Phoebe's lady-in-waiting. She would devote her life to that. In time, Ah Po took over the management of the household more or less as the governess.

We survived the war as refugees mainly sustained by the careful and progressive sale of Phoebe's personal collection of jewellery. It must have been hard on her, but Wendy and I did not feel any hardship at all. We were too young to understand and we were always well fed and given everything that mother and Ah Po could provide. We had not tasted anything better and had nothing to compare against. The food, accommodation, the self-made toys and the general way of life were regarded as the norms. It was ironically a happy childhood and I made many little friends.

We had the generous help of Uncle Robbie, the husband of my father's eldest sister Auntie Hesta. Uncle Robbie was the son of Sir Robert Hotung, known then as probably the wealthiest man in Hong Kong. We took up temporary residence in the Hotung house in Macau as our halfway house before settling into more humble rented premises. There were five of us – mother, my paternal grandmother, the ever loyal Ah Po, Wendy and I. I could not tell the difference between the respective qualities of the homes. I suspect Wendy probably could as she was two years older.

By the time I started kindergarten, mother had to make a choice between the Chinese or Portuguese streams. English schooling was not on offer in the Portuguese enclave. It must have been a virtual no-brainer for mother who obviously chose Chinese for us. We were placed into one of the best-known Chinese schools, Pui Ching.

The simple life in Macau was to me extremely enjoyable. We made toys from ice-cream sticks and mineral water bottle tops. I spent hours with my friends on the beach picking shells and used those as pawns for childhood challenges much as the more fortunate would use marbles. I would wander on those beaches until Phoebe sent a frantic Wendy to find and bring me home. I would get a hiding almost daily, but that did not seem to make me repent. Those were days of complete heaven to me and I did not have a care in the world. Phoebe was a loving mother and she never even hinted to us that she had any problems. She bought whatever she could afford or what was available in the market to ensure that Wendy and I had the best she could provide. We were lucky to have her as our super mother.

School was school and it was a place to play in. Of course, we had to learn things as well and that gave rise to the foundation of my ability to deal with written Chinese which has served me to this day. We were reared by Ah Po who spoke Cantonese with us all the time. Chinese was therefore very much my mother tongue as English should be. We were to a large extent bilingual right from the start. When I was about five in Pui Ching, the school gave us a year of introductory Mandarin. A native of Peking (Beijing now), Miss Huang, taught us precise Mandarin accent or Peking diction; I suppose a parallel would be King's English in the United Kingdom. This became embedded in my head even though I did not appreciate its significance at the time.

Almost three decades later, when I saw the need to speak Putonghua (the name given to modern Mandarin by the Chinese Communists in 1949), I was surprised that the dialect came to me easily. Miss Huang had given me a firm foundation.

Whilst I went about my early school days oblivious to the troubles of the world, Phoebe endured serious hardships. There were five mouths to feed, a household to maintain, two small children to care for and educate, a deceased husband and limited savings other than a collection of personal jewels. Banknotes were useless and had no value during wartime. We survived on her jewellery and almost on that alone for a while. In later years, Phoebe would always encourage young women to accumulate jewellery as the most reliable form of investment. She always gave traditional Chinese gold and jade jewellery to her daughters and grandchildren. Her logic was sound – when banknotes, bonds and other monetary paper instruments would lose their value, there would still be a market for jewellery. We lived on that, but surely that would not have been sufficient to see us through the war, no matter how frugally we lived. I did not have a notion – until my teenage years when mother told me – that throughout the war years in Macau, my dad's half-brother MC Hung had been sending her money from Bangkok.

MC had fled to Siam (or Thailand) at the outbreak of the war to avoid capture by the Japanese. He did his best to escape being a POW. He was in fact in the Royal Hong Kong Regiment, a volunteer corps manned mainly by local Hong Kong residents who were Eurasians, Portuguese and other non-Chinese minorities. Luck would have it that MC did not take the front line because he was suffering from a bout of jaundice at the time. It turned out that his regiment was decimated by the invading Japanese forces in one of the most one-sided and brutal battles in the defence of the colony, at Wong Nei Chong Gap. MC was not about to stretch his luck by remaining in the colony, and he made his way to Siam.

He slowly built a successful and rewarding business in Bangkok during the war as a rice merchant. He learned to read and write Thai and was deeply immersed in Thai culture and society. He absorbed a deep knowledge of the rice trade in the lucrative Thai market which dominated Asia then in rice exports.

MC always had the determination to perfect anything he set his mind on, and his attention to detail at work later became a legend with the Wharf Company in which he plied his trade on his expertise in rice. The man had the highest degree of integrity and that had a decided influence on me when I later got to know him and love him as a stepfather.

"I might have been put into prison by the Almighty to test my tolerance, my patience and my resolve"

3

PRISON LIFE (2009-10)

I lay on the hard bed in my cell and reflected. What explanations could there be for me to have adjusted so quickly to prison life reasonably well?

Well, perhaps it was the war? We had to make do with simple things then and never took things for granted, a far cry from those born after the war who would be dependent on materialistic things for satisfaction. We never had that when we were growing up. In fact, I was virtually born "into the war"! Not quite prison, but I suppose not a great deal of difference in terms of what we had in reality when we were in Macau!

I had been in Stanley Prison five months. Initially, I found it difficult to sleep on the rock-hard bed, but I got used to it. The food was bland and tasteless, but nutritious enough. There was no coffee and no alcohol, so I detoxed quickly and actually felt the better for it. There were daily outdoor sessions for exercise. Unfortunately, we ran into the most oppressive summer in July and August with temperatures in the cell reaching 37 degrees or above. Sweating was like a constant waterfall. In a matter of six weeks, I had lost 17 kilos. Arriving in Stanley at over 90 kilos, I had dropped to under 74 kilos and looked thin as a rake. I was worried about this rapid weight loss, but in fact it made me healthier.

Physically the lighter weight made life easier. The hardness of the bed no longer bothered me so much. It was easier on the knees when I walked or jogged. I found the simulation of the golf swing actually allowed a fuller turn and a better follow-through. A couple of my more rotund friends who visited me commented on my weight loss and I suggested they come to the Stanley Spa & Resort for guaranteed success, far better than the expensive health farms in Thailand!

I had also grown accustomed to the daily diet. With integration into routine work in the workshop, it led to a degree of camaraderie with friendly inmates, and the days passed more quickly. Mentally, I had become more philosophical. I decided not to harbour bitterness against anything or anyone as that would only be self-destructive. Instead, I geared myself towards positive thinking to the exclusion of self-pity or negative thoughts. This left me with clearer focus on preparing my appeal in concert with my legal team.

Throughout my prison term, right from the start, senior representatives of the British Consulate visited me regularly to lend moral support. These visits, perhaps once every couple of months, gave me the chance to talk to someone with a good sense of understanding. They also assisted in my needs when called upon to do so. I cannot express my gratitude and appreciation enough for the attention the Consulate gave me. I am now fully convinced that there can be no consulate that operates more efficiently with the same degree of care as that of Her Majesty's.

With time, the appeal papers were carefully prepared and refined. By the fourth month, these were ready for filing with the appeal court, and this step was taken by my lawyers on my behalf. Within the same period, I also managed to deal with the majority of my personal finance and banking requirements – a tedious and time-consuming process when my only means of communication was by means of handwritten letters albeit without the ability of keeping copies. Once these legal and financial issues had been tackled, my mind was placed at rest and I was relieved by the way these earlier outstanding issues had been put away, at least for the time being.

Those months of focus under considerable stress had given me a state of mental calmness. I was encouraged by my own ability to concentrate and the capacity for hard work even though I was in prison. It reinforced my belief in myself and I thought there was life in the old dog yet!

Quite naturally, having been at the top of the corporate pile, I was not accustomed to mingling with the majority of the inmates whose backgrounds were so different from mine that there was a degree of disconnection between them and myself. Most were there for drug-related offences, homicides, arson and such felonies, with not too many for white collar offences. The majority of them could not relate to what I stood for. I did not expect them to.

My fellow inmates were mostly local Hong Kong Chinese, and it was strange for a start that I was categorized as a foreigner simply because I held a British passport. In recognition of the actual situation I was in, I somehow managed to adapt to the fold. This required the readiness to behave in a similar fashion as them in terms of manners and speech. I started to act like the Romans and began punctuating my Cantonese with crude and foul adjectives. Once this happened, I became more acceptable as one of the crowd. The language was atrociously rude. Never had I been in the company of people who swore with such regularity – every utterance was invariably punctuated with impolite references to the mothers of their friends. The Cantonese people of a certain class use foul language so often that at times these are used almost as terms of affection, which I suppose could be similar to English phrases such as "Are you alright, you old bugger?"

For similar reasons, I was allocated Western diet as my British identity dictated. This meant no Chinese food, despite being born in Hong Kong. I was caught in the web of the system. I used electric shavers almost for the first time in my life as wet shaves involved a complicated process of going to the hospital for such. All washes, whether on the washbasin or shower, were with cold water which turned icy during the winter. When one got sick and stayed in the hospital, the regimented routine of inspections did not abate and one was awakened to sit up, however sick. We never got paid in cash for our work in the workshops, but we were given pay-sheets whereby one could place orders for purchases of snacks, drinks or cigarettes etc. from what I would call the prison tuck-shop.

There were all sorts of quirks, many of which seemed simply bizarre. Understandably, the rules had to be made for the majority. However, most of the officers were not at all inclined to use their discretion when unusual circumstances demanded. No unusual decisions, no mistakes! Telephone calls had to be applied for and approved even though the prisoners paid for these. Because of the environment we were in, most people would avoid telephone calls except for emergencies. Rules would however not be bent and we still had to apply for approval even in emergencies. By the time these were approved, it would normally be too late to meet the emergencies, especially during weekends when most things came to a stop.

There were simply no salt, pepper, sugar, or soya sauce, not to mention spices of any kind. These were taboo. There was no coffee at all. I never could find out why this was. This might be their way of "controlling" a healthy diet? But surely, these are not harmful if not taken in excess?

Similarly, because we were in prison, there was hardly any consideration for our comfort if only to a tolerable degree. During the summer months in our cells, the temperature often rose to around 37 degrees. There were no fans and ventilation was poor. I generally went through over two T-shirts drenched with sweat every night. If we slept at all, it was due only to pure exhaustion.

Health supplements were simply not permitted. In my case, even my family was not permitted to bring these in, despite having explained that these had been my daily requirements for almost 10 years. I was 70 years old, but I was treated just like a 20-year-old inmate.

There were many such antiquated rules even though we were well into the 21st century. We however did not have any choice. We just had to knuckle down and accept them, no matter how absurd these rules appeared.

As for general atmosphere and realities, I gradually found that all the phobia of prisons held in the outside world was nowhere near the truth. The fear of being beaten up or sexually assaulted was far over-exaggerated. So long as I was polite to my fellow inmates and befriended them, there was nothing to fear. In fact, despite the crimes they had committed, I found the majority extremely nice, generous and kind, and had no problems getting on well with them.

There were two particular good friends I made there. One was Mok Swee-Chuan, a Malaysian Chinese who shared many good hours with me as I knew the Malaysian/Singaporean way of life through my long stint there in the 1970s and 1980s. The other was Wendy Kurnia, an amateur Indonesian scratch golfer who played internationally for his country. Wendy was a very talented sportsman and we certainly had many common interests. Both of them were in there for drug trafficking. I wish them well.

The chores in the workshop did not require any brainpower. Both the officers and my fellow inmates were amazed by my willingness to submerge myself in the menial work at hand and the smile that went with it. One learns how to mentally enjoy work whatever its nature, and I got on with it on the acceptance that those tasks had to be faced daily. There was nothing to be gained by grumbling.

It had occurred to me that I might have been put into prison by the Almighty to test my tolerance, my patience and my resolve. That thought became the mental driving force which enabled me to endure the ordeal.

Perhaps I started then to revive my fervent Anglican Christian upbringing and moved closer to God.

To occupy myself, I read a lot. I also felt the need to communicate with members of my family as a measure to stay close to them. I was however appalled by the denial of the use of the telephone (except in emergency) and the Internet. This resulted in letter writing by hand which went out with the 1980s. It was the only way to communicate and I just accepted that as a fact of life. With my family being the main source of supply, I delved into novel after novel. In a matter of six months, over 50 novels were polished off. It made up for the years when I had been too occupied to find time for reading. This enhanced my self-discipline and motivation.

To keep out of trouble, I minded my own business and followed all the rules and regulations. I was always polite to the officers and my fellow inmates. In return, I found reciprocal courtesy and willingness to help within reason and provided I did not expect too much. Prison life could be relatively calm and peaceful so long as some basics were followed. I did not encounter any personal threats or violence whatsoever, contrary to common belief on the outside.

There were ironic moments too. As a Justice of the Peace, I had been visiting most of Hong Kong's correctional institutions for many years, including Stanley. It had always appeared to me that these prisons were generally well run with reasonably happy prisoners. Discipline seemed to be good and cleanliness and general appearance of the premises and facilities were satisfactory. From the inside, things were not what they seemed to me when visiting as a JP. Not to put too fine a point on the matter, things looked great to a visiting JP because there was always ample time and opportunity to prepare for a "good show". One wonders what it would be like on impromptu visits!

There was humour too. Just before one such JP visit, the officers were telling us that we had the right to raise complaints with the visiting JPs.

A lone voice rose from our group: "There is no such need. We have our own in-house JP here!" On this occasion, the officers did share in the laughter.

There was a fresh-faced young officer who appeared. He seemed a young and innocent new recruit. One morning, he approached me and asked if I was the JP that he had heard about. I replied in the affirmative. He then asked very politely how he should address me. That was amusing to me and my fellow inmates who were milling around. My reply was the only one I could give: "Young man, you should just address me as 341863!"

"I was advised that I only needed to tell the truth and Ray would do the rest"

4

PRE-TRIAL

A midst this process of self-recognition and assessment, I went about the detailed consideration of my appeal strategy with my legal team, in particular my good friend and counsel Kevin Egan. Under friendly advice, I had every intention of engaging the best lawyers to defend my case in District Court. Within my own circle in the "Hong Kong Establishment", this meant the reliance on big name barristers and eminent QCs or SCs (Senior Counsels, as they are called after 1997 in Hong Kong). This was the very route I followed.

I had asked to be represented by a top SC known to be good in ICAC cases. However, the protracted period of over two and a half years of investigation had drained me financially with mounting legal costs, and the diminishing recurrent income caused by enforced resignations from various fee-paying directorships. I found myself in a cash flow dilemma of not being able to afford the hefty fees demanded by the SCs.

Just at that time, my friend Kevin Egan had a chat with me at the bar of the Foreign Correspondents' Club. Kevin offered to act for me, not quite pro-bono, but close to it. He would do it for a fee level perhaps best described as "forgiving". Kevin was well-known for his deft handling of ICAC cases. I did not go to him initially only because he was himself involved in a case of some discomfort with the ICAC. When Kevin offered his help to me, he had by then extricated himself from his own legal bother. Quite naturally, I jumped at his offer.

As a matter of courtesy, I spoke honestly to the SC about my cash flow predicament and Kevin's offer. He behaved in a gentlemanly fashion and suggested I should run with Kevin, wishing me luck at the same time. By that time, there was only a matter of eight weeks before the hearing. I took comfort from Kevin's commitment that he would give priority to my case. Within days, he had already prepared a well researched and considered opinion which impressed me no end. We were to all intents and purposes ready. Unfortunately, we then realized that my scheduled hearing date would clash with another case on Kevin's diary. He did however tell me not to worry as it was his intention to ask for a re-schedule of my hearing dates at the pre-trial review session.

The presiding judge at the pre-trial review was however not at all accommodating despite Kevin's assertion that I would have problems appointing an alternative counsel within such a short time remaining. The judge refused to budge and she insisted on adherence to the original hearing dates which left me only 16 days to find an alternative counsel. Most respectable barristers would already have their diaries filled at that late stage. I was left in the lurch and was truthfully in a state of panic.

Again, Kevin came to the rescue. He gave me a suggested solution which I readily accepted. A member of his chambers, Ray Pierce, had just finished a case ahead of its estimated duration and he was available. Kevin introduced Ray to me on a Saturday morning at the FCC. Ray appeared to me as a confident, dour Scotsman – a good start I thought! Ray had received his brief from my solicitors only two days before but had already got a good handle on the facts of my case.

That impressed me but frankly I did not have much of a choice. I took what was on offer and Ray was to work very closely with me to prepare. We had another 11 days remaining before the trial.

There were two other advantages attached to the reliance on Ray. Firstly, as he was in Kevin's chambers, it was much easier and quicker for my files to be transferred to him. Secondly, Kevin had been briefed by Kevin Steel of Robertson's, my solicitors. It followed that all it took was for Kevin Egan to hand my case to Ray under advice to Steel without the need for time-wasting correspondence and conferences. It became a natural continuation of the preparation process.

My hearing was to commence after two changes of barristers and solicitors. But we were ready. I was to enter the trial with a high degree of optimism and confidence. It was agreed between my legal team (Egan included) and I that a great deal would depend on the evidence I would give when they put me in the witness box. Our collective anticipation was that I had an excellent chance of acquittal. I was advised that I only needed to tell the truth and Ray would do the rest.

I was in a buoyant state of mind because of my legal training and accumulated experience on my feet derived from years of warding off hostile questions when facing investors and research analysts in my investor relations role with my group of companies. I had after all earned widespread acclaim as being quite sharp in that line of work.

The years of legal and corporate experience would come in handy after all. We were ready for the trial.

"Despair was not the word to describe my state of mind then. The more appropriate word was anger"

5

THE TRIAL

I was charged with accepting an advantage. The inference was that the money I had *borrowed* from a third party was corruption money for agreeing to propose a candidate for full membership in the Hong Kong Jockey Club. The candidate was already a Racing Member of the Club and would thus have already gone through the stringent vetting process. I was merely proposing her for the upgrade to Full Membership. This charge was based on the surmise that a passage of money between the candidate and the third party was somehow linked to the loan to me.

The hearing began in a sedate manner with all the preliminaries as expected. Prosecution witnesses were called and they answered as predicted. When read together, we gathered that the prosecution would try to string a story together somehow. We tried to follow the thread and had a pretty good idea where they were heading. I was not an active player in the proceedings until Ray put me on the stand on the second day.

Ray began with a line of questions on facts which were not contentious at all, designed merely to establish my background, my place in society, my career milestones, my civic contributions and my family details. He then traced in greater detail the facts of the case. All in all, after the first couple of days, the post-mortem was that we were OK.

Throughout the trial, there was a gathering of my close supporters who were mainly my good friends, notable amongst them Jim Mailer, Murray Burton, Jock Mackie, Ted Thomas, and Nick Brown. My youngest two daughters Katish and Natasha attended when they could. Gail only came at crucial sessions as I did not want her exposed to the media or to embarrassment. There were not many sessions that were "crucial", thus Gail never attended until the summing up. Kevin Egan, who could not take the trial, sat through most sessions when he was free to keep an eye on the proceedings.

My cross-examination by the prosecution also began calmly, almost a repeat of Ray's examination-in-chief. I gave the same answers. Then came what the prosecution must have regarded as the meat of the evidence. I answered by simply telling the honest truth consistently. I could see the prosecution counsel getting frustrated as he was trying his best to break me down. The debriefing which took place afterwards again suggested that we went OK.

The following morning took on a different mood. As he could not break me down on the facts, the prosecutor kept on repeating that in his opinion, I was lying. I took it that he could say nothing else but that. In my humble opinion, that was the sum of his case – to just suggest that I was lying. At no time did the prosecution produce any solid evidence to support their counsel's suggestions.

The judge adjourned the case pending his judgment for about three weeks. To all intents and purposes, the hearing was over. Both counsels had summed up.

Before we all made our exits from the court, there was an air of optimism in our camp comprising all my friends, Ray Pierce, Kevin Steel the solicitor, my family, Kevin Egan and myself. The majority voice suggested quiet confidence that I would be acquitted based on the evidence before the court. We simply had to be patient and wait out the three weeks.

The day in court for the judgment was a total bombshell. All those in my group who attended, one and all, were shell-shocked by the judge's verdict. Gail was in New Zealand as she did not even think she needed to be around in the belief that I was totally honest.

The Deputy District Judge found me guilty on all counts, strictly on his own opinionated theory that I was guilty without regard to the hard evidence at hand. Egan branded it "conviction on suspicion". I was not really in the mood to jest around. My head was swimming, but I could at least exert enough control over my appearance to maintain my dignity, yet mindful that the judge's decision was so blatantly flawed that it called for an appeal against conviction.

After a very brief meeting with my lawyers, I was unceremoniously handcuffed and driven away to the Lai Chi Kok Reception Centre to spend the night there prior to transfer to Stanley Prison early the following morning. Because of the delay of my departure from the District Court, the media had already dispersed by the time we came out, thus saving me from being harassed by the press. It did not matter. The press already had the story. It was all over the evening news on television and radio. By the time I arrived at Lai Chi Kok, there was almost a welcoming party amongst the inmates and officials.

Despair was not the word to describe my state of mind then. The more appropriate word was anger.

Incarceration was hard to accept, but that indignity was nothing when compared to the destruction of my reputation in society and how people would see me in their eyes. I would have a criminal record attached to every move I would make from then on, to impact on issues to do with jobs, travel, the ability to hold public office, board positions and to practise in any professional capacity. Decades of hard work and high achievements were destroyed in the instant that the judge needed to pronounce verdict.

The impact of my conviction shocked Katish and Natasha who were in court with their respective men Dan and Ben. Gail was in New Zealand and the girls had to call her. I could only guess how upset she must have been as all of us had expected an acquittal. Poor Gail caught just about the first flight out of New Zealand to return home. What happened subsequently was hell for Gail as she had to pick up the pieces of the home and family without me and without real warning. She reacted with great courage and resolve and I am so proud of her. Katish was a tower of strength and showed a degree of control and calm that I did not expect. No doubt she must have been cut up inside but did not show it. My three elder daughters were all overseas and they were advised by Katish as I understand. To me, the turmoil created for them must have been even greater than mine. The media did not offer those in Hong Kong any respite either.

After about three months in prison, I thought about all the possible avenues that could be used as grounds of an appeal. Egan was working along similar lines concurrently. After a legal conference held in Stanley, Egan, Steel and I agreed that they would send the draft grounds of appeal to me for comments.

On receipt, I found Egan's draft virtually word perfect save for a couple of minor factual corrections required. Egan was always hands-on and extremely thorough. I approved the draft but it was not yet ready for filing until checked against the full transcripts of the trial. These transcripts had been requested from the court but receipt was being awaited. The matter was thus put on hold pro tem.

This wait was fortuitous because another close friend, Barrie Barlow SC, who had shown interest in my case, had researched an important issue concerning the assertion in court that I was purported to have acted as an agent of the Hong Kong Jockey Club, a point which Ray Pierce had conceded and which was a central issue of my conviction. I had never been comfortable about this concession because I simply did not see myself as an agent of the club. What I did was make a "recommendation" in the application form that the candidate was, in my view, suitable for admission as a member of the club. It was upon the discretion and the final decision of the club's stewards or management whether to accept my recommendation or otherwise. Surely that did not look like an agent to principal relationship to me.

Barrie wrote to my solicitors, out of the blue, a comprehensive letter including his research and his opinion to dispute the decision of the judge on this agency issue. He volunteered his willingness to argue this point in appeal court for me, leaving the pure "criminal" issues to Egan. I took up Barrie's offer with Egan and he was comfortable with Barrie's suggestion. As they both said, they were just happy to put their best efforts forward to help a good friend.

The grounds of appeal would thus include the agency point. The improved grounds of appeal were finalized and the document had the weight of force and merit. It was filed on 12th November 2010, and we simply had to wait to hear from the High Court on the scheduled hearing date.

"John should do exceedingly well in his pursuits once his interest is awakened"

6

EARLY LIFE

I had never been a model student in my younger days. School days were for day-dreaming or spent on the sports field. To me, the saying "school days are never dull" should be put into practice and every day should be fun. Classroom work never came into play. The routine was either obstreperous pranks or reveries into yonder!

Following the footsteps of my father Walter and many others in our family, I went to the famous Diocesan Boys' School. It was modelled on an English public school in that boarding was available and most of the masters were British. We were brought up with a strong emphasis on the use of English, and spoken Chinese was not encouraged in school, a far cry from today where most of the teachers are locals. Sports were considered an important part of education and the school produced young people with confidence, to the point that some others might regard as arrogance. It was definitely a bit of an institution. As we look around Hong Kong society nowadays, it is amazing how many higher-ranking and successful men came from DBS.

The Christian religion was an integral part of my upbringing. I was baptized from an early age with the Church of England. In school, religious knowledge was a subject we all studied and weekly church attendance was strongly encouraged. I was to attend service at St. Andrew's Church in Nathan Road every Sunday and, after my confirmation at the age of 12, I acted regularly as an usher in church. It was in those early days that I started to gain a reasonable understanding about the value of belief and that regular church attendance would teach me the discipline so much needed in life as a whole.

Discipline was stressed not only in the classroom but in everything we did. In sports, we were all inspired to be competitive and to have the will to excel. As a result, the school teams performed generally with distinction in inter-school competitions, especially in athletics. Under the leadership of the master Jimmy Lowcock (later to become headmaster), the school won the inter-school athletics championship many years in a row during my time there.

As for me, a reputation of being always capable of providing hilarity at will ensured that I had plenty of attention from my schoolmates. The majority of the teaching staff did not share in the enjoyment. There was no ill intent or evil motives in what I did. It was just good clean fun. Perhaps a few of the more liberal-minded teachers shared some quiet chuckles at times, but they never made that public.

Cricket was my first love. It was the only activity that could capture my total attention. In that sense, it was my first real discipline. I dove into cricket with relish. From a very early age, I was obsessed with the game. I read books on it, dreamt about it and lived it. By the time I was 10 or 11, I had already accumulated so much knowledge on cricket that I was a virtual dictionary on the more publicized aspects of the game. By the time I was 14, some friends gave me the nickname of "Wisden".

With such devotion and a semblance of natural talent, I was good at the game too. Through every grade at school, I normally topped both the batting and bowling averages and was a reliable slip fielder as well. Groomed when captain of the junior team, I progressed to the 1st XI by the time I was just 14, and later became the youngest school captain just before I turned 15. I was to continue captaining the school for four successive years.

Undisturbed by the occasional spurts of academic attention as demanded by examinations, I still focused my energy on sports. I was one of the better tennis players, good enough to make the school team. In athletics, I used my lanky frame to hone myself into the school high-jump champion when a senior.

Life was totally predictable. Year after year, I managed to just scrape through the exams, but became more and more a name on the playing fields. Obviously, I was awarded school colours for many disciplines. Captaincy at cricket also taught me to be a good leader and a team player and it improved my inter-personal skills. Confidence followed as a natural consequence.

Education and personal development are of course inter-connected. Confidence and achievements attained in one area often benefit the other. In my case, the success achieved in sports did rub off in the classroom and I was to realize that if I could achieve such a high level of success in sports, there was no reason why I could not do the same in academia provided I was prepared to give classwork the same degree of commitment. It was upon this recognition that I managed better in my senior years.

The school played in the open Hong Kong Cricket League. We met strong oppositions from the leading clubs, the Police, and the Army, Navy and RAF from the British Forces. In those dizzy days as a teenager, I found myself week after week matching the art of captaincy against experienced men many years older than me. I was only 15 or 16 but had to pit my wits against them. I was to prove their equal, at least on the cricket field.

When I was 17, to the surprise of most in the cricketing fraternity, the school ended the season second in the Saturday League, losing only to the winners, the Army. I had a great season topping the school averages in both batting and bowling and featured as well in the top list of league averages. The experience of leading a team to success gave me further insight into strategy and leadership. Perhaps I came of age as a sportsman then.

Despite the lack of concentration in the classroom, some masters took a liking to me and I in turn responded. Indeed, I did better than normal in the subjects taught by masters who were partial to my sporting pursuits and extroverted behaviour. As luck would have it, those masters all taught arts subjects rather than sciences, which suited me well as science and mathematics were already destined to be condemned to the sphere of hopelessness in my world of learning.

In my school certificate year, it suddenly dawned on me that I was about to face my first external examination as a serious test of my academic ability. The realization shocked rather than inspired. In the final analysis, the school certificate was then, as it is now, an interim hurdle more designed to trip rather than to encourage. It did nothing positive to further anyone's career on its own. On the other hand, it was an obstacle which had to be surmounted without which one simply could not progress to the next level. It was thus a necessary evil. In short, the certificate was of no help, but if one failed, it could mean the end of secondary schooling. I met that with deep apprehension.

My command of English had always been above average, as were the attendant arts subjects such as history and literature. However, the certificate demanded at least a pass in one of the sciences or mathematics and there was not a chance in hell that I could bring in one of those. That was eventually proven to be the case. In all, I passed eight subjects including Chinese as a second language. In addition, I had high grades in English, literature and history, but as predicted, I could not manage to pass in any of the sciences nor mathematics. I was not certificated and school policy dictated that I must repeat the year or leave school. Neither alternative looked too appetizing!

There were no other options open to me. I grabbed the bull by the horns and took the matter direct to the headmaster. He was kind enough to see me. My contention was that my sciences and mathematics were so weak that even if I were to repeat the year, there would be no guarantee that I would pass on a second try. I argued that on the opposite end, my arts subjects were so strong that I had every chance of passing these well at 'A' level. I pleaded to be allowed to bypass taking the school certificate at 'O' level again, and be permitted to enter sixth form for 'A' level arts – and promised to swat for biology and pass that at 'O' level in those sixth form years. This was totally unorthodox and unheard of but I had to try it for size!

It was such an outrageous proposition that the headmaster first laughed out loud at it. However, having thought about it for a day, he thought there might be some logic and merit in it. He then acceded to my request and as he said, his agreement to such an unusual request was only in response to an unusual set of circumstances. He was swayed by my sporting contribution to the school and what he saw in my leadership quality. In his opinion, those attributes should not be wasted, an assertion that he embossed by appointing me Second Prefect of the school in my sixth form year. That was my first taste of the power of persuasion. What was more, I knew then that the substance of an argument was less important than the quality of its presentation!

The years passed and I duly passed my three 'A' levels with some ease with good grades in literature and history. I did manage to pass the 'O' level biology but only scraped by. I received a conditional acceptance into Hong Kong University despite my late application. The condition was not because of my 'A' level marks, but rather the marginal pass in biology.

To short-circuit what could develop into a drawn-out process, I approached the Vice Chancellor, Lindsay Ride (later Sir Lindsay). The VC was an ardent cricket lover, as most Australians would be. He thus knew me well as we had played against each other many times. After a nice chat, he handed me a deal in good humour. He said, "John, if you agree to captain the university at cricket and be active in athletics and tennis, I will give you a place in the English Faculty with Edmund Blunden. I hope that's OK with you?" How could I reject such an offer!

I entered HKU knowing full well that I would be there for only a year. This was because I did not even realize that HKU did not offer a law faculty then. When the penny dropped, my application to a British university was too late for the academic year. This meant that I had a year before England and what better way was there than to spend it at HKU?

My applications to British universities were acknowledged. My qualifications were basically adequate, but unknown to me was the requirement of passing Latin at 'O' level. I had never done Latin before, which meant a crash course during my HKU year. Through an introduction, I studied in private tutorials under Father Gallagher, an Irish Jesuit. It was to be twice a week and this was the serious bit in the year at HKU. Otherwise there was no pain at all.

Whilst studying English in the main, I did English Literature, Logic and Psychology. I had to make a show of it as I was after all supposed to receive some academic benefits from my year there. I attended some lectures, but not all. I also showed some inclination towards the more interesting sessions, but truthfully my mind was not always there. In my head, what I had to do was to live up to my commitments to Lindsay Ride and I went about those activities with gusto.

Those were halcyon days. I could do all the things I loved without the burden of having to pass examinations at the end of the year. I was going to England anyway.

In the university sporting circles, I had a year of unadulterated triumph. The HKU cricket team was led to their highest standing in the league table for years; I made the university team for tennis and reached the final in the men's doubles; and most notable of all, I was crowned the overall athletics champion or *Victor Ludorum* by winning four events and coming runner-up in the half-mile, breaking the university high jump record in the process.

The Dean of the English Faculty was a well-known scholar and poet called Edmund Blunden. Blunden was also an extremely keen cricketer and an exceptionally nice gentleman. He knew me well and had shared a glass of sherry with me after matches on a few occasions. He was sorry to lose me when I told him I was England-bound. Having lectured me on English for a year, he was only too aware that I had not given my maximum effort to his subject. I then asked him for a testimonial before my departure to England. He gave me a glib write-up as follows:

"Fundamentally, John has an excellent command of the English language, but somewhat lacking in literary substance at present. He should do exceedingly well in his pursuits once his interest is awakened…"

That was to prove prophetic!

"To me, the more apt description was the French word 'patron'..."

7

EARLY TWENTIES

At every stage of my younger years, I never lacked enthusiasm. At each turn, I approached challenges with the strong resolution that I would put my best foot forward. Somehow, these commitments never really lasted. My 'awakening' referred to by Blunden would have to wait until I started working in the commercial world.

The weekly tutorials with Father Gallagher paid dividends. I did some serious cramming for the exams because a Latin pass was crucial to my admission to a law degree course in England. As a matter of interest, Latin is no longer a compulsory subject for law these days. Two of my daughters, Samantha and Natasha, both read law at universities. They were not required to pass Latin, but I did have to in 1960.

The results for 'O' levels would not be published until August, by which time I was already in London. Two offers came in from different universities. I opted for Birmingham as they had a top reputation in law. The faculty was headed by Professor Hood-Phillips, the author of the constitutional law textbook used by all the universities. I had passed Latin and could get in. I took up residence at Chancellor's Hall in Edgbaston which pleased me no end as I would be residing in the very district of the Warwickshire County Ground where test cricket was played.

The wickets in England played differently from those in Hong Kong. It took me a little time to adjust to those conditions. My batting only needed minor adaptation as I batted with bat and pad close together with a preference of playing forward anyway. But I found that I was short-pitching my medium pacers and was often punished. It took me a while to get used to bowling a fuller length and by the time I had adapted, half the season had gone. On the other hand, I had a wonderful season with the bat, scoring an aggregate of over 1,500 runs for the university and for Southgate Cricket Club in London during the summer holidays.

The pattern of my priorities did not change. Cricket dominated. The additional call of competitions in high-jumping and tennis tournaments meant that my lectures had to be compromised because these competitions often took place during weekdays. It was as though university life was designed as a test over the question of choice. We played sports for the university, often requiring our time mid-week when lectures were being conducted. We could not possibly do both. We were supposed to strike a good balance. In my book, if we did that to the letter, we would probably do badly in both. Yet, if we chose one, we might as well forget the other. Hobson's choice really!

Despite exercising a degree of temperance, the distractions of extra-curricular activities did take its toll on my legal studies. My first year results fell marginally short of requirement. I was recalled from London to meet Professor Hood-Phillips and his words have been etched in my mind ever since – "It is commendable that you made so many runs and had so much athletic success in your year here at university. We give you credit but you still have to pass examinations. I suggest that you come back from London to re-sit the two subjects during this summer before the next term." I did not. Instead, I decided to read for the bar by joining Gray's Inn in London.

Over the next several years, I religiously attended the compulsory dinners during the dining terms at Gray's and by the end of the third year,

I had satisfied the requirement of attending the requisite 12 dining terms of three dinners each. I sailed through Part I of the Bar Exams quickly and attended lectures conducted by the Council of Legal Education at Chancery Lane.

I had entered the world of the law largely on the influence of my family – many of my uncles were practising lawyers. Uncle Archie (Archie Zimmern) was regarded by many as my mentor. To me, the more apt description was the French word 'patron'. Archie was really my patron and guiding light in many areas, from cricket to the law, from general counselling to exposure to the adult world, and extending to playing golf and tennis together. He did more than he needed to for me.

Archie played cricket for the Colony as a wicket-keeper cum batsman. He showed me the rudiments of the game when I was very young. He was a barrister and became a QC, followed by appointment to the High Court Bench. He ended his legal career as The Hon. Mr. Justice Zimmern. Some might consider Archie to be somewhat pompous and overpowering in his demeanour. I thought otherwise. To me, he was a straight-talking man with a big heart. I held him in deep affection.

If there are regrets in my life, one of these would be the effect on Archie when I defected from the law to the commercial world. I suspect it would have greatly disappointed Archie, although he never showed this sentiment to me at any time. Archie continued to be my fiercest supporter and I could see his pride after watching me play the innings of my life as an opener in the Hong Kong Trial match which led to my selection for the Hong Kong Colony Team in 1970.

The bond between Archie and I filtered through to his entire family and this close relationship is maintained even today. My wife Gail and the children have stayed close to Archie's family after his untimely demise when he was only 64. Auntie Cicely, Annabel and Hugh are very dear to us, as are Annabel's husband and daughter Peter and Louise. Hugh is actually the godfather to my son Sean. How uncanny!

Soon after my move from Birmingham to London, I was married to Gloria Baker in an old church near Oxford. As a married couple, we settled in rented accommodation. Our first daughter Lesley was born the year after the wedding, followed by second daughter Tracey 15 months later. The apartment became too small and we moved to a house in Petts Wood in Kent. From there, I had to commute by train every day, 30 minutes each way to Holborn where I would spend the day at lectures in Chancery Lane or read in the library in Gray's Inn.

This was my routine, but keeping it was not easy due to the distraction of having a young family. I took every minute I could spare to spend with my two little girls and enjoyed my time with them. My interest in sports was not going away and when I was not in physical participation, I would be a keen spectator. My love for horses came to the surface roughly at that time mainly because opportunities were there. I learned to ride in Bromley, close to Petts Wood, from a retired colonel and became a reasonable rider by the time the winter ended. I was at least good enough to trek safely through the woods on my own.

My love of horses went beyond riding and it extended to the wider equine world. Horse racing was of particular interest, not so much for the punting but for the excitement of watching the superbly balanced thoroughbreds charging down the track in absolute splendour. From Petts Wood, the Lingfield, Sandown and Kempton racecourses were within close reach and I took the opportunity to attend meetings there. In this way, I gradually moved into the bloodstock world which held me in wonder. I have derived so much pleasure from this interest throughout the years and that knowledge was gained from those early years in England.

Domestic bliss with my young family dominated my daily life back in the early 1960s. Sporting diversions provided the spice. By nature, I have always been a people's person. There is a need for me to be amongst family, friends and associates. A drink with friends or "the lads" after a game of cricket or a wee dram at the 19th hole of a golf course are there to be enjoyed. In fact, these sessions must be treated as integral parts of cricket and golf. A modicum of single malt after a day's work with business friends and colleagues is a part of business life.

Law practice, in particular at the bar, seemed to me a lonely profession. I found it irritating when I had to stay in to read law books and prepare papers when my cricketing mates spent time having drinks at a nice pub somewhere. I thought hard and it came to me, purely as a personal preference, that perhaps I might be more cut out for the commercial world where I would have regular interaction with people.

I had completed the entire course of the Bar Finals and sat the examinations, but my inclinations were not really there. When I discovered that I had to re-sit the entire exams despite failing only two of 12 subjects, I lost heart. Efforts became half-hearted and before long, the law was abandoned. I turned instead to the commercial discipline.

I tried all sorts of things, from being a buyer in a department store in Bromley to telephone sales; from peddling insurance to anything that would give me some commercial exposure. Realistically, I was on the lookout for the right opportunity, recognizing that I had to have some patience and experience first.

The opportunity came when MC, my stepfather, pointed me to a chance at the Hong Kong and Kowloon Wharf and Godown Company Limited in Hong Kong. This opportunity made me sit up and when officially offered the job by the then General Manager, Gerry Forsgate, I was ready to meet this new challenge. This also meant I would return to Hong Kong, the place for which I held the fondest memories, not to mention the chance to be close to my mother again.

My mother Phoebe was the kindest woman I have ever known and I found myself thinking of her often while in England. The last mile home was indeed the longest mile.

"John's habits are totally those of a 'gweilo' but he has the business sense of a Chinaman"

8

MY PARENTS

My decision to join the Wharf Company was due almost entirely to the influence of MC Hung, who was then the Chinese Manager of the company by name, but in reality, the comprador.

MC had inherited the comprador position from his uncle at the West Point branch of Wharf before the war, on the former's retirement. By my entry into Wharf, I had become the third generation of Hung presence, spanning an uninterrupted period of some 90 years from my grand-uncle's start to my retirement in 2002. This little fact was regularly played up as an interesting PR snippet during the later stages of my career.

MC was one of two brothers born to the second wife of my grandfather at a time when it was fashionable in Asia for a successful man to take more than one wife. MC's mother was a nurse in a hospital in Canton (now Guangzhou). She took up with my grandfather whilst nursing him when he was unwell during one of his China business trips. When MC and his elder brother were very young, their mother died and the boys were installed into the Hung household. In those days, my grandmother did not have much of a say, and I understand she begrudgingly agreed to accept the care of the two boys but never with the same degree of devotion as she gave to Walter.

MC therefore grew up as "brother" to my father, Auntie Hesta and Auntie Phyllis. The story went that when Walter was courting Phoebe, MC was often entrusted with the job of delivering love letters to my mother on Walter's behalf. I gather that MC was quietly infatuated with mother starting from then. When the war broke, Walter was already gone. Perhaps MC felt a sense of responsibility towards Phoebe, Wendy and I. This could have arisen from a mixture of loyalty, family responsibility and brotherly love. I would never fully understand nor would I care to surmise. His Bangkok rice trade prospered. We returned to Hong Kong in 1945, followed shortly thereafter by MC from Bangkok.

Phoebe spoke to Wendy and I one morning. She was intending to marry MC and asked for our opinion. I could not tell how Wendy felt, but I thought it was the best thing to happen. What could be wrong with my mother marrying my favourite uncle? Although I did not realize the significance at the time, how convenient that was in the practical sense. I had gained a father that I never had, yet I did not even have to change my name. To differentiate from our reference to Walter as "daddy", we were to call MC "pop".

It was not all smooth sailing. Grandma was filled with anger that her stepson would marry her daughter-in-law. She probably had reasons to be upset but her view was also coloured by bias and old-fashioned disapproval. Walter was her son and MC was not! In consanguinity, I suppose a measure of antipathy is not all together unexpected. I would not stand in judgment over the behaviour of my forebears.

This rift was to escalate to a serious family break-up. Grandma, who had always been part of our household, decided to move out. She was given a house at Seymour Road by Auntie Hesta. Phoebe was naturally hurt by all this, yet still decided that she would do all the right things. Each weekend without fail, Ah Po was to take us to visit Grandma. Grandma and Phoebe never really spoke face to face extensively again other than the occasional polite greeting.

MC was to care for us as though we were his own. He saw us through our education all the way to tertiary and professional levels. As if that was not enough, he even paved the way for me into the Wharf Company which was to become my life-long career for 34 years. They say that if you lived with someone, you grew to be like him in some ways. I soon learned to share MC's values which were in essence "work hard, play hard and never waste a moment". At work, he was a man of detail. I recall after returning from England, he turned out an accounts book and told me exactly to the penny what he had spent on me in all the years that I was in the United Kingdom. It was simply amazing.

His work as comprador demanded that he kept a number of separate bank accounts. His responsibilities included making the monthly payment of the wage roll to the entire labour force, which numbered well over 1,500, and thereafter reclaiming the total from the company. He was also responsible for collecting all warehousing receivables and then turning over the proceeds fully to the company. In essence, he was virtually the guarantor for the company. He had to be diligent and ultra-careful, but then MC was so vigilant with things under his care that this responsibility did not bother him at all. The job appeared to have been tailored for him.

The comprador's role was to act as the go-between for the Western management and the locals. He received very meaningful commission through the handling of huge sums of money but bore the burden of heavy responsibility. These were qualities that MC had in abundance and the role fitted him like a glove. With his intimate knowledge of the rice trade, he was the perfect man to head up West Point as the branch operated the largest group of warehouses, or godowns, for rice storage in Hong Kong. 80% of West Point was concentrated on the storage of rice, accommodating over 50% of the entire stock of the staple grain on which the Hong Kong population depended for their daily diet. MC befriended all the large rice merchants and made this business virtually his own.

This so impressed the Wharf board that they offered MC the role of comprador of the Wharf Company, not restricted to West Point only. MC was to move from a branch to control the whole. This led to the establishment of Chee Wo Hong, which existed solely to discharge the comprador role. In that outfit, MC took on a partner in Leung Chi To who was to take responsibility over labour relations and operations.

When I first joined Wharf, they placed me under MC at Chee Wo Hong, although I was to be trained to an intense schedule for the first four months. I did not feel comfortable in the Chinese environment of Chee Wo Hong; the old Chinese gentlemen still wrote long-hand Chinese on ledgers and used the abacus for calculations. I reasoned that I had to grin and bear it for a while, even though the atmosphere was way too foreign to me after my many years in England. The training involved basic familiarization with the different segments of the core Wharf operations. These were to be addressed one by one on a monthly progression. Weeks were spent physically in godown keeping, tallying, dispatch of transportation, stevedoring and acting as overseer on-board for loading/discharge of ships in mid-stream. I went then to the Shipping Desk which was responsible for the dispatch and recall of lighters/barges. I started at the very bottom rung and greatly valued this experience. This was an aspect of my "education" which I would not have traded with anyone. It formed the fundamental platform from which I was to move upwards to better things, yet I would never forget those days and the people that I worked with and learned from, their aspirations and frustrations. It made me a far better man-manager than I would have been had I missed that experience.

I recall a superintendent of shipping, George White, an old hand on stevedoring and shipping who acted as my principal instructor at the Shipping Desk. He called his staff together and said sternly to them: "Listen up. You will do your utmost best to impart all your knowledge and experience to young Mr. Hung here. You'd better take this seriously because in less than six months, you'll all be calling him 'Sir'!"

Through this training process I became aware of the stress encountered by the junior staff, an awareness that was to make me sympathetic to the needs of employees in general even though I myself was destined for top management.

I would never know whether it was the intention of management or MC's wish that I was to inherit the comprador role. Regardless, I was not at all interested. As no one had given me a definition of my future, I was in fact getting quite wary that they might expect me to do so. Having been Western-educated in England, I could not see a good fit for me in essentially a very Chinese outfit like Chee Wo Hong. My mind was firm that I could not remain there. I was not opposed to the Chinese business mindset, only that Chee Wo Hong operated in what I considered an antiquated way.

Many of my friends had observed throughout my career that I was an odd specimen not frequently found. In fact my best friend, the late Bernard Chow, used to jest "John's habits are totally those of a *gweilo*. He plays cricket, goes horseracing, drinks and swears in English. However, after working with him for years, I find that he has the business sense of a Chinaman." The word *gweilo* is Cantonese slang for a foreigner in Hong Kong. It means foreign devil.

I reasoned the comprador probably existed when there was a language and cultural barrier between the Europeans and the locals in Asia. With the Europeans gradually integrating into the local scene and the younger generation Chinese returning from Western education abroad, that barrier was gradually being eroded and dismantled and the role of the comprador would soon be a thing of the past. I believed then that the comprador could well be phased out not far beyond 1970. The two sides were now capable of dealing direct with each other.

My mind was in turmoil as I was torn between loyalty, gratitude and respect for MC on the one hand, and the knowledge that I was not in the correct place in Chee Wo Hong on the other. Unpopular though it was, I applied for a transfer from Chee Wo Hong to central administration. In effect, I was seeking a Western career in preference to a Chinese one. The General Manager, Gerry Forsgate, fully understood that I wanted a "real job" instead of fretting in an antiquated system.

It is never easy to work for one's father. If I did things right, it would be attributed to the advantage I had with his advice and guidance. If I did things wrong, I would be regarded as useless. Some might even sneer "John can't even do things right despite having his father to help him". It was a no-win situation from which I had to extricate myself. I needed to start standing on my own two feet.

My legal background was another reason for Forsgate to accede to my request. In 1968, it was the dawn of the container revolution. Forsgate and the Commercial Manager, Douglas Bland, saw the need for the shipping documentation and the company's Conditions of Business to be completely revamped from the old version originally designed for the breakbulk cargo. I was asked to re-draft the whole lot.

I was transferred under the supervision of Douglas Bland. I can clearly recall the elation of finally being placed in a job which could fully utilize my natural talents. However, much as this move was pleasing to me, it was hurtful to MC. Mother actually asked me how I could do that to MC after all he had done for me. How would you explain something like that to someone who loved and nurtured you? I did speak to MC. He gave no answer but never raised the question again. In retrospect, it was a decision I had to make. Much as I hated upsetting MC and mother, I did the right thing. They were to see that in due course.

My first job under Bland was in Shipping & Forwarding as a junior Shipping Executive. From 1969 to 1972, my ascendancy in the company was meteoric. In a matter of just three years, I had risen through four grades. It was at that point that perhaps I had finally been "awakened" in the context of Edmund Blunden's words!

"I did not question the wisdom of your decision, but only the process through which you reached it"

9

FIRST SPELL AT WHARF

Wharf was the leading warehouse and shipping terminal operator in Hong Kong. We operated 13 breakbulk berths alongside the praya adjacent to the Star Ferry Pier on Canton Road for a full linear kilometre. The site in the centre of the fragrant harbour was prime property in Kowloon.

The management was mindful of my training and ability. Bland moved me to answer the numerous claims received, most of which related to the loss of cargo discharged from ships or stored in warehouses. The company relied on our Conditions of Business to refute claims and it was a known fable in town that it was an extreme rarity to succeed in any claim made against Wharf.

I can recall that when Ben Line received an ex-gratia "without prejudice" settlement for a miserly sum of some HK$400, my cricketing friend Hamish Muirhead, who was also the head of Ben Line, decided against cashing the cheque. Instead, he had it framed and hung it in his office. Hamish called it the treasure of a lifetime.

We felt there was ample justification in our rejection of these claims. Firstly, the loss of cargo was often not outturned on discharge ex vessel, and there were generally good reasons to conclude that damage or loss arose from extraneous circumstances beyond our control. We held the legitimate view that risks should in the first instance be borne by the claimant's insurance companies. Otherwise, we would be placed incongruously in the position of underwriters when no premium had been paid to us. The Conditions of Business made it easier for us to reject claims by invoking clauses therein, but there were good logical commercial reasons behind the drafting of these clauses.

In a matter of just over two years, I was promoted to Deputy Commercial Manager under Bland. My portfolio had been substantially enlarged. In addition to claims which were largely delegated to Andrew Milliken, I was relieved to concentrate only on the more complicated cases which might involve litigation. I was then also exposed to other aspects of terminal management and operations as Bland's right arm.

From about 1970, Hong Kong companies began to feel the pinch of high cost. The wide variety of fringe benefits or perks hitherto given to senior executives was being trimmed. Inherited from old colonial days, senior men could save the majority of their salaries because the company covered a wide array of perks like housing, car and driver, gardener, entertainment, utilities, education, leave passage etc. The high aggregate cost of emoluments began to worry the boards and top managements in the increasingly competitive world. Shareholders of listed companies started to question the necessity of such perks. More and more, the terms of employment became increasingly cash based.

It seemed to me that each time I was promoted up a rung, some of the perks were removed from that grade. As I went up the corporate ladder, it appeared that I had gained very few additional benefits. Was I perhaps born just a little too late?

In the late 1960s, Wharf was without question the leader in Hong Kong for terminal and warehouse operations. Our tariffs were always taken as the benchmark for other smaller operators to follow. In terms of the container revolution, that was no exception and Wharf was obviously the pioneer in Hong Kong, and I was an integral part of that management team. The advent of containerization was an important breakthrough in the system of global cargo transport.

The arrival of the container as a unit of distribution effectively replaced the breakbulk form of transport which had survived generations of sailing ships, steamships and gas-turbine ships with the derrick/winch combination of lifting and material handling. This was replaced by container cranes either fitted on-board vessels or the giant "portainer" cranes fitted dockside on shore.

In a speech I made in 1971 to the Rotary Club, the scope of which was so wide that I could either just skim over the surface or go hammer and tongs into every detail, I defined "containerization" for the benefit of the Hong Kong shipping community as "the movement of goods from point of origin to point of destination in a single unit of distribution which is compatible to various forms of handling, including road vehicles, rail wagons, ships and even aircraft". This speech later formed the basis of my thesis used for the application for membership of the Chartered Institute of Transport. I was exempted from sitting the qualification examinations and accorded the MCIT.

Douglas Bland was keen to prepare a new set of documentation to meet the changing needs, and once my revision of the Conditions of Business was completed, I was asked to devise this to the best of my ability under reference to Bland himself. I set about doing so at once, but this took time and care. It would be unwise to rush through this project.

In the meantime, the very first combo-container ship to arrive in Hong Kong, the *Port Elizabeth*, berthed alongside Wharf's berth at Tsimshatsui (now Harbour City) in 1969. I was proud to have played an active part in this momentous milestone in Hong Kong's maritime history. Looking back, the arrival of *Port Elizabeth* signalled the turning point of Hong Kong as a major container handling hub in Asia. The subsequent record-breaking container handling figures at our container port in Kwai Chung all emanated from that small beginning. After almost four decades, Wharf has continued to preserve its heritage by maintaining a strong foothold in this trade as the majority shareholder of Modern Terminals, a leading container terminal operator of Hong Kong.

Higher management exposure raised my status in Hong Kong transport and shipping circles. Invitations to speak at functions came frequently.

In reinventing the shipping documentation to cope with the containerized world, I recognized the necessity that the traditional bill of lading and shipping order had to be replaced. The replacements needed to be user-friendly, appropriate for operational efficiency, acceptable to bankers and underwriters and of course to the shipping lines. I went through a painstaking process of drafting and design of documents, testing these against loopholes, amendments, submitting the final drafts to bankers for comments and then refining again. The entire process took some six months before these were put into operation. Adaptations from international standards had to be made to accommodate the peculiar shipping practices of Hong Kong. The Transit Warehouse Receipt used today at the container port in Hong Kong in fact emanated from that process done in 1970.

Hong Kong was plagued by a Colony-wide strike by the lightermen at that time. Without lighters constantly at work, cargo destined for export soon piled up. Import discharged cargo held in lighters could not be landed. Ships had to wait in the harbour for berths to be made available as ships were helpless without lighters in mid-stream. The port came to a virtual standstill.

An invidious choice faced me in one of those problem days. Our container berths at Canton Road were fully occupied. The strike had slowed the turnaround of vessels, thereby causing longer occupation of berths. The port was jammed up by fully laden lighters. It was almost an emergency state of affairs. There was a combo-container ship from Sealand in port waiting for a berth. We did not have one available. The problem was that all the Sealand cargo had been received and stowed into containers ready for loading on board. Douglas Bland was away and I was in charge. Something out of the ordinary had to be done.

I recalled that we had a gentlemen's agreement with our main competitor terminal at Whampoa Docks to help each other in the event of emergency. This had the blessing of Bland. The situation that faced us then was just such an emergency. I spoke with John Meredith at Whampoa Docks and arrangements were made at once to dock the Sealand vessel at Whampoa and we would move all the containers there by road. Sealand was happy and the vessel was satisfactorily turned around. Meredith waived the dockage charge as a friendly gesture, obviously to be reciprocated in future when the boot was on the other foot. It was a win-win situation for all as far as I was concerned.

In the absence of Douglas Bland, the Finance Manager Bill McLuskie obviously outranked me. He saw from his window on the top floor a trail of containers on articulated vehicles being moved out of our premises. I was summoned to his office to explain. I did not have any difficulty explaining what had happened. After all, I had saved the company from red faces and made our best terminal customer happy. Pretty ingenious, I thought.

McLuskie did not agree. He wanted to know whether the additional cost of haulage would mean that we had suffered a loss. To me, even if we had just broken even, that would have been enough, and I knew we did not lose money. Added to that, because the Sealand ship went elsewhere, we also avoided a chain reaction since the next berth vacant could be allocated to another waiting ship. I kept calm and told McLuskie that if he gave me 30 minutes, I would work the calculations for him. He agreed to wait.

My assistants did a quick assessment and I returned to McLuskie's office. The actual costing showed that we had made money even after incorporating the cost of road haulage. Further, the profit was not at all bad because we did not have to pay dockage. To me, my decision had been totally vindicated. Then came the classic from McLuskie – "John, I did not question the wisdom of your decision, but only the process through which you reached it." I just looked blankly at him, but suppressed the laughter!

Tongue-in-cheek though it was, on reflection perhaps McLuskie had a point. The logic of his remark did make sense, if not in the context when it was said; at least it was a discipline that would be useful if one had the time to go through that motion. In reality however, I simply did not have the luxury of time to use slide rules and calculators when the decision was made amidst negotiations with Meredith and handling our operational staff under the severest of time pressures.

It was at that time that we were targeting the Orient Overseas Container Line for a terminal contract. I called the OOCL office in Hong Kong and spoke with CH Tung, long before he became the first Chief Executive of the HKSAR. I was told that on matters of terminal contracts, the decisions were taken by their London office rather than in Hong Kong. I was given the name of Capt. Stone to contact in London. When I arrived there and called, I was advised that I was being expected and that Capt. Stone would meet me for lunch at the Dorchester.

I duly arrived at the Dorchester Bar and ordered my usual whisky soda as I waited patiently. Twenty minutes on, there was still no Capt. Stone. After a further 10 minutes, I thought it was time that I should ask the bartender whether he had seen a Capt. Stone. He looked at me in a bemused manner and said "Of course, Capt. Stone is a regular here and he is sitting just four seats from you to the left." Capt. Stone obviously overheard and came immediately to greet me. It was a classic. What Capt. Stone was looking for was a pure Chinese person, while I was expecting perhaps a blue-eyed blond Englishman. As it turned out, I look more Western than Asian, and Capt. Stone was in fact a Chinese gentleman who chose to anglicize his name! The Chinese surname "Shek" actually means "stone". Capt. Stone and I became good friends and OOCL did come to our terminals as our contracted shipping line.

The container revolution was in full swing by the end of 1971 and I was comfortable in my job. Challenges came daily. The unexpected always happened, yet I felt deeply entrenched in my role. Just as I was settled, the offer came for a transfer to Singapore. This was most unusual as the Wharf Company had never before been confronted by a need to second people overseas. Wharf had bought a 33.3% share in a company called Singapore Warehouse Private Limited; 50% was held by leading local businessman Ong Chay Tong, and the remaining 16.6% was held by the Hongkong Bank in Singapore. Wharf had the management contract.

I was called upon to lead the management in Singapore with my colleague Bernard Chow in support. We were to assemble a management team, complete the projects and market the entire facilities. These projects would include a newly designed 14-storey container warehouse based on a Wharf blueprint, all to be done within a very tight timeframe.

It was a daunting task as I had to be virtually on my own. Although I was filled with excitement, I was at the same time only too aware this would be a case of sink or swim and there was nothing in between. I was just 33 years old. After much thought, I accepted the challenge on the basis that if one did not go out on a limb, one would not gather any fruit. I left for Singapore in February 1972, to be followed by my family when the girls Lesley and Tracey completed their school year in July, naturally accompanied by Gloria and baby Samantha.

This was the best decision I made. The exposure to higher echelons of management and boards of directors was to force me into fast growth mode. The maturity and business acumen that I was expected to display would separate the sheep from the goats. Which way was I to go?

"I could not exactly explain why, but my mind was wrestled in contradictions"

10

SINGAPORE (1972-86)

My local partners from the Ong family, in the persons of Ong Choo Eng and Steven Ong, met me at the Paya Lebar Airport holding up a long placard which read *Selamat Datang*. That was the welcome to over 14 years in Singapore – Wharf had indicated that I would only be there for a few years!

I was installed immediately into the Wharf-controlled Marco Polo Hotel. As it was the weekend, I made a beeline to the Singapore Cricket Club on the Saturday morning. It was a venue familiar to me as I had first played on the Padang in 1960 for the Combined Hong Kong/Malaya Universities against a Singapore XI, and again in 1971 when I was with the Hong Kong Colony team. At once, I met a few people that I knew and a few more friendly faces were introduced to me as the day went on.

It is never a problem in cricketing circles to strike up a lively conversation. By about 5pm, when Anchor beer was flowing freely, the chat had become more animated and all inhibitions had disappeared. Suddenly, the captain of the Friendly XI announced that someone had just cried off and they were one short for the Sunday match. Would I like to play? I did and the baptism was quick. My membership was rushed through and I became a regular within a fortnight.

Spurred on by friends, I also began to take up golf seriously again, not having touched a club since I played briefly at Birmingham and in Ceylon. With lessons from professionals, it was not difficult to play off a handicap of 18. However, if I played cricket the day before, the slice would creep in. My standard of golf remained at the same level so long as cricket remained my priority, which it did.

Planning at work began in earnest for the container warehouse. The earlier-completed Blocks 1 & 2 needed to be filled. I had assembled a project team with an architect, a civil engineer, a quantity surveyor and so on. This required detailed financial projections to support submissions to bankers. As my time was dominated by project and finance management, Bernard Chow was empowered to handle administration and more importantly sales and marketing. This teamwork brought satisfactory results.

Then one day as I was walking along Orchard Road, I ran into Bruce Valentine, a colleague at Wharf on vacation in Singapore, who related to me the shocking news that Douglas Bland had died suddenly on the operating table in Hong Kong. Douglas was my first mentor at Wharf and I would definitely miss his challenges which were intended to energize my development as an executive. His unexpected passing was a tragedy to the Bland family and to the Wharf Company. Douglas was a renowned artist specializing in modern abstracts outside his career at Wharf. He used to quip that work at Wharf was just his hobby. He was a man of immense energy and his creativity did not end with the canvas, but extended to his business imagination as well. His driving force and plain refusal to accept defeat were qualities that brought much success to the company. He was obviously going to be missed.

By being virtually Douglas' deputy before leaving for Singapore, I should have been the favourite to succeed him, and I naturally contemplated a probable recall. That thought was troubling as I had arrived in Singapore not even three months earlier, and the containers with my personal effects had just been unpacked. My corporate future had to be defined quickly since my family would shortly be leaving Hong Kong to join me unless there was a change of plan.

Hong Kong's decision came to me a couple of weeks later. Bill McLuskie, who was Forsgate's deputy then, called me on the telephone. The decision was that I must remain in Singapore. It was felt that Wharf had a responsibility to the Singapore shareholders, especially to the Ong family. Accordingly, management continuity was important. My withdrawal would have sent all the wrong signals on the Wharf commitment to the Singapore venture. It was the right decision. I could not pin down exactly the cause of my sentiments, but my mind was wrestled in contradictions – relieved that my personal life was settled by not having to move physically again, but strangely deflated perhaps because Douglas' position had probably been in my sights subconsciously for some time?

On hindsight, remaining in Singapore was to prove best as major personal developments would come, ultimately leading to a highly successful and exciting career within Wharf, although not before some frustrating years.

The economic climate in Singapore was soft. In the interim, we had to build an effective support management team with local Singaporeans trained in Wharf culture and methodology. The two traditional warehouse blocks needed to be filled in a tough buyers' market. There was a target average rental rate to aim for, but this seemed realistically out of reach. Wharf HQ suggested that we should perhaps fill the vacant space by providing storage service as custodians for reward through the use of godown warrants as practised in Hong Kong.

The godown warrant system had worked like a treat in Hong Kong for decades. Import cargo was pledged to banks for financing by importers.

Such cargo would be stored by Wharf and godown warrants were issued to the order of the bank. Cargo would only be released if instructed by the order party (i.e. the bank), normally only after the importer had redeemed the debt owed to the bank. I reasoned that this system would only be successful in Singapore if the local banks would accept Singapore Warehouse on trust in the same way as bankers trusted Wharf in Hong Kong. This proved a huge barrier as Singapore Warehouse simply did not have Wharf's size, pedigree and track record.

The godown warrant system, in its true classical form, never took off in Singapore and we were left to store free cargo not requiring bank finance by storage clients. These customers generally did not have the quantity and recurrent turnover to justify long-term occupation of space. This meant we were taking in only small quick-moving consignments on the basis of "money for old rope" and not much more. Bernard and I worked tirelessly against the odds. In reality, the warrant system was not worth keeping in view of the very limited revenue it generated. The operational costs of staffing and administration were too high to justify its continued existence. We wound down this operation and spent our time focused on the leasing of space instead with full steam ahead.

Rental income was needed for cash inflow, much required to justify bank funding for the container warehouse project. Leasing made reasonable progress but occupancy had only reached 65% by the end of the first year of 1972. We had to tighten our belts.

We were fortunate to have the Hongkong Bank as a shareholder. They supported us through thick and thin, and their support later permitted the company to gear against a leverage of an incredible seven times, then unheard of in any major commercial development in the private sector in Singapore.

Cost cutting became an art. Unoccupied floors were closed with water and electricity supply cut off. Elevators were re-programmed. We piled and laid the foundation of the container warehouse for 14 floors but would only build seven in the first phase. Funding required for Phase I was re-calculated downwards, reflecting a corresponding reduction of interest payable. The exercise was well thought through. I could not help but remember McLuskie's remarks to me in Hong Kong. Perhaps I had "gone through the process" properly this time?

Despite cost cutting in operations, we continued to feel the pinch. Additional measures followed. Non-core services were outsourced, and the headcount of junior staff was trimmed to absolute minimum. Additional austerity measures were progressively introduced.

The Chairman, Ong Chay Tong, asked to see me one day. He observed that as I dealt effectively with all top-end executives, whether expatriates or locals, and I had first-hand experience gleaned from Hong Kong's container operations, I was vital to the leadership of the company. On the other hand, could Bernard's position be localized to save a sizeable amount in personal emolument cost?

I found this proposition hard to defend as most young educated Singaporeans were quick on the uptake and they also had the advantage of local knowledge and connections which were probably superior to ours. I had to conclude reluctantly that Bernard could be replaced by two local hires, one on finance and administration and the other on sales and marketing, because even the aggregate cost of these two would be less than Bernard's total expatriate package. This meant that I would need to adjust my own portfolio of focus but that would not present too many problems.

With all the pros and cons comprehensively evaluated, Ong wrote to Forsgate. Things moved at lightning speed thereafter. Within two months, Bernard was withdrawn and repatriated. We hired Yeo See Kiat as Finance and Administration Manager, and Miss Boey Chee Kiew as Business Manager.

I was extremely sad to see Bernard leave with his family. Bernard and his lovely wife Amy had become very close to me. In my first months in Singapore, when I was on my own, Amy had always welcomed me into their home. I saw the births of their two children. Bernard was my "partner" and was extremely likeable with a wicked and often corny sense of humour. The Chow family was later to become a favourite of my wife Gail.

Bernard sadly passed away in 1999, and I was asked to deliver the obituary during his funeral service. Bernard's wonderful and happy personality will remain with us in our family.

"… how was I supposed to know? He said nothing and they all wear batiks!"

11

STRAITS TIMES IN 1970S

We simply had to mark time pending a rebound of the economy which could take two months or two years. The container warehouse project was put on hold as we pushed to complete the leasing of the first two blocks. In that relative lull I had more time for cricket and golf.

The first thing was to acclimatize to the heat of Singapore. Initially, when I opened the innings at 10.30 in the morning, I would get to 30 or 40 relatively quickly. Always known to see the ball early, I usually outscored my partner but the oppressive heat then got to me and I would invariably lose my wicket to tired shots before reaching 50. It was extremely irritating to play against the locals who would go through the entire day under the sun without much sweat. This acclimatization process took almost the entire season.

Golf courses were equally hot, and I would play 14 or 15 holes reasonably well and would then collapse in the last few. To me, it was preferable to tee off in the afternoon to benefit from the cooler conditions in the final stretch rather than start in the morning as it would get progressively hotter towards noon. By the second season, my body began to adapt to the heat more like a local and the heat no longer bothered me to the same extent. That season became my most successful since England, scoring over 1,000 runs with two centuries and a healthy average. The golf handicap also went down to about 12.

One morning, my Traffic Manager came running to me and said a man was in the premises demanding a large sum of money for "protection". He strenuously protested when I asked to see the man, making the point that such sensitive matters should be handled by the locals and that it would not be wise for me to expose myself over such issues. I however wanted to go out on a limb for satisfaction. Foolhardy though it might have seemed, I always liked taking calculated risks.

A very thin man appeared, looking decidedly nervous. I spoke English and my Traffic Manager acted as interpreter in Hokkien. I saw the telltale veins on his arm with needle points clearly visible. He asked for a ridiculously large sum. Whether his demand reflected "market rate" or otherwise I would not know. I counter-offered about one-third of his demand and told him to "take it or leave it". To my surprise, he asked for a calculator and then punched a few numbers before answering me. He accepted my counter-offer in principle but wanted the total sum adjusted to a strangely odd number. I asked why. Apparently, the figure had to be divisible by 39 as they were a group of 39 people. I demanded from the man a photocopy of his identity card, his address and telephone number.

To me that was the only course I could sensibly take. I went to the Chairman, Mr. Ong, to seek his advice. He fully supported my action when I explained that we could not afford to upset the entire group of 39 as they could badly disrupt our business operations. There were over 500 people who came to work for our tenants daily, many of whom were females, some of whom could easily succumb to threats and thus stay away from work. Let us imagine that if we had asked the police to arrest the man, there were still 38 of them left! What else could we do?

How was I going to expense this payment though? Hong Kong would never condone such actions because they would never understand the local conditions under which we operated. In fact, I had many problems getting Hong Kong to refrain from applying "Hong Kong standards" to Singapore. Chairman Ong directed that the project's main contractor should carry the cost of the money paid to the man, as the stability of the site was just as important to them as it was to us. The problem was solved when the contractor agreed to this. This was done out of the best intentions in the world and in the interest of the company. To quote Shakespeare from the *Merchant of Venice*, Bassanio said "To do a great right, do a little wrong." I had to back my own instincts when I took that decision.

One morning some months later, we discovered that three of our cement mixers were missing from our site. Our Traffic Manager and other executives were busy looking for the insurance policies and thinking of reporting the loss. I stopped them in their tracks. Instead, I asked the Traffic Manager to contact the thin man and to ask him to come and see me. The man duly arrived. I asked him where was the so-called protection if our large cement mixers could go missing? I told him he was duty-bound to return the cement mixers by the next day.

By 7am the next morning, all three pieces of machinery reappeared on site. The man came in at 9am out of breath and seemed short of sleep. He complained of the extreme difficulties he had gone through to recover the mixers because the machines were not taken by his people but by another group from another area in Singapore. He stressed that he was a man of his word and would fulfil his promises regardless of the degree of difficulty involved. I thanked him and thought how true it was that "honour amongst thieves is more binding than a legally executed contract". We would have no further "accidents" from then onwards on site.

Nothing too eventful happened in Singapore for years thereafter. It seemed that McLuskie, who had been elevated to General Manager on Forsgate's retirement, was not partial to risks. For years, the container warehouse project was put on hold despite the growing impatience shown by the senior Mr. Ong. We continued to mark time. By then, Blocks 1 & 2 had been almost fully let. The project team was left twiddling their thumbs. Nobody at Singapore Warehouse was too happy. The professionals in the team were not earning the progressive fees that they had expected. I was stuck in the same position since my arrival from Hong Kong. My salary was essentially frozen for five years since the annual percentages of increases were only just sufficient to cover inflation. We were a disgruntled lot!

I estimated that I could just about cover my duties and responsibilities by spending perhaps only say 40% of my time on them. Rather than sit around and moan, the project team members and I decided that we should perhaps use the window of free time to sharpen our golf. At least this would give relief to our frustrations at work. We played an average of three rounds per week which was possible because of the close proximity of the courses to the city in Singapore. Quite naturally our handicaps went down. Putts missed before started to drop. Iron shots went straighter. We kept our sanity through the camaraderie of golfing pursuits, and the wining and dining that went with it. Our spouses were encouraged to take up the game. Later, my then wife Gloria actually became the Ladies Captain of our club. She played steady golf in a tidy way, much in keeping with her character.

We continued to tread water without going anywhere at Singapore Warehouse. No discernible progress was made. The Ong family ceased to be as friendly and accommodating as they had been earlier. Visible impatience showed. I acted as the conduit between Mr. Ong senior and Hong Kong. When my efforts to urge positive action failed, Ong took it upon himself to write directly to McLuskie.

McLuskie was never one to be easily swayed when he had the bit between his teeth. He dug in and the more he did so, the more Ong senior was irritated. As this wore on, Ong began to turn awkward and the only way he could vent his displeasure was to place obstacles before me. He resorted to the tactic that since we were not moving forward, we must press for increases of rentals and further cut operational headcount. I was literally caught in the crossfire. Ong was the Chairman of Singapore Warehouse but McLuskie was the boss at Wharf. The pressure was inescapable.

I was given temporary relief by an unexpected interlude. Prior to leaving Hong Kong, I had been in charge of a serious claim made by the Bank Negara Indonesia in respect of one lot of cargo held to their order under godown warrant. It involved the alleged loss of some 30 tons of nutmeg oil purported to have been delivered from our warehouse on an unauthorized basis. We contended that the release had been made against a properly executed delivery order, which they claimed to be a forgery. We also suspected that the contents of the packages were not nutmeg oil but probably prohibited substances which had since been smuggled out of Hong Kong furtively under clandestine operations. How else could 30 tons of nutmeg oil have gone missing from the face of the earth? And why would such a huge quantity of nutmeg oil (equivalent to a high percentage of the world's annual production output) be shipped to Hong Kong where the nutmeg trade was really negligible?

The case was extremely complex and the files were left open when I left Hong Kong in 1972. The Bank decided on legal action and the case was up for trial. I was recalled to prepare and testify for Wharf as the defendants. The total liquidated damages claimed were in the millions, a very serious sum indeed in those days.

When I went to court, I was shocked to see it was presided over by Mr. Justice Zimmern – my "Uncle Archie"!

When I was called to testify, the examination-in-chief by Oswald Cheung QC went pretty well by our estimation. The turn then came for my cross examination by a leading QC, a well respected and highly skilled cross examiner called Henry Litton. He was a senior when I was a kid at school. Incidentally, Archie and Oswald also attended the same school. It struck me then that all the central players were old boys from the Diocesan Boys' School, yet some of us were on opposite camps. Regardless, Litton was certainly not about to spare me.

The session began with mild questions on the clarification of facts. Then it became pointed. When a veiled suggestion was given against actual facts, I began to explain forcefully and perhaps in an argumentative tone. The bench intervened. Mr. Justice Zimmern said "Mr. Hung, permit me to remind you that your position in court is simply that of a witness for the defendants. Please just answer yes or no, or at most keep it brief." I stopped in my tracks and did as I was directed.

Auntie Cicely had a giggle with me when she heard this story. Archie never raised the issue again. He ruled for the plaintiff against Wharf.

The case took me out of Singapore for two weeks. I returned to Singapore to the same problems I had faced two weeks earlier. There was no point losing sleep over the impasse. There was not much I could do anyway.

After a few months, I was told that Archie and Cicely might be visiting me soon. As a High Court judge in Hong Kong under colonial rule, Archie was to cover the Assizes in the Asian circuit which included Brunei. After hearing the case, Archie and Cicely took the opportunity to visit me in Singapore en route back to Hong Kong.

Of course I went to Paya Lebar Airport to meet them. I waited at the arrival gate and saw them coming towards me. It was great to see them and I gave them the *Selamat Datang* treatment. We walked together to the waiting limousine, followed by a smallish man carrying two large suitcases. We reached the car. Instead of placing the suitcases in the boot, the uniformed chauffeur sprang from the driver's seat, turned to the small man and said "Allow me, Sir! That's my job, not yours!" The man who carried the bags was in fact the Brunei High Commissioner in Singapore.

In a look somewhere between embarrassment and shock, Cicely said quietly to Archie: "I'm embarrassed of course. But how was I supposed to know? He said nothing and they all wear batiks!" This sort of thing must have happened to Cicely before, I suspected!

"If you would refer to that clause, it tells you that you must never intimidate your employers"

12

FAMILY IN 1967 RIOTS

Gloria and I were married when we were both very young. I was reading law and she had just completed her tertiary course in Home Economics in Bath, Somerset. We had known each other ever since we were children. The wedding took place in the Parish of Stoke Talmage in the County of Oxford, England. This was because the father of Gloria's best friend was the parish priest.

Our first daughter Lesley was born in 1964. She brought me the first taste of fatherhood and I doted on her even though she was a highly strung baby who took some handling. Before her first birthday and in anticipation of our second child, we moved to larger accommodation from our flat in London to a house in Petts Wood in Kent. In the following year, amidst a snow storm, Tracey was born.

Tracey was very different from her elder sister. A smile was always on her face and she slept soundly. There was definitely a mischievous streak in her, but with her rosy cheeks and curly hair, she was cute and lovable. She challenged authority even then, and was decidedly precocious.

Together, they made a delightful pair. I had the energy to take them to see animals in the countryside, roll around the grass with them and they returned my devotion with their attachment to me. There was nothing I would not do for them. We even surprised them with a West Highland Terrier puppy for Christmas when Tracey was less than a year old. We called the dog "Marsh". Marsh became very much my dog and she followed me everywhere when she was not sleeping on top of Tracey in her cot!

In January 1967, the family flew home to Hong Kong. We arrived to a huge welcome from our parents. Phoebe and MC were all over the girls as were Gloria's parents Tom and Doris. We were quite thankful that the girls were taken off our hands for a while as it gave us some respite after the incessant demands on us as parents in England.

My job with Wharf started on 1st February. By April, sparked off by industrial disputes and fanned by the Red Guard influence of China's Cultural Revolution, riots broke out. The Red Guards called for a purge of all employers and people of privilege. The workforce walked out. The Wharf management had no alternative but to put into practice the wholesale firing of over 800 employees. Rioting spread throughout the Colony. The wife of a senior European diplomat was manhandled out of her car by a mob. Letter bombs were sent through the post, left on doorsteps, or simply left at random in the streets. The bomb disposal squad of the Royal Hong Kong Police Force was kept very busy.

Whole hell had broken loose! What had we done by leaving England and pulling up our roots there?

People thought Hong Kong would never recover. Markets plunged. Expatriates left the Colony and returned home. A high percentage of Hong Kong's much valued Portuguese community emigrated to Canada, the United States and Australia. Some Westernized local Chinese did likewise. It was in essence the beginning of Hong Kong's much publicized "brain drain".

We were despondent. We had just unpacked our personal effects shipped from England, lifted our anchor to take a chance in Hong Kong and what did we find? It was frightening. The children were watched at every step. They were not allowed to pick up anything anywhere for fear that the objects might explode! It was as bad as that.

In recognition that the industrial action was probably inspired by a small number of agitators, Wharf took action. A few supervisors who were known troublemakers were promoted to junior management. Well guarded vehicles were provided to transport executives around and they were dropped off or picked up directly at doorsteps. Most significantly, we established two "Reinstatement Tribunals" to vet all discharged employees with a view to re-employing those who were proven victims of threats. These tribunals were chaired by Gerry Forsgate in Hong Kong, and the Deputy General Manager John Henderson took the Kowloon tribunal. I was drafted into Henderson's tribunal to assist.

These sessions usually began with a short address by Henderson before we saw the applicants individually. In one such session, the militant-looking group waved the Mao's Doctrines booklet, commonly known as the "little red book", at us amidst chants of defiance. Henderson calmly put up his hands for silence and then referred them to a clause in the little red book and said "If you would refer to that clause, it tells you that you must never intimidate your employers"! Round One to Henderson – there was no question about that. We eventually re-hired approximately 600 out of the 800.

The riots of 1967 turned out to be Hong Kong's first demonstration of its resilience against extreme adversity and its amazing ability to rebound. The same pattern was to recur again and again in response to every crisis for years until the Asian economic meltdown in 1997.

Within a matter of months, the riots had died down. Both the property and stock markets fully recovered. Transport systems returned to normal. The streets were safe again. Everyone breathed a sigh of relief. For us, any tinge of regret for leaving England was forgotten. There was a life as good right there in Hong Kong as could be found anywhere.

My involvement in Henderson's tribunal meant that I had been exposed to the rank and file of the company. Gossip was rife that I was the "young Mr. Hung". They associated me with the Chinese because of MC, thus I was one of them. The respect or regard, which I did not really deserve, was on the face of almost every employee thereafter. That did me no harm at all.

The little girls grew nicely and started kindergarten. In Lesley's case, she even started junior school in September 1967 at the Diocesan Girls' School, the institution that most female members of our family had attended, including Phoebe, her sisters and my sisters Wendy and Evelyn. The girls also joined ballet lessons and Lesley was good at it but Tracey showed little interest. They were kept busy but that did not deprive them from having fun. Most weekends were spent at 'Phoebus', MC's weekend house in Sai Kung in the New Territories.

After a longish period of quarantine, Marsh was flown from England by arrangements made by agents. Marsh had been taught well on her habits. She was not to do her "business" unless outdoors. The plane journey took close to 18 hours with transit stops between London and Hong Kong. Marsh flew separately from us as most members of royalty did. We went to the cargo depot to meet her on arrival at Kai Tak Airport. She was in her small box when offloaded. When she was let out, much as she wanted to run to us, she could not help but squat down and release a stream which ran the length of the tarmac – 18 hours of rainwater accumulated in the clouds adequate to create a flowing torrent! Marsh was really sweet and was obviously trained to be a creature of habit!

By the end of 1971, our third child was born. Samantha was our third daughter in succession. She was a contented baby, very easy to care for. In any case, unlike the first two born in England, we had home help in the person of Ah Sum. As Gloria worked as a teacher, Ah Sum was virtually the nanny to Samantha. Consequently, Sam was to learn Cantonese long before she understood any English. Her habits were all Chinese and chopsticks were the only "weapons" she knew for meals.

Six years between Tracey and Sam meant that the elder two treated Sam like the baby that she was. As we both worked, Sam was totally dependent on Ah Sum, but since we lived upstairs, Phoebe did not mind lending a hand with the girls. Tracey often sneaked downstairs to see her grandparents. This was her ploy in disguise as what she really wanted was to share MC's soup. MC did not seem to mind at all. In fact, he reciprocated by pretending to come up to watch football on TV with me, but really it was to play with Tracey.

Lesley would stick with us as any self-respecting first born should. They were all very different but I loved them all.

By August 1972, the family joined me in Singapore. In the first few days, I took them around to show them the town. They got settled in the house, which they all liked, and were taken to my normal haunts; places like the supermarkets, retail malls, hotels, restaurants, and of course the Singapore Cricket Club and the Tanglin Club, the latter being their preference as Tanglin was a better family club and they had a great pool and an excellent casual local restaurant.

We went to lunch one weekend to a smart Western restaurant. The elder girls loved it as they could have their milkshakes, burgers and ice cream etc. Sam looked totally puzzled at the table setting and said aloud "Why are there no chopsticks and bowls?"

Sam was a real country bumpkin and she also looked quite dopey at times. Little did we know then how Sam would eventually turn out. My immediate task was to Westernize her because if she spoke no English, she could not possibly assimilate into the life of an expatriate in Singapore where the medium of teaching, even in kindergarten, was English. I spoke only English to her. Even when she answered me in Chinese, I would revert to English. In Singapore, the Chinese dialects commonly spoken were Hokkien or Teochew, but not Cantonese. She needed to speak English if she was to get into school.

Sam learned very quickly to the extent that from then on, she refused to speak Chinese. She has never used Cantonese again to this day. It was at that time that I thought Sam might have a brain! When she approached her teens, we were to discover that she was in fact academically quite brilliant without the need to study much at all. There exists a photographic memory in that head of hers!

Just as I had settled with my young family, I was sadly informed of the very sudden and unexpected passing of MC due to a "pancreatic failure" after having been committed to hospital in an emergency.

I returned to Hong Kong at once. During the journey from Singapore, I reflected on my time spent with the man who effectively brought me up, a man who had shared so many common interests with me, a man I had missed so much when I was in England, and a man who I had deeply respected, admired and regarded as my best friend.

"Once an issue has been checked and passed by your old man,
you know your backside is covered"

13

STEPFATHER

MC died at the relatively young age of 64 for one who kept to clean living and physical fitness like a religion. As he often said, he was an expert on health. He did not smoke or drink. He did not even keep late nights. Life deals surprising turns. His time was up, as they say.

His passing really shocked Phoebe. She had now lost two husbands and the suddenness of MC's passing left her totally unprepared. Apart from Wendy, the rest of us were all living overseas. As the elder son, I took charge of the funeral arrangements and saw to the dignity of the burial service. After a few days of comforting mother to the best of my ability, I had no option but to return to Singapore although I had held out to mother that I would always do what I could if she ever needed me. Phoebe had always been a proud and self-sufficient person. I knew in my heart that she would not call.

From the very first day MC became my stepfather, he took me as his own. He was appreciably younger than Walter, thus our age difference was only just a little over 20 years. He was still young at heart and fit as a fiddle. He was a strong tennis player and mad about the game. He began teaching me tennis when I was about 10. I was a lanky youth and not at all coordinated before puberty. He thought I had talent but that was not at all evident to me.

After I turned 11, tennis took a back seat to cricket. I only took to the courts with MC once or twice a month in the cricket season but played more during the summer. My cricket progressed fast as I grew to six-feet-two and was able to acquit myself well even in adult company. Regarded as one of the best schoolboy cricketers in the Colony, I of course made it my priority.

I grew in strength and height and the general improvement in agility rubbed off on my coordination. Suddenly, to the surprise of MC, I no longer played tennis like a "small boy". He took great pride in my improvement as I developed a big serve and a sharp volleying ability at the net. My ground strokes were never great, but good enough to chip returns back to the feet of the incoming server. My doubles play was far superior to my singles. MC and I entered many tournaments as partners and we were a formidable combination. If we both held our serves, it meant we only had to break our opponents once to win a set. We had much success doing that.

It used to drive mother mad because our matches never ended on court, but continued in the evening at home. MC was also a great one for the deft volleying touch. He insisted that we should volley at each other in the dining room "to improve our touch and control". Mother would scream at us saying there were glass cabinets and ornaments about. But we never broke a single item in years of volleying! The foundation was to prepare me for eventual inclusion in the university teams at HKU and Birmingham.

On holidays and weekends, MC would tag me along to look at second-hand cars and properties. He loved cars and would change these at will whenever he spotted a bargain, often ending up with four or five cars at home. It was his passion. As for properties, he also targeted peripheral lots for investments. On one such occasion, he took me to Sai Kung, off a little village called Sheung Yeung, to see a plot of land. All I saw was long grass but MC bought the plot. After the grass had been cleared, I then saw the wonderful sea view it had. The plot was to become a weekend house with a full-sized tennis court. The house was named 'Phoebus' after mother. We did many things together, well surpassing what he ever did with his own son, my brother Michael. The close age difference between us was the factor.

He hurt his right arm once and had to lay off tennis for six months. Not content to stay away totally, he tried to train himself playing left-handed. Endless hours were spent knocking balls against a wall. Within about four months, he could play left-handed reasonably on court. His persistence and determination were amazing.

When I was already at Wharf, MC suddenly decided he wanted to play cricket. I was astounded since I did not know he had played before. It turned out that he had a solid defence and was lethal with his cross-batted shots which he called forehand cross courts (pulls) or down the line (cuts). He opened the batting for the KCC Hornets and they won the Saturday league.

There was an occasion when I played against him. He was facing the first over and I had the new ball. Without labouring on too much detail, the first five balls all wrapped him on the pads and he survived two strong LBW appeals. I removed his middle stump with the sixth and final delivery. Mother, who was watching, was livid with me and said "How could you do that to your father?" I gave no answer, but MC said he was responsible because he was the one who had instilled the competitive spirit in me. Mother was silenced but muttered that we always ganged up against her.

One Christmas, I mentioned that I intended to take a short holiday in Greece during the forthcoming Easter break. MC's face turned sour, he rose from his seat at the dining table and walked off in a huff. We all wondered what was troubling him. Mother later told me that MC was upset because he thought I had no right to speak so freely about flying all over the place when I was not yet earning. I thought he was ridiculously sensitive, yet years later I saw things in the same light when our daughter Katish went on about going here and there for her Spring break from Georgetown University in Washington DC. Fathers would be fathers. They do think alike, whilst children behave the same even from different generations.

Although I had transferred earlier out of Chee Wo Hong, I never lost sight of what MC did there. One year, he was about to take a month's leave out of Hong Kong with mother. When arrangements were made for me to cover his absence, I was given his full power of attorney. McLuskie challenged MC's decision and said I was too junior to cover MC's affairs. MC decided to confront McLuskie in front of Forsgate and simply asked Gerry, "If you were going away, would you give your personal power of attorney and signing rights of your bank accounts to Bill or to your son Brian?" It was a no-brainer. Enough said!

I realized the seriousness of my responsibility in handling the Chee Wo Hong affairs and ensured that Wharf settlements were promptly paid in MC's absence. The receivables came a little late, but I still effected full settlement even though it meant divesting some of MC's equity investments. As a family, we had to be seen to be whiter than white.

Never a trader because he did not like risks, MC was however the soundest executive anyone could wish for in a team. Forsgate once said to me: "Once an issue has been checked and passed by your old man, you know your backside is covered."

Calculated risk-taking in the family would thus fall to Phoebe. Although she looked disinterested in business, she did actually have a sharp mind and her assessment of investments in the stock market was surprisingly sound. She was perhaps not as wealthy as she could have been because she constantly gave things away to people less fortunate than herself. She really "couldn't give a damn" about the accumulation of wealth, as her favourite actor Clark Gable would say in *Gone with the Wind*.

Phoebe was to me a virtual saint although I thought she was overly generous to some people who perhaps did not deserve her kindness. MC used to furtively complain in jest to me about Phoebe concerning her almost indiscriminate giving of gifts to people milling around her. MC called these people "parasites" and he had a secret code with me to describe the gathering of these people. He termed their presence as "MPB" standing for "manifestation of parasitic beings"!

MC and I did however acknowledge mother's generous heart and agreed she was a super human being despite her occasional gullibility with the MPBs.

14

Singapore Fling

At home, the children had been suitably installed into English-language schools which were purpose-designed for expatriate children in Singapore. Lesley went direct into United World College for secondary schooling and Tracey went into Tanglin School. Young Samantha started going to playschool. Gloria did not work and spent her time attending cooking classes or golfing with her lady friends.

Singapore was an awkward place for expatriate wives, especially those who had professional qualifications. They were essentially dependents of their husbands and it was well-nigh impossible for them to obtain work permits unless their qualifications were such that no local Singaporean possessed. As a teacher, Gloria had to resign herself to a relative life of leisure to which she was not accustomed.

When I left for Singapore, Marsh fell very ill. Gloria surmised that the dog suffered from a broken heart as I was nowhere to be found. Marsh was lost and confused and then became so ill that she had to be put down to prevent further suffering. I was saddened as Marsh had been with us for some 10 years.

The girls wanted another dog and pleaded with some reason as our home was certainly big enough for a dog to have more than adequate space. We eventually gave in and acquired a canine friend for them in the form of a frisky beagle. We named him Basil. Basil was terribly intelligent and energetic but utterly eccentric.

We often used to entertain outdoors. In typical Singaporean style, we had large parties on the lawn where large quantities of beers, wines and spirits flowed in a friendly casual tropical atmosphere. Guests would help themselves to buffet dinner and booze from the free-standing bar set up on the edge of the lawn. Ashtrays were provided at strategic positions but nobody seemed to use them. Cigarette butts were strewn on the lawn wherever people were standing. Those were great evenings, particularly when the guests were predominantly cricketers and their ladies.

The mornings after would be hard work in gathering the numerous empty soft drink and wine bottles and mountains of beer cans. One such morning, we noticed hardly any cigarette butts, and then we saw Basil eating the remaining butts one by one, and he was still only a puppy. In time, we never had to clear cigarette butts. Basil would be the vacuum cleaner. He had acquired a taste and he loved it.

After a Monday evening cricket meeting, the boys and I were having a quiet drink at the bar in the SCC. I was called urgently to the phone. My daughters were in severe distress because Basil had been knocked down by a car outside our home and died. I rushed home at once.

By unanimous decision, we were to give Basil a Christian burial. I could not deny that to the girls as they were already under much grief. I called my cricketing friend John Martens who worked for the Primary Production Ministry and was expertly advised of the rule that a hole of at least four feet deep must be dug before an animal could be buried therein. Starting at 8pm, I commenced digging in complete darkness save for a small light which shone from the kitchen window. Excavation with a simple garden spade was hard work, made only slightly easier by the mud which was gradually being made softer by the driving rain. It took me close to three hours before the burial site was made ready. I was drenched to the bone and developed an aching back.

Prayers were conducted by Lesley. Tracey prepared the deceased by wrapping him in choice blankets. Needless to say, a favourite toy or two were thrown in to accompany Basil to heaven. With the burial complete, we refilled the hole. By gentle persuasion, the grave was permitted to harden overnight before a wooden cross was to be placed on the select site in the back garden. No headstone was required, by negotiated agreement!

My chronic bad back might have started then.

Problems at work did not abate. Ong and McLuskie were still at odds over when the container warehouse project could commence. I was the "sacrificial lamb". This awkwardness persisted for a further 12 months before McLuskie would give the green light for piling to start with a prescribed slow build-up of floors. The building had to reach the top first even though the upper floors would be left unfinished because the container-lifting equipment supplied by Demag of Germany could only be installed if the "engine" is placed at the top of the building. The hydraulics for the traversing movements on each floor to move the boxes onto the platforms could then be installed floor by floor. Upfront cost would thus be inevitably expensive and not strictly apportioned equally by floors at the beginning of the project. In short, we had to pile for 14 floors although we intended to complete only seven floors in Phase One.

I also knew that apart from this "preparation" phase, things would move slowly and I did not expect any acceleration until more time had elapsed. Spare time would still be there for my sporting pursuits to continue.

I entered the Cricket Section Committee of the SCC, first as the Hon. Secretary, later as Vice-Captain. As the season ended, we were to learn that I was to be the new Captain of the club, hopefully to lead a strong team to win the league championship the following season.

Being situated at the crossroads of the Far East between England to the West and Australia/New Zealand to the South-east, Singapore was geographically a place teams would pass through unless they preferred to use the Hong Kong route. It was a city where leading touring teams chose to stop to break their journeys in half. Similarly, we were in relative close proximity to various cricketing centres, thus permitting financially affordable tours. All of us involved in the club took as many opportunities as we could to maximize our cricketing exposure. It was the sporting life.

The New Zealand World Cup squad passed us on the way to England for the big tournament. Their strong team, captained by Geoff Howarth, was one of their better sides including names such as Burgess, Coney, Lees, Cairns, Hadlee, Chatfield, Bracewell, Boock and the double cricket/ rugby international Brian McKechnie. The New Zealanders, though obviously superior to us, could not get us out as we ended on 160 for 7. The game was drawn. A month later, New Zealand came third in the World Cup.

A humbling incident happened when we played the Derek Robbins XI at the Padang captained by the former England captain Mike Denness. I faced the spin wizard Intikhab Alam but could not read his deliveries and felt stupid. My batting partner suggested that I should perhaps just play every ball as an offbreak. I duly struck the next two balls through extra cover for fours. Denness then eased from gully to a position between slips and third-man. The next ball pitched on the same spot. I went for the same drive. It was a ball that spun the other way, took a thick edge and the ball flew straight down the throat of Denness.

On the way back to the pavilion, I walked past the bowler's end and heard Intikhab say to mid-off "There's one born every minute" – sucker that I was! These pros always worked us amateurs out. It was just a matter of time.

The expatriate community in Singapore was extremely transient. People came for a couple of years and most of them then left. Much of this phenomenon was caused by the difficulty in obtaining work permits or the ability to renew these. Because of the strict immigration restrictions, the Singapore Cricket Club, traditionally an expatriate dominated institution, also suffered constant membership changes. Not many stayed more than one tour or two of two to three years. The 1st XI had the same fate and the composition of the side would rarely be settled. Losses of people were however generally compensated by new arrivals. Somehow, we always had a decent team comprising mainly expatriates with a few local Eurasian stalwarts. Of these locals, two exceptionally talented cricketers stood out in the persons of Reggie da Silva and John Martens. Both became great friends of mine.

The club touring team that went to Australia was similarly composed in terms of player mix. We landed first in Perth which was probably the wrong start as Western Australia had the hardest and fastest tracks. In the first match at Scarborough, I faced Sam Gannon, then a test left-arm quick with a nasty late inswinger off just short of a good length. I was given a real baptism and was hit inside the pad on the knee twice on the same spot. I could not walk and had to sit out the next two matches. Aussies are hard men, but I do admire their winning mentality.

Melbourne daily *The Age* called for the team sheet the evening before our match against the Melbourne Cricket Club at the famous MCG, but when they saw the list of Western names, they asked us "Where were the Singaporeans?" We explained that we were not the national side but the Singapore Cricket Club composed almost entirely of expatriates and just hoped the confusion had been cleared up.

We were put in to bat the next morning. I took the long walk of 130 yards to the middle. I played and missed the first two balls which both took a vicious movement off the track towards slips with the next turning sharply in the other direction. I glanced at the scoreboard and saw a flashing red light against the bowler's name. He was none other than Max Walker, the then Australian test fast medium bowler – some experience!

There was no respite when we played North Melbourne the following day. We had read earlier that Frank "Typhoon" Tyson had slowed down to only a "gale" then. Tyson bowled off only eight paces at us, but if that was just a gale, I wondered what a typhoon would have been like.

We reached Brisbane and looked forward to playing on the Gabba against the Queensland Cricketers Club. It was a big disappointment as the match had to be abandoned because of a waterlogged pitch after a downpour.

Anyone who says that all professional cricketers are only after money would have to face up to me. This is far from the truth, especially when we refer to Dennis Lillee, Rod Marsh and Graeme Wood, three test players from Western Australia. They agreed to come to Singapore as the guests of the Singapore Cricket Club and all we had to do was secure the support of Qantas to fly them and their wives from Perth, put them into complimentary hotel rooms at the Wharf-owned Marco Polo, and pick up their F&B bills at the club. They did not ask for a single penny of fees, for a solid week of coaching, running clinics, visiting schools and so on. Prior to their departure, we even staged an exhibition match pitching the Singapore team against a DK Lillee XI made up of the three of them and eight former internationals from Asian teams. This provided an even and competitive game and I played in the Lillee XI.

The General Manager of the SCC called me one morning. "Skipper, you'd better come down. Keith Miller is at the bar." I introduced myself to the all-time great. He looked at me and suggested that we had met before. I said that he must have been mistaken. As he had been covering the Ashes for the *Daily Mail* in England, I asked him how quick were the fearsome Australian pair of Lillee and Thomson? "Well John, I suppose their quicker ones would be up to the pace of Ray and I." I declined to comment.

After chatting for a while, Keith said, "I know – it was 1954." I asked him what happened in 1954? "I did say I knew you, John. It was in 1954. You were that lanky young bugger in shorts who bowled me at the nets, weren't you?" Of course he was right. I just didn't think that was significant enough for him to remember. In truth, Keith toured England with Lindsay Hassett's famous Australians. When they passed through Hong Kong, they played an exhibition match at the old HKCC ground on Chater Road, right at ground zero of Central. I was 15 years old, wearing shorts and thick horn-rimmed glasses and thin as a rake. I did bowl at the nets where promising youngsters were permitted to. But how on earth could Keith possibly relate me to that "boy" when I was almost 60 pounds heavier, totally grey and wore thin metal-framed glasses and a rather smart business suit?

Keith added "Ah! You must know that I never forget a face of anyone who bowled me, even if at the nets." He had a reputation for having a memory like an elephant. But this was ridiculous! Regardless, it was a pleasure meeting Keith... again.

"You have to be clever, Sir. This is a hot country. Why stop at the lights when we are under the shade of a large tree here!"

15

QUIRKS OF THE SINGAPOREANS

Progress on the projects at Singapore Warehouse remained slow. We had almost resigned ourselves to a long wait before McLuskie would give the go-ahead to speed up the construction of the container warehouse. In the interim, we recognized the need to streamline the management as best we could.

Site excavation and preparation for piling had however started and things were trundling along on site. Singapore being what it was, there were constantly strange things happening which kept us alert but strangely these sometimes also kept us amused. It was a mixture of acceptance of the absurd blended with a smile. In the face of frustrations at work, we needed a sense of humour to maintain our equilibrium and positive outlook. We had to be philosophical about some of these eccentric and bizarre local traditions and practices. Since these instances all made such a deep impression on me at the time, I hold a keen sense of recall as I scribe a few of these stories.

Not long after my arrival in Singapore, I hired a Malay driver called Razak. He was more than a driver to me. Rather, he was my driver, valet, marketing man and local tour guide all rolled into one. Needless to say, I relied heavily on him and the scope of services he provided seemed endless. On outward appearance, Razak was a real gentleman, neat and smart in his uniform, held a good deportment with a likeable personality to top it all. In reality though, he was street-wise and knew exactly how to butter me up.

One day, Razak was driving me back to my office after lunch at the Marco Polo Hotel. As we approached a set of traffic lights, Razak stopped the car about 50 yards behind the vehicle we were following thus leaving a big gap between the two cars. I had to ask him why he did that. He answered in a matter-of-fact way, "You have to be clever, Sir. This is a hot country. Why stop at the lights when we are under the shade of a large tree here?"

My drivers never lasted long with me. They tended to change jobs just for the sake of a few dollars more. I tried to persuade them to stay, but I soon accepted that this was the way things worked. Changing jobs was the norm with them. Following Razak, I hired Rashid who was extremely eccentric. He was nowhere as suave as Razak, but he had his own bag of tricks. Nothing pleased him more than going out to buy lunch for me on occasions when work tied me to the office. He knew that if he bought lunch for me, he would get a free lunch too. Rashid did not stay long either.

Another short-term driver later, Donald was my fourth and last driver in Singapore, but unlike Razak and Rashid, Donald was Chinese and he stayed with me for years. He was an unlikely man to be a driver in the sense that he was too well educated for such a job. He was born into a well-to-do family in Penang and attended a famous school there. He met with misfortune as all his savings were lost in the Gemini chit fund scandal in Singapore. Because of his background, Donald knew many people in high places, including senior government officials and business executives. On one occasion when he was waiting for me at the Singapore Cricket Club, I could not locate Donald at the club car park even though my car was there. When I made enquiries with the security guards, I was told that Donald had been invited into the Men's Bar by a prominent member. Initially I was quite irritated by that, but when I went into the Men's Bar to find him, Donald was having a merry time with a good friend of mine. I softened up as I was told that they sat next to each other decades ago in school.

Being a virtual compulsive gambler, Donald was a superstitious man. Whenever he saw a road accident, he would insist on stopping our car so that he could copy down the number of the damaged car. He believed that these numbers were lucky for the 4-Digit lottery. On one such occasion, a car was actually overturned on the side of the road. This excited Donald even more than normal. He took down the number and told me that this time he would put double his stakes on the 4-Digit because his bad luck would also be "overturned" as he muttered in his Singlish accent that the car had "turned turtle"!

It was amazing to me that many Western-educated Singaporeans used very typical and sometimes old-fashioned English jargon in their daily speech. Spoken with a heavy Singlish accent, these utterances could sound quite hilarious at times.

Many funny stories were rolled into one when we encountered the mystery of the tree spirit at Singapore Warehouse. Way after the event, I discovered from general conversation with Singaporean friends that the belief in tree spirits was quite widespread in that part of the world.

A large old tree was standing on an open area in the Singapore Warehouse compound on the exact location of the designated throughway for the passage of vehicles. Container handling and haulage were after all our bread and butter. I wanted the tree cut down. None of the Chinese workmen was willing to perform that task as they felt the tree was sacred. Despite my persuasion and arm-twisting, we just could not get anyone to do that job. I then commissioned outside contractors to cut down the tree and this was done over a weekend.

The Monday following, an accident took place when a construction worker fell and was severely injured. People immediately attributed it to the tree being chopped down. They downed tools. When I came to the scene, I was told that unless we prayed to the gods with offerings to appease the tree spirit, accidents would continue to occur. I was advised that when in Rome, do as the Romans. My staff arranged for a Buddhist ceremony to be performed with a full complement of holy papers, roast suckling pig, attendance of monks etc. This ritual was performed on a Saturday and we all thought that peace would return.

A few days later, another accident occurred. Panic spread once more and there was uproar among the workforce. It was at that time that our old Tamil watchman came forward. The watchman had been with the company on the same site for decades, and he told us we should have asked him before we conducted the Buddhist ceremony. He was not surprised that the tree spirit remained annoyed because, to his knowledge, the tree was not a Chinese tree but an Indian one as it was planted by members of his Tamil clan years ago. We had prayed to the wrong spirit!

The watchman volunteered to arrange an Indian ceremony the following weekend with all the necessary trimmings to pray to the Indian spirit. When it was all over, I was told there was a cost overrun during the ceremony as they had to buy more goodies to satisfy the Indian spirit. As it was related to me, when they first prayed, the Indian spirit was extremely angry about the unauthorized felling of the tree. It was lucky that the spirit's feet (the tree roots) had not yet been totally removed, so it was still possible to seek forgiveness. The additional offerings together with the humble apologies that accompanied the Indian prayers were finally accepted as the spirit felt that the soul of the tree could now move away in peace, thus permitting us to remove even the roots with the spirit's blessing.

I did not know what to make of all this and thought it wise to resist passing comments. No further accidents happened thereafter!

As we anticipated the completion of the container warehouse, we had planned for certain areas within the complex to be used as offices for the tenants' administration activities. It was therefore necessary to provide toilet facilities that were suitable for executive use. At that time, all the toilets in the warehouse were the hole-in-the-ground type for squatting. We thought it necessary to upgrade these to the sitting type with proper toilet bowls and seats. These were duly installed. A couple of weeks passed and we were appalled to see that the toilet seats had footprints on them or worse still, some toilet seats were actually broken by frequent trampling. Old habits die hard!

When we were preparing the foundation work, the site had to be excavated first to remove unwanted boulders or any foreign materials. There was considerable excitement one day and the rumour reached me that we had discovered a few bright green gems which were thought to be emeralds. Hey, we were sitting on a mine and there was no need to build a warehouse! The value was on our doorstep and the returns would be almost immediate! I had to see these gems for myself. They looked great all right. The colour was indeed bright green and the small objects were translucent.

An old-timer on site then told us that the site used to be a dumping ground for broken drinks bottles. Over the decades, those bits of embedded green glass from the broken bottles had created an emerald rush in the 1970s at the tip of River Valley Road! You should have seen the faces of disappointment amongst the workforce. To a few, that was another instance of being cheated by false hope.

"The thrill of watching one's own horse win is a feeling hard to describe. It far surpasses even backing a 50 to 1 winner on someone else's thoroughbred."

16

SPORTING LIFE

Advice came from the High Court in December that my appeal hearing date had been set for 19th May 2010. It was to be a six-month wait. Kevin Egan advised against an application for an accelerated earlier date. There was no reason to question Kevin's views.

I did a quick calculation in my head. If we won the appeal, I would be released in May. If unsuccessful, I would then have a further five months to serve until mid-October at which point I might have to consider whether to take the case all the way to the Court of Final Appeal. There were many balls in the air and it would be wiser to just get on with life and avoid speculation. I thought I should adopt a state of mind in the same manner as I would build an innings. Look at 25 runs first, then to 50 and set forward milestones as I went along. There was no better way for time to pass seemingly faster.

I found things to occupy myself. I read novel after novel; wrote many letters which drew replies and thus made the correspondence self-perpetuating. Whatever time that remained was used to write this very book. It was a good time for writing as my mind was clear from pressing problems since the appeal preparation had already been completed.

In between writing letters and this book, I read more for inspiration. I was particularly taken by Jeffery Archer's *Prisoner of Birth* because it described prison life in England. It was uncanny to read how much our prison resembled the British version in Archer's book. On reflection however, this was not altogether surprising since Stanley Prison was built by the Colonial Government in 1937, and only subsequently upgraded and marginally modernized. I could actually see in Archer's words the description of the cell which I was occupying.

Numerous things in Archer's book reminded me of the very environment I was in, from the regimentation to the dining arrangements, and even the recreational time that we had for exercise. We were either on the football field or on the basketball court. Those who did not play were free to engage in tai chi, aerobics, jogging or walking. It was at those times that I longed for the opportunity of playing the sports I favoured such as golf or tennis. Naturally these were not available but that did not prevent me from thinking of my sporting pursuits in the past.

I gave up competitive tennis as a serious sport long ago although I continued to enjoy the occasional knock-around with friends. In fact, I had many happy hours with Katish and Natasha on the tennis court when they were young. My wife Gail even said that I had remained light on my feet and moved well on court even when I approached 50. Competitively however, I simply could not fit everything in and was frankly too lazy to run hard around the court as I got older. Athletics was a thing for youngsters and I gave up high-jumping once I was 23 years old, which coincided more or less with the start of married life. During my athletics days in Birmingham, I also threw out my arm with the javelin and my career as a bowler was over. With no bowling to worry about, I turned myself from a mid-order batsman to an opener and honed my craft in playing the line with the body right behind. It was to make me a specialist opener, a role that was to bring out the best in my cricketing ability in the years to come.

Golf took more and more a central place as I had to anticipate that my cricketing career would come to an end sooner or later. Eventually, I gave up cricket at the age of 47 because I could no longer see as well when fielding close in, even though my batting was still satisfactory. In fact, even in my swansong, I still managed to score 61.

There was another ready replacement for cricket right there, a pastime which I did not have time for earlier. I could take up horse racing in earnest. In my days in England, I had shown keen interest but had to suspend deep involvement because of career and family demands, not to mention cricket. I was never too interested in National Hunt over chases and hurdles. Flat racing was my passion as the classic version of thoroughbred racing.

I joined the Royal Hong Kong Jockey Club as early as 1970. The word "Royal" was dropped after the handover of Hong Kong in 1997. Little did I know that it was that small beginning with the Jockey Club that eventually had the indirect effect of landing me in Stanley Prison. It has left a sour taste, but I would admit that in the 1980s and 1990s, the Jockey Club did provide the opportunity for me to have some great moments in racing.

The thrill of watching one's own horse win is a feeling hard to describe. It far surpasses the backing of even a 50 to 1 winner on someone else's thoroughbred. It could, I suppose, be compared to seeing one's own son performing well in the sporting arena. New Zealand gave me the first taste of success as an owner but Hong Kong would give me many more.

New Zealand ownership came in the form of a partnership. This was quickly followed by the formation of a syndicate in Hong Kong. Zippalanda was in fact the first horse put into training in Hong Kong by the syndicate of that name. The Zippalanda Syndicate raced the 2YO (two-year-old) griffin which placed second twice in his first two outings. Things looked very promising for the following season. Unfortunately he went lame during the summer break and died after an operation.

Zippalanda was replaced by a well-bred Argentine colt, Sirocco, whose sire Shy Tom came from the bloodline of the super Blushing Groom. Sirocco was to give us the greatest pleasure owners could wish for.

Sirocco had a Class 1 career in Hong Kong, winning eight races from a 3YO to 7YO. He earned close to HK$10 million in stake earnings. However, his most notable achievement was his amazing consistency as he was rarely out of the first three places. He was as honest as they come and one of the most durable horses I have seen, lasting a continuous five consecutive seasons and a winner in each. He had such a calm disposition that he remained entire and was never gelded, an exceptionally rare condition in the Hong Kong racing scene. He was then sent to the New Zealand racing centre Karaka on retirement to stand in stud.

The syndicate continued successfully to expand the string of good horses and the next one was Sharki, a New Zealand bred colt ex Cape Cross out of Ricamo. His short career in Hong Kong was impressive, winning his first race and being a winner four times by the end of his 3YO season. Sadly, he developed a strange dry coat and had a knee problem which caused us to retire him after his 4YO season. Sharki was handed as a gift to Cherie Archer, our manager in New Zealand.

Upon settling in the New Zealand environment, Sharki started sweating again and there was hope that he could perhaps race again. Cherie placed him with a lady trainer, Natalie Tanner, who trained her horses on the beach. Sand training was supposed to be easier on the knee. Resumption of racing looked promising. As required by New Zealand Thoroughbreds, Cherie changed Sharki's name to "Who Knows" and the horse's second career began. Who Knows, kept fresh and sound by the "magician" Natalie, found success which surpassed even his excellent record in Hong Kong. Within a season, he won thrice on the leading New Zealand tracks and his rating rose to 106, higher than what he had achieved in Hong Kong. Who Knows remained in training and even though we no longer owned him, I was thrilled to see this incredible story unfold.

The syndicate currently has Zephyrus in training. All the horses in the syndicate are named after trade winds around the world. My own horses, starting with Headingley and followed by Sabina, are named not surprisingly after famous test cricket grounds!

"The acquisition of Wharf by Sir YK was history in the making and the year was 1981"

17

NEW LEASE OF LIFE

The "stop and start" nature of the container warehouse project had its consequences. One could not simply press a button to start a project that had been placed in hibernation for such a prolonged period. Planning details had to be revived, approvals needed re-applications, the original critical path which had been disturbed had to be re-worked, materials had to be re-ordered and the workforce had to be re-assembled. In other words, allowance had to be made for lead time again.

This was what happened when the decision came from Wharf to start the project. The project team was excited by the proposition. Physical progress was to begin at last, but the rift that had developed between the majority shareholders and the management was no longer easy to mend. This might have gone too far.

Then we heard the strong rumour that Wharf had become the target of a hostile takeover by shipping magnate Sir Yue-Kong Pao, or Sir YK as he was popularly known.

Sir YK hailed from Ningpo, a seaport on the east coast of China, a distance of only 70 miles to Shanghai as the crow flies. We are told that at the time of the Opium War, Britain considered Ningpo one of the strategic ports in China. Indeed, it was one of the five ports opened internationally as a result of the Treaty of Nanking. By that same treaty, Hong Kong was ceded to Britain as the main settlement prize, but Ningpo was probably more developed as a port than Hong Kong at that time.

People from Ningpo were known to be the shrewdest businessmen to come from China. They were renowned for being tough negotiators. Sir YK certainly lived up to that reputation in his dealings, which were legendary.

Sir YK was a banker in Shanghai. He moved to Hong Kong after Mao's Communist regime took control of the country in 1949. He then gradually grew his investments in ship-owning. It was widely believed that he built up Worldwide Shipping with the staunch support of Michael Sandberg (later Sir Michael) of the Hongkong Bank. With the bank's support, Sir YK expanded his fleet to a staggering size of some 27 million tonnes. By way of comparison, the high-profile Greek shipowners had fleets reputed at about 7 to 10 million tonnes each, way short of Sir YK, who was later referred to as "King of the Seas".

With such a reputation, Sir YK's attempt to wrest control of Wharf from the Jardines group was big news. The local press played him up as a kind of Robin Hood. Up till then, large British firms such as Jardines and Swires were regarded as impregnable. Naturally, the incumbents at Wharf and Jardines did their utmost to defend themselves to ward off the takeover. Whilst this process lingered, everyone involved even remotely was kept alert by this affair. I was in many ways sheltered, being out of place and out of mind, far away in Singapore.

For six to seven months, the Wharf HQ in Hong Kong seemed to have forgotten about me. No one corresponded with me at length from Wharf. When I wrote, I received no meaningful response. It felt as though I did not exist. I found myself working in a vacuum and decided the only way was to take my own initiatives to run Singapore Warehouse as best I could. As in that magnificent movie *Dances with Wolves*, I felt just like

Kevin Costner at the deserted outpost in the West when everyone else of any importance was back East.

Back in Hong Kong, Sir YK kept a step ahead of the Jardines defenders all the time. He had flown back to Hong Kong from London via Air France on a weekend. Having secured the financial support of the Hongkong Bank, he went on television and announced his revised offer for Wharf shares on a Sunday evening. By noon on Monday, Wharf was his!

The acquisition of Wharf had made Sir YK a local folk hero for penetrating the shield of the British corporate stronghold. He had taken control of a large associate listed company from under the nose of the most famous, powerful and long established "noble house" of Jardines. It was history in the making and the year was 1981.

The news was officially announced within Wharf of course. The change of regime and the new management team were made known. Sir YK's son-in-law Peter Woo was to head the management as Deputy Chairman to Sir YK. Bill McLuskie stayed as General Manager whilst the long-term loyal aide of Sir YK, Gonzaga Li, was appointed Deputy General Manager. Even at that time, Wharf was already a large company and the digestion process needed time and attention. It was therefore no surprise that the silence from our Hong Kong HQ would continue whilst they were engaged in the complex corporate absorption exercise.

Peter Woo paid a visit to Singapore a couple of months later. It was the first time I met Peter and we clicked almost at once. We grew closer over the years and became good friends in time. We played golf and tennis together and had a great deal to talk about. I was later to become one of his closest and most trusted aides and the one to advise him on many of his personal exploits and sensitive corporate moves.

When he first touched down in Singapore, he had obviously already done his homework, at least to the extent that he knew who were the long-serving executives. In his own words, he regarded me as "very senior" and considered I was perhaps wasted in what he thought was a "limited portfolio". He saw that my bilingual ability gave rise to a huge advantage insofar as I had all the attributes of an expatriate and yet was able to deal with the Chinese on an equal basis.

The respective styles of management of Jardines and the Pao group were vastly different, as were their philosophies. Wharf, under the umbrella of Jardines, tended to put their executives in a highly structured hierarchy with each man confined to his pigeon-hole and working within that defined scope. It was a structure that encouraged self-protection of territory to preserve job security. The new regime on the other hand encouraged individual creativity and innovation. There was no bar whatsoever against suggestions from anyone on any subject. We were encouraged to think "out of the box" even as teamwork in execution was widely preached.

In just a couple of days of discussions with Peter, my eight years of frozen promotion came to an end. My scope of management was widened considerably. From being pigeon-holed in Singapore Warehouse only, I was made Chief Representative of the Wharf Group in Singapore; appointed to the board of the Wharf listed subsidiary in Singapore, Hotel Marco Polo Limited; given a brief to seek investment opportunities throughout the Asean region; and appointed a director of Gordon Land, a joint venture between Wharf, Hongkong Land and Sino Land. The call was "work hard, think laterally, create opportunities and achieve success – then you would be rewarded". Essentially – no holds barred.

I recalled that about a year earlier, Sir YK had assembled the top 20 executives in Hong Kong and told us in no uncertain terms that he already held about 30% of the company and hinted that it would only be a matter of time before he would have control. I was made acutely aware then that Sir YK would soon be our master and recognized even then that he always got what he wanted once he set his mind on a specific target. I held him in admiration and in awe.

This was a new phase in my revitalized career which had taken a long time to materialize. I sorted out the Singapore Warehouse management with a slight re-shuffle; examined the Asean region's investment climate and narrowed down the preferred target countries to Thailand and Malaysia, and then set about going into macro studies on these countries. I would zero in on the detailed identification of potential projects in due course.

The container warehouse project was finally progressing and planning began for its launch with marketing as the main objective. The attraction of a brand-name anchor tenant was considered vital to serve as a magnet to draw in others. Blocks 1 & 2 were enjoying over 95% occupancy and we waited eagerly for the rental reversion cycle to permit the increase of our monthly gross. Things looked rosy.

It was on a fact-finding trip to Penang with Peter that I really got to know the man well. Away from the pressures of home, Peter was thoroughly relaxed and enjoyed what Penang had to offer. We played our first tennis game together there, enjoyed some local cuisine, listened to a local band with a singer that sounded like Kenny Rogers and generally let our hair down. It was then that we began to understand what made each other tick. In retrospect, that Penang trip did a great deal to cement the relationship between Peter and I which led to many years of corporate success thereafter.

After Penang, I began to identify new investment opportunities, and some promising projects started to surface in Malaysia and Thailand, more specifically in Bangkok. With Peter's endorsement, I was to embark on more detailed fact-finding on projects and opportunities for investments in these two target countries.

"You see, Michael Sandberg and I actually agreed the deal about 3 o'clock earlier today"

18

KING OF THE SEAS

Two opportunities emerged in Bangkok. The first involved some old warehouses owned originally by Sime Darby for conversion, the zoning of which was open for discussion. The other was a mega property development which I code-named Siam City where the idea was to create a huge multi-purpose complex comprising residential, commercial and retail elements. The opportunity came to us because the promoters had heard of Wharf's reputation in the successful development and operation of Harbour City in Hong Kong, which Siam City would attempt to mirror.

Investing in Thailand for the first time on our own was a daunting prospect especially if it involved huge capital. Unknown factors were there and we had to get acquainted with the local rules. I assembled a team of advisors from people that I had known before who also had roots in Thailand. They assisted me greatly in the process.

After a round of due diligence on the country risks and the assessment associated with large developments, we concluded that the amount of management time and attention required for the Sime Darby project was too heavy and the estimated returns not sufficiently rewarding. The balance was simply not there and we decided to pass on that proposal.

Total focus moved to Siam City. Property laws, regulations, restrictions and approvals had to be studied. The legal position in relation to land titles had to be checked with lawyers locally. Documentation on land titles seemed too simple for us to have confidence. It was just a paper with many chops but we were told that was how things were. Different market segments on residential, commercial and retail had to be examined and understood. Supply and demand projections in Bangkok needed to be prepared and sensitivity variations tested. All these would aggregate into a major exercise over a considerable period of time. I was to make 17 trips to Bangkok from Singapore over the following year and a half. Peter was kept constantly updated, but we agreed that the project should be kept privy between ourselves. Neither Peter nor I wished to excite others before the time was ripe. After all, we had not even formed a firm view ourselves whether the project was a go or no go.

The natural passage of time threw up many points of clarity and solutions to earlier problems. It was hard work, but we were encouraged by the progress. It was only a matter of time when we would reach the point where Peter and I were comfortable with the jigsaw. To me, it was exciting as we were effectively pioneering uncharted territory. The prospect of the project looked more and more lucrative as we moved forward.

It was about then that Sir YK first visited Singapore since his takeover. I met him on arrival at Changi International Airport. As we drove into town, Sir YK provided me with a taste of his amazing power of observation. As our car sped past a stretch of HDB blocks of residential apartments, Sir YK said those blocks were wonderful and I was curious because we had similar developments in Hong Kong. Before I could ask, Sir YK explained: "Look John, there is absolutely no laundry hanging from those balconies at all. I shall have to inform our own government in Hong Kong of this." I had driven past those HDB blocks numerous times. Never did it occur to me this was a significant issue. In truth, I never even thought about it. I suppose that was what made Sir YK great, and I ever so ordinary.

At the rooftop of Block 2 of Singapore Warehouse, Sir YK could take a bird's eye view of our entire site and its surrounds. He was impressed with the development but noticed a group of decrepit structures close to the northern boundary of our property. I identified those as the squatters we had attempted to clear for many months, but had failed thus far as we had found it difficult to gain government assistance. Sir YK understood and muttered something about playing golf that afternoon with an extremely high-powered friend of his. I had no idea who his friend was. On the Monday that followed, a group of senior government servants came to Singapore Warehouse and offered their help with the squatter clearance and it was achieved within a month. I just wondered!

Singapore Warehouse had a medium-term cash excess of some S$10 to S$12 million if I can recall. Peter Woo asked me to read the market and give him my recommendations. By the time that my proposal had reached Hong Kong, Peter had gone abroad on business and Sir YK picked up my papers instead. I had recommended we should go short on Singapore dollars and long on US dollars. Sir YK surprised me by calling, as I had expected Peter. He however supported my recommendation and asked me to proceed. He then instructed me to place some S$55 million. I reminded him that we only had about S$12 million, but he asked me to call Worldwide in Singapore to arrange inclusion of their funds in the equation. I gulped and said something to the effect that I had not thought of such a large sum when I gave my recommendation. His quick reply was, "Listen young man, if your reading is wrong, we should not put a cent on it. But if it is correct, why should you worry about the amount?" For about two months, I watched the currency market with bated breath. Thank goodness I was proven right in the end. Of course Sir YK's logic could not be faulted.

By that time, I had been exposed to Sir YK enough that nothing would surprise me any longer. How wrong I was – I ain't seen nothin' yet!

Mr. Ong was in fact the Asian Business Advisor of the Hongkong Bank in Singapore. Whether that was a help to him or not, I would not know, but Mr. Ong suddenly made a bid to acquire Hongkong Bank's share of 16.6% in Singapore Warehouse. I got wind of this and called Peter Woo. We could not afford to let this happen because if the sale went through, the Ongs would hold 76.6% to our 33.3% and they could then make our lives miserable. Peter agreed and I called Nick Carp at Wardleys to prepare a rival bid for us. Nick promised to revert after the weekend.

On Monday morning, Nick suggested we should offer what he considered a "more than adequate" amount. I called Peter but found that he was in hospital because of a broken ankle sustained while playing basketball over the weekend. In his stead, Sir YK dealt with me. Sir YK thought I should go back to Nick and ask him to look at the proposed counter-offer again, but making sure that Nick understood that the amount must be enough to guarantee success. I was to say "YK Pao does not lose battles." Yes Sir!

Nick revised his recommendation upwards but sounded reluctant as he maintained his original recommended amount was really sufficient. I reverted to Sir YK with Nick's 12% increased sum. Nick only relented because he knew that people who lost deals would probably not work for Sir YK again!

Sir YK asked me to draft a telex offer for his approval. After reading my draft, he called and said it was good, but he wanted to include two additions. First, he added a further 10% on the price. I protested and got a terse reply: "a couple of million may be a lot to you, John, but to me it is a drop in the ocean. We can't lose this one. Just do it." The second thing was to add a clause to say the offer would lapse at 5pm. It was then about 3.30pm. I asked whether I could send the telex but he told me in no uncertain terms that it must not be sent until 4.45pm. For the next hour and a quarter, I must have smoked ten cigarettes and bitten off all my nails. At 4.45pm, I pressed the telex machine and the offer was sent.

Surprise? At 4.55pm, John Hill (the CEO of Hongkong Bank in Singapore) replied by telex: "John. Re your telex of 4.46 pm today, offer accepted, subject to contract to be completed this evening. Rgds. John." Mission accomplished. We had the 16.6% and a total of 50% to equal the Ongs. I called Sir YK to break the news.

He was calm and controlled. I was floored by his reply: "John, thank you for your hard work. But I already knew. You see, Michael Sandberg and I actually agreed the deal at about three o'clock earlier today."

I was totally deflated and asked why he did not tell me. His answer was that he was afraid we would leak the information but he had to leave me to deal with John Hill because the deal was under our Singapore jurisdiction. I just sighed. Later I called John Hill and he told me a similar story as related to him by Sandberg. I went down to the Singapore Cricket Club, not sure whether to celebrate or drown my frustration. Nick Carp appeared and joined me over drinks for reasons that neither of us could really pinpoint, nor did we really bother to.

On reflection, everyone should have been happy. We all saw the master at work!

Stories, books and articles have been told and written on Sir YK Pao and his exploits. There is not much need for me to say any more. I cannot even try to suggest that I am any form of authority on such a great man. That would be too presumptuous of me. However, one thing is for certain. Sir YK was a rare genius within the realms of his own pursuits. To me, it seemed these talents were born in the man.

He had an incredible knack of business timing. He knew exactly when to build ships, when to come ashore, when to turn his landed property investments back to the ocean again. Each time he made those decisions, he picked the perfect time.

Sir YK was the only person to call me "young man" when I was already this side of 40. He constantly chided me on my smoking. He did not seem to mind my cheeky humour and my leaning towards the unorthodox, so long as I took my work and my health seriously. He was tough but fair. He would give clear instructions and set deadlines. Then he would leave you alone to the task without bothering you in the interim. I knew however that I must deliver the goods on time and with good quality. If I failed just once, the trust might no longer be there.

Sir YK was a master at boardroom play. Having watched him at close quarters, I would not like to be on his opposing side. Even though I only served him for a few short years, it was a huge privilege during which time I learnt an awful lot.

Much of what I learnt was from general observation of how Sir YK conducted himself in business and the tactics he used in dealing with people and situations. It is not easy to pinpoint actual examples. It will suffice to mention a few of the basic principles that he seemed to employ. Firstly, it was preferable to receive an offer rather than make one; delay decisions for as long as possible, as additional information may come to hand in the duration; once decisions are made, go for broke; and believe in one's own assessment of a solution regardless of the size of the transaction. These appeared to be the basics, but then the final effectiveness would depend on deft execution which separated the men from the boys. It was Sir YK's expert handling and his superb sense of timing that made him what he was.

When Sir YK passed away, Peter asked me to coordinate all the correspondence and condolences received. Until it happened, I had no idea what this meant. Letters, telegrammes, cards and telexes came in the thousands. These came from dignitaries all over the world – from heads of state, prime ministers and presidents, captains of global industries, academic laureates, senior businessmen, chairmen and CEOs, and people of the highest standings from just about every walk of life in every developed country on the planet. He was a globally respected figure.

His funeral entailed the use of several specially decorated blocked-off floors at the Hong Kong Funeral Parlour, with full CCTV facilities. There were thousands of attendees and mourners. Special personnel had to be at hand to act as ushers and to keep order, dignity and decorum.

The funeral service was a solemn affair. The family for some reason decided to entrust me with the onerous role of being the master of ceremonies, conducted bilingually in both English and Cantonese. In recognition of the solemnity and importance of the occasion, my nerves were consciously suppressed as best I could to ensure that things went without a hitch. Looking at the front four rows seated before me, I observed at least eight heads of state, perhaps 60% of the money in Hong Kong and many other luminaries. I shuddered.

In the midst of discharging my responsibility, I somehow managed to dispel stage fright. Sir YK would have expected that from me. My mind was dominated by the honour bestowed on me to have been chosen by the family to stand there... to send off this great man.

*"Wharf had invested S$3.5 million... and walked away with
S$61... a capital gain of 16 times PE"*

19

THE SALE (1982-83)

Construction of the container warehouse was completed. Wharf held 50% of the company and had management control. We might have held a strong hand, but the joint venture was far from harmonious. Under the old regime, at least the Ongs could trace back to the spirit behind the joint venture and argued on the basis of the original intentions behind the drafting of the agreements. With the new regime effectively under Peter Woo, we had the convenience of ignoring what had taken place in the past, and simply kept the relationship going in strict accordance with the shareholders and management agreements to the letter. Inevitable confrontation was on the cards despite outward courtesy shown by both sides. It was only a matter of time.

McLuskie had left Wharf a short time after the takeover. Peter Woo took full charge without any opposition, supported by Gonzaga Li. As for Singapore and Asean business, I was often consulted, a far cry from the former regime. Coordination with Hong Kong was closer and it was teamwork all round with nobody flying off on a tangent.

Sir YK came into my office in Singapore and noticed a framed calligraphy of a single Chinese character hanging behind my desk. He asked whether I put in practice the meaning of the character. My reply was "I've had to in the last several years to keep my sanity, Sir." He nodded and I took it that he understood my sentiment. The character was 忍 meaning "patience", "endurance" or "sufferance".

Perhaps my period of enforced patience and endurance might be coming to an end, I thought. The Ong/Wharf differences gave me cause to believe that one party had to buy out the other. They just could not continue to co-exist. There were too many clashes in terms of culture, basic approach to business, the question of patience, and contrasting beliefs in systematic approach as against gut feel.

I did not have to wait too long. We just sat tight and waited for the Ongs to make the first move. I had learned from Sir YK that it was always preferable to respond to a proposition than to instigate one. Their first interludes came in the form of casual chats between Ong Choo Eng and I. We were just shadow-boxing with each other, I guess. Choo Eng was the project manager of our construction projects and he had a strong influence over the local workforce, a role not too dissimilar to that of a comprador as I knew it. He was my golfing mate and we got on really well and were fond of each other. Yet we both knew where our loyalties lay.

Choo Eng was not yet committed to making an offer, yet I felt there would be no smoke without fire. A couple of months passed and whilst there was a great deal of "political posturing" from both sides, we remained patient and kept all our options open. We were actually prepared to move the discussions along if they wished, but thought it best to keep things close to our chest and hold the trumps. I did not know whether Peter was a buyer or a seller, but I suspected that perhaps Peter did not know that himself either.

The offer eventually came in the form of a written bid for all our shares, presented by merchant bankers on their behalf. We entrusted our work to Richard Orders of Baring Brothers. Richard was a good cricketing friend of mine and an extremely capable banker with high technical skills.

The offer was rejected as a matter of negotiating posture. However we genuinely felt that the financial consideration put up by them was only just a notch up from being derisory. They only gave value to the property's market value and ignored over seven years of management efforts, the design of the Wharf-invented container warehouse technology, and the successful marketing by the Wharf executives that had filled all three blocks to virtual full occupancy. Further, in any acquisition by one party to take out the other, there must always be a premium for control.

We wanted to flush out what they were really after. We were not too worried whether we were either buyers or sellers so long as we secured the best deal. We gave them the litmus and succeeded in drawing out the real intentions. They were buyers. A meeting in the presence of our respective merchant bankers was arranged to take place in Singapore.

The bilateral took place in their bankers' office. It was a long-winded process, too painful to relate in detail. It suffices to say that what began as a courteous exchange of guarded niceties soon degenerated to ruthless haggling on principles and the values attributable to individual items. Their wish to acquire our shares was not wavering, and we simply pressed for the highest possible price. The deal had to be closed right then and there and signed off. We could not afford to allow the momentum to slip. In the process, I detected a tinge of Sir YK in Peter's boardroom play.

The transaction took all of four hours to be concluded. The Ongs would buy all our shares for S$61 million, with completion in two months together with orderly management takeover.

Wharf had invested a mere S$3.5 million some eight years earlier, funded the development at seven times gearing from bank borrowings, completed the construction, marketed and filled occupancy in all three blocks, repaid the majority of the bank loans and then walked away with S$61 million – a capital gain of S$56 million or 16 times PE in eight years. Some deal for any corporate!

Once this transaction was completed, the joint venture came to an end. Singapore Warehouse became a wholly-owned asset of the Ong family and they could do what they liked with it. Ong Choo Eng became Managing Director and I gave him all the help he needed during the handover process. He had been my good friend and colleague for eight years and there was every reason we should have remained so despite our parting of ways. Mr. Ong senior appeared in a better mood and his previous hostility faded away. The company organized a wonderful banquet to send me off, attended by most of the staff and board directors. That left me in no doubt that they valued my contribution and camaraderie. They were a group of friends I would miss.

Peter wanted to repatriate me once I came off Singapore Warehouse. He said there were important things to do in Hong Kong. However, there were other issues in my mind, not least the project in Bangkok and a few smaller opportunities in Johor Bahru across the causeway from Singapore. It would be far more convenient to cover these from Singapore than from Hong Kong. After I explained this to Peter, he agreed to consider my views.

My life had always been affected by fortuitous events. It happened again. Wharf had for some time invested in the ownership of hotels, some in Hong Kong and others in Singapore, the Philippines, Bangkok and Vietnam. From the Jardines days, Wharf's management had entrusted hotel management to the Peninsula Group under the Hong Kong & Shanghai Hotels banner. That had remained the pattern which nobody had questioned until the new regime came into being.

Wharf contended that certain measures conducted by the hotel management were perhaps improper. Allegations were made which required us to delve into detailed fact-finding. Severe discomfort between the two groups was being felt. Whilst all this was taking place in Hong Kong, it would be in Wharf's interest if I were to remain in Singapore to keep an eye on the Marco Polo which was considered the flagship of the Wharf hotels, and it was also a Singapore listed company. My repatriation was thus postponed.

One thing led to another. Peter had done a transaction with Sino Land and Hongkong Land in a three-way joint venture in Singapore called Gordon Land and I was appointed to the board. The large project in Bangkok gathered momentum and I was deeply immersed in that. The view was to move this forward quickly as Wharf could not afford to leave me locked in this project any longer than necessary. I was instructed to prepare a detailed presentation of the project to seek Sir YK's blessing and then place it before the Wharf board.

Sir YK was abroad when I arrived for the management meeting in Hong Kong. Peter and I went through the salient points and we were ready. The next morning, we learned that Sir YK had apparently returned via Bangkok. When we greeted him, he vaguely commented that Bangkok looked dusty and disorganized to him. Ever sensitive to Sir YK's moods, Peter and I thought it wiser to defer the Bangkok presentation until a more opportune time. I recall making the cheeky remark, "OK. Let's wait till the dust settles in Bangkok!"

We held off for a more favourable day. However, that day never came because even before the "dust settled", another developer went along and the mega development started construction without us. We had put in a tremendous amount of time and effort yet it did not bother us too much. We had to be philosophical about these things. It was never wise to chase deals. There would always be other opportunities around the corner. In addition, what we had learnt about Thailand would no doubt stand us in good stead sometime in the future.

I was to remain in Singapore at a time when my first marriage broke up. This situation had been brewing for quite a while, at least as it seemed to me. Gloria and I were married when we were both very young and we were just two young people in love. As time went by, our respective values changed. I was driven by my career ambitions and she maintained that the family and the children came first. Neither value was wrong, but under pressure, one thing had to give way to the other at times. This state of affairs was all too common in the modern world. In my case admittedly, I spent weekends at cricket or golf and also travelled extensively for business reasons. Business requirements demanded regular attendance at dinners and cocktails which Gloria did not enjoy and soon she declined attendance more frequently than not. I got used to the idea of going to these functions on my own to the extent that my friends and associates often wondered where my wife was. The fact that expatriate wives found it difficult to secure work permits to work in Singapore probably contributed to the problem as there was no teaching job to keep Gloria occupied.

To be fair, Gloria was a good wife and mother. No one could accuse her of being otherwise. It was just a case of two people drifting apart with opposing values and priorities. In retrospect, our characters were really chalk and cheese. I was every inch the flamboyant extrovert, and she was the quiet introverted homely being. My life had evolved but she had remained the same girl I married almost two decades earlier when we were only in our early 20s. The lack of mutual compromise brought the relationship under strain and when I became involved in an affair with another woman, the marriage came to an inevitable end even though that extra-marital relationship did not last the test of time. In my opinion, we were both at fault to different degrees although the direct cause of the final break-up was visibly mine.

"She was not Mediterranean, but had actually a South Pacific Polynesian look"

20

GAIL

Adjustment to the life of a bachelor took some getting used to. I moved into an apartment on my own; something I had not experienced since my Birmingham days. Ironically, this did not disturb my work output at all. If anything, I put my heart and soul into the office and my productivity actually increased. I took refuge by focusing on work to the exclusion of personal problems.

When off work, there was little point sitting alone in my apartment and moping. It seemed sensible to keep myself occupied and socialize at clubs and mix around with friends. Obviously, this had its attendant drinking which was expected. As time went on, I realized that a surfeit of food and drink could not be perpetuated, and a conscious effort had to be made to scale down or risk a burnout by over-indulgence.

On one particular evening, I was having a pleasant drink with my close friends Michael de Kretser and Beth Kennedy. They were committed to a social gathering later that evening at the Singapore Polo Club and asked me to join them, suggesting they had an American lady to introduce since I was not attached to anyone at that stage of my life. I did not really take the meeting of the American girl seriously but reasoned that some solids in my system would not be out of place and Beth and Michael were hilarious company anyway.

At the Polo Club bar, the American lady was absorbed in deep conversation with a mutual friend, which was just as well. I would rather have a quiet drink prior to dinner. My hosts were then joined by a lady friend who appeared quite detached. She stayed at the bar when others were scattered. When we talked, I had an inkling that she might have thought I was brash. After dinner, I invited my hosts to the Marco Polo Club. Most were game but the lady declined.

To my surprise, she did come to the Club later. Her name was Gail. I could not make out her nationality but thought her mysterious. Her appearance looked to me Mediterranean, yet she did not speak with an Italian nor Greek accent. Her English, if at all slanted, was mild probably because she had been anglicized in the English-dominated expatriate community in Singapore. She was probably equally curious about my ethnic background as well.

I called her the following morning but she sounded short and blunt. I took her out of my mind. In the afternoon, she called and politely said she should thank me out of courtesy for her enjoyable time at the Club. I intimated I would call her soon. When we had a simple Chinese dinner in Johor Bahru a couple of evenings later, I found her relaxed and gracious company. She had a great sense of humour. The evening also dispelled any idea that she might have thought ill of me. The answer to my puzzle was also revealed. Gail was in fact a New Zealander from the Bay of Islands with a Pakeha (or European) father and a Maori mother. That mixture gave her the dark hair and olive skin, and her sharp features were obviously from her dad. She was not Mediterranean at all, but had actually a South Pacific Polynesian look. To me, she was an attractive specimen of a woman.

The rest is history. Within a week, she had agreed to become my wife and has remained my best companion for over 30 years. She has been my joy, my strength and my inspiration. There can be no man more fortunate than I. Gail has brought domestic stability back to my life, returning me to a semblance of mental and physical equilibrium, thus putting an end to my brief but somewhat unruly interlude as a bachelor.

My move to Singapore in 1972 was intended for perhaps three years. By the time we left for Hong Kong, I had stayed over 14 years. By then, I was fully entrenched into the Singapore way of life; qualified as a Permanent Resident; installed as a member of leading clubs and well established in the corporate circles and society at large.

Wharf's demand for my return finally happened when I was made aware that continual stay in Singapore would not be in the interest of my career. I had to agree even though I was a little wary of how the family would settle in Hong Kong.

After a couple of years of dispute which involved a legal tussle, the Hong Kong & Shanghai Hotels decided to settle out of court by way of termination of the contract for the Peninsula Group to manage Wharf-owned hotels. This meant we had to assume management at a moment's notice. Wharf had anticipated this outcome and had already formed Marco Polo International. Key positions were filled by recruits wrenched from other leading hotel groups but although this had been done, to leave the new company without "leadership" would be to invite disaster. Wharf decided that a Wharf ethos had to be inculcated and our own culture developed. This task was left to the "old" hands of Wharf. Gonzaga Li was made President and I was appointed Director of Operations.

I initially drew debilitating remarks from the "professional" hoteliers such as the vice-presidents and the general managers. They quite rightly claimed superior knowledge of the trade, even at times questioning my authority. To me, management was management and there is no rocket science attached. Once the essential principles of management are understood, it would not matter whether it was hotels or warehousing or transport or retail that had to be controlled. It is all to do with methodology, discipline and most importantly man management. I decided to take regular physical checks and inspections in rooms, public areas, back of house and F&B outlets. These activities acquainted me with the physical realities so that I would not be blinded by the spin and excuses forwarded by the senior staff.

I took them on. I told them that my role was to observe through the customers' eyes and my criticisms had to be corrected by the vice-presidents of any particular discipline as that was not my job but theirs. They had to put things right. In the following year, I gave them constant critique but did not interfere in the manner in which they tackled the problems. They were just expected to produce results. We ended the year with excellent results and slowly developed a good reputation as a hotel management company.

Every hotelier almost without exception believes that he or she is an artist. I played to their ego and they responded with their best foot forward. The group grew in maturity and soon developed its own culture. I was then released to return to the Wharf corporate HQ. When the new president was recruited to take over the hotel group, the Wharf ethos in the hotel management had already been assured.

My next job was to lead the transport division. The portfolio included Hong Kong icons like the 'Star' Ferry, the Hong Kong Tramways and the Cross Harbour Tunnel with also the Western Harbour Tunnel close to completion. I had held many positions within the Wharf Group, but none of the others was more trying and less financially rewarding than the transport division.

The job itself was hugely complex. Hurdles and landmines were everywhere in the form of government regulatory obstacles. There were unions, political lobby groups and the need to appease the fare-paying public. Decision making was always shackled by these negative forces, yet the division's annual revenue from the government-approved ferry and tram fares were minuscule in terms of percentage contribution to the Wharf bottom line.

I had always regarded it to be the height of disproportionate injustice for the position of the head of transport to be placed so low by the group management. The limit on the fundamental financial rewards of the division head was justified by group management under the guise that the division did not offer sufficient contribution to group profit. To me, this did not make good sense as the man did not ask to be there and he simply could not make miracles in the face of realistic limits stipulated by the government. The man who did this job consequently never got the recognition he deserved. It had to be the most absurd criterion to judge a man's performance in a large organization!

Five of the strangest bedfellows came together to form a joint venture called the Hong Kong Cable Communications (HKCC) to bid for the first cable television franchise offered in Hong Kong. It could be argued that the five partners would bring a vast array of expertise to the party, yet one could detect even at an early stage that every member had its own self-interest at heart. A large group of Wharf executives was deployed there and I was one of them with the portfolio of planning the network build.

Amidst an atmosphere of constant bickering amongst the partners, we went ahead. Most were prepared to put their differences aside pro tem. HKCC somehow managed to surprise all by successfully warding off the strong competition. The cable TV franchise was ours.

Planning is always easier than execution. With the project already in hand, the bickering resumed to an extent that resembled a Roman Senate in the days prior to the fall of their empire. Disagreements were not just between opposing sides, but there were at times five different views on a single issue. The brevity in which I recount the atmosphere then understates the pain felt by those concerned. Although Wharf had voted to preserve unity right to the end, the board collapsed the joint venture by the majority vote of 4 to 1. Discussions with the government resulted in an announcement that HKCC had withdrawn from the cable TV project by mutual consent.

It was a massive disappointment to the industry, to the government, to the expectant viewing public, and most of all to Wharf. The government did not re-offer the franchise pending a comprehensive re-think.

The surviving cable team led by the never-say-die Stephen Ng stuck to the task relentlessly like a Rottweiler and eventually convinced government to award the franchise unilaterally to Wharf. I played no part as I had already been re-assigned to the newly formed Property Development Group led by Gonzaga Li.

This property development unit had a brief to establish quickly an arm specializing in the business of property trading as opposed to long-term investment, a discipline which had been the core bread and butter of the Wharf Group. Strangely, property trading had hitherto been neglected. A small group of Gonzaga, Florence Chan and I formed a nucleus which gathered gradual momentum. This was the seed of the business Wheelock Properties would inherit at a later date under Ray Tse.

I was moved again to the bid team for Container Terminal #8 at the Kwai Chung Container Port. The team which had been assembled had all the disciplines required, with a civil engineer, a financial accountant, and various support units seconded from Wharf. We hired specialist professionals such as Halcrow and MVA traffic engineers. We did a good job but failed to win the bid.

I kept moving from portfolio to portfolio, all the time gaining more exposure and wider experience. By the end of this merry-go-round, there was no longer any part of the Wharf group in which I had not been involved.

"You deserve that, darling. It needed that push, didn't it? Isn't it about time?"

21

MAIN BOARD

As my move from Singapore to Hong Kong was so sudden, I remained on Singapore payroll for some time. This was done to avoid complications on my emoluments and tax etc. Thus I was working in Hong Kong as an expatriate. As I was still technically residing in Singapore, it would not be convenient to stay in private accommodations in Hong Kong as a visitor. This meant that I had to reside for the time being in a hotel until officially relocated. This became a severe inconvenience when Gail and the children arrived. To reside in a hotel with a young family was far from ideal, even though we had a unit of two suites and an extra bathroom for use as a mini-kitchen with a microwave so that we could at least rustle up simple meals for the children instead of total reliance on the hotel room service menu.

The residential awkwardness was something we could tolerate, but the more disturbing factor was my earnings which were clearly inadequate for our needs. In 1972, when I was transferred to Singapore, the terms were that I would be paid in Singapore dollars at the then prevailing exchange rate of HK$1.95 to S$1. It was rounded off to HK$2 to S$1 for simpler calculation. In the 14 years in Singapore, all adjustments, annual or otherwise, were done in Singapore currency. In 1981, there was a change of regime from Jardines to Pao. When I was repatriated, as explained above, I remained under the Singapore payroll for the rest of the financial year. When the time came for me to come under Hong Kong employment conditions again, I was rudely told that I would be paid in Hong Kong dollars which I had assumed would be in accordance with the original exchange rate of HK$2 to S$1. How wrong I was! Human Resources told me that I would be remunerated at the then prevailing exchange rate of HK$4.30 to S$1. This meant that my monthly salary would be effectively slashed by more than half! Was it a case of top management not knowing what Human Resources was doing? To me, whoever took this decision was of no interest to me. What mattered was that my income had been cut by more than half, to an extent that the move had set me back for years. It was certainly not the type of incentive that one would expect for an executive rattled up as being on the ascendancy.

Naturally I was thoroughly agitated by this, but as there was heavy pressure at work, I concentrated on my job rather than moping over the emoluments issue. However, I knew then that I must be on the lookout for alternative employment opportunities as we could not continue to live from hand to mouth over the longer term. I had always been a fiercely loyal person however I was treated. I reasoned that so long as I received a salary, I would be duty-bound to give all that I had to the job. If one was unhappy, there was always the exit door. The principle was: if you don't like it, then leave. I held the belief that management should know what was right and what was wrong. At least, they ought to.

Gail and I were blissfully happy on the domestic front which compensated for the inadequacy of my income to an extent. Being sociable people, we made many friends. Living in the thick of Harbour City, there were numerous F&B outlets to try out and entertainment was never too far away. At the weekends, the whole family would make for the New Territories or more specifically the Clearwater Bay Golf & Country Club, which had many facilities suitable for young children. We also put the girls into tennis lessons and I spent many hours of enjoyment with them on court.

Both girls were slotted nicely into Beacon Hill, a primary school run by the English Schools Foundation. Things had settled and Gail's job with Keith MacGregor at Cameraman did help a little with the aggregate family income. We made do but without much to spare.

The advertising legend of Singapore, Ian Batey, was planning the expansion of his business reach to Hong Kong in both advertising and public relations. Both these disciplines had been massively successful in Singapore including the well-branded "Singapore Girl" series for Singapore Airlines. The Batey Group had already earmarked the heads for both the advertising and PR arms for Hong Kong, but Ian felt they both needed leadership by a seasoned person established in the commercial circles of Hong Kong and one who had a conceptual flair in the communication field. I was thought to be just that man.

Over a friendly dinner between Ian and Caroline Batey with Gail and I, the seed was sown. I was to join the Batey Group, act as Managing Director and Deputy Chairman of Batey Hong Kong with 50% of the Hong Kong company shareholdings. The plan included a push into China when the timing was right. The deal looked exciting and I relished the challenge. Having met the designated heads of Hong Kong advertising and PR, we drew up the agreements and these were duly signed and attested and my shares were fully paid up.

My resignation was submitted to Peter Woo. What transpired thereafter was pandemonium. Gonzaga and Peter took turns to speak with me. I had no intention of withdrawing my resignation. I did not mention too much about seeking another career, and merely suggested that I was perhaps getting stale in the same company and needed a change. Persuasive language was used, such as questioning my loyalty and even touting the line that I should have been mindful of being the third generation of Hungs in Wharf. Even Sir YK had a go at me. It was virtual torture and I was not even near Guantanamo Bay! Finally I had to reveal to Peter that it was the inequitable exchange rate issue that had forced me to look outside the group to Batey.

Peter was visibly sympathetic but suggested that I should have aired my grievances personally to him to prevent it from escalating to the level that I had to resign. I appreciated Peter's gesture. He told me they would call me for more discussions the next morning.

The new package offered to me was staggeringly attractive. However, the change to amazing generosity did seem to be an admission of the previous injustice. I did not enjoy this sinister thought in my mind and thought I should have been more gracious in my sentiments. In retrospect, the fact that this had happened was a slip in governance in corporate coordination. It was an anomaly that should not have happened. In the context of this, I have to give full credit to Peter for taking the decision to put things right without delay. The Chairman's attitude augured well for the future as it showed the group's recognition of the contribution of its more promising executives and top management's willingness to correct mistakes for the sake of improving the group as a whole. The attractive package came as such a surprise that I needed time to reflect and to discuss with Gail. I told them that I would respond as soon as I could.

The new package indicated that my salary would be increased four-fold; my appointment to the Wharf main board would be immediate; my bonus would be based against the new salary at year end; my accommodation would be upgraded to a house on the Peak; and I was to be awarded meaningful share options. Apart from pecuniary and fringe benefits which were enticing, my ego was also tickled. Of course the first thing to do was to speak with Gail. Typical of her, Gail said "You deserve that, darling! It needed that little push, didn't it? Isn't it about time?"

Gail has always been a frightfully honest straight-shooter. She calls a spade a spade and never minces her words. This could be a little off-putting to someone who did not know her well, but it is really a likeable trait as you always know where you stand with her – always black or white and rarely grey. She would not take nonsense from anyone nor would she expect others to tolerate insincerity from herself. She has immense strength of character and is thoroughly streetwise in everything she tackles. Yet underneath it all, she has a soft and kind heart and always empathizes with the feelings of her fellow human beings. I have learnt a great deal from her over the years.

To curb my excitement, Gail reminded me that before I could firm up my acceptance of the new Wharf offer, there was an absolute need to speak face-to-face with Ian Batey. After all, my agreement with Ian had already been sealed and dusted. I gave Peter my verbal acceptance, conditional upon release from my obligations by Ian Batey. Peter gave me compassionate leave of absence and I went to Singapore with Gail to meet Ian.

By the time I saw Ian, he had already a sixth-sense feeling that some circumstances had changed. My quandary was met with complete understanding and sympathy. Being a gentleman and a true friend, Ian actually advised me that Wharf's offer was too good to refuse. He was prepared to tear up the agreement as if it had never happened and at the same time undertook to return every cent that I had paid for the shares. Ian was of course a businessman and he might have seen that his cooperation would put him in high regard with Peter. This did happen. Soon the Batey Group was engaged as the designer of the logo for Marco Polo International Hotels.

With the Batey affair behind me, I settled down as a main board director of Wharf Holdings. It was the end of 1990 and my eldest daughter Lesley was getting married in England in November. Gail could not travel as she was seven months pregnant. I set off to England with Katish and Natasha. They were 12 and eight respectively at that time.

"You should know that the moment you put dollar signs in front of numbers, mathematics start to make sense"

22

FINANCE DIRECTOR

The journey to England was the first overseas trip that I had made with the girls on my own. It was also their first trip away from Gail. Excitement dominated their minds as they were looking forward to visiting England for the first time. This lasted until the first nightfall when we were dining in London. Katish remained in perfect control, but Natasha began to pine for mother. Tears fell on her pizza and it took the combined efforts of Katish and I to pacify her. It took a good cry to get things out of her system and she was fine for the remainder of her trip.

I was very keen to have the girls well presented at the wedding. Our good friend Maria Melville came to the rescue. She just took the girls off my hands and off they went to Harrods. A couple of hours later, they returned, both fitted with lovely dresses, and we were ready to travel north the next day.

Despite my reasonably good knowledge of English roads, there were the occasional missed turnings as I had not driven to the wedding destination before. We eventually reached Flookburgh in Cumbria by late afternoon and checked into the small hotel that Lesley had booked to accommodate all the overseas guests. I was almost immediately called to attend the final wedding rehearsal and left the two girls under the care of Tracey's husband Robin. Tracey had to go with me since she was the matron of honour. When we returned to the hotel, I found Robin at the snooker table but to my surprise, Katish and Natasha were happily dining with my former wife Gloria who had a way with children. They looked very comfortable sitting together there.

We retired to our room and Katish wanted to call Gail and I obliged. She spoke with Gail and then passed the telephone over to Natasha. Suddenly I overheard, "Mummy, I don't know why Dad is divorced from Gloria? She's ever so nice!" I grabbed the phone and heard the mocking remark from Gail, something to the effect of whether I was having a happy reunion! Innocent children would say what went on in their little heads, but then, why ever not?

It was a cold and overcast November day in the Lake District of England. Lesley and I arrived at St. John the Baptist Church in freezing wind in a vintage car that leaked. Lesley wore a lightweight wedding dress and she must have felt the bitter cold. The ceremony went without a hitch and I had gained a son-in-law in Andrew Tattersall. The wedding banquet was a happy occasion and it was also the first time that many relatives had met Katish and Natasha. Thanks to Maria, the girls were beautifully turned out and behaved politely throughout, yet not at all shy or inhibited. They were their natural selves. I was so proud of them and they were, in my pink-spectacled eyes, the belles of the evening and I knew that would have pleased Gail.

On return to Hong Kong, I saw clearly where Wharf was heading. They say "cometh the hour, cometh the man". Peter was very likely the right man heading up Wharf at that time. Whilst Sir YK was undoubtedly the visionary who engineered the acquisition of an empire through the deft handling of an expert entrepreneur, what he had left was a group so large that it required systematic and methodical top management. It was no longer possible to manage such a vast and diverse business through gut feel alone.

Having been trained in modern methods of management through Columbia Business School in New York and Chase Manhattan Bank, Peter was well equipped to manage a large group by reliance on modern management methods, systems and vision. It may just be my personal opinion, but I sincerely believe that whilst Sir YK was the correct leader in his time, Peter was perhaps even better suited to run a huge conglomerate.

Sir YK and Peter were products of different generations. Sir YK grew up in a world where Hong Kong was transforming itself from a manufacturing-based commercial society to a service-based economy. It was early days in that equation and the climate was one of hardship and the need to fight through tough barriers. Sir YK was a master in that environment. By the time Peter took over the corporate empire of Wharf, Hong Kong had already been transformed into a commercial centre of some sophistication. Corporate governance was the call of the day, and the regulatory regime had begun to become a necessary administrative requirement as demanded by the stock exchange, and later accentuated substantially by the Securities and Futures Commission.

Due to the high-profile recognition commanded by Sir YK not only in Hong Kong, but internationally, imagine the quandary Peter must have found himself in: having to uphold the family traditions, being compared to Sir YK and yet having to withstand the pressure of running a huge group professionally and successfully. He had to be his own man and have the singleness of mind to focus on what he must do. He did that extremely well.

Peter had ideas in store for me. He felt the share price of Wharf did not reflect its true value. In his estimation, the Group's assets and earnings stream deserved higher recognition. He wanted to use all my efforts to drive up the share price and threw the challenge at me. Having been personally involved in every operating division, I held a big advantage because I knew the fundamental support each division would give to

the Group financially. It was a case of promoting the operating divisions'
combined power so that the aggregate would substantially lift the share
price of the parent Wharf.

There was nothing I liked better than a dare. OK then, let's get on
with it.

To give me the necessary credentials, I was appointed Wharf's Finance
Director. This brought an amusing conversation between my mother and
I when she called me from London. "John, what's this I hear from my
sisters in Hong Kong that you've been made Finance Director? That can't
be true because you can't even add one and one together."

"It's absolutely true, Mom, but don't be too surprised. A Finance
Director doesn't have to add one and one. Others do that for you.
Besides, you should know that the moment you put dollar signs in front
of numbers, mathematics start to make sense to me."

"As usual John, you're impossible – always talking nonsense!"

The challenge started in earnest. The Wharf share stood at $6.95. The
first step was to digest the annual reports for the previous 10 years to
bring myself up to speed, then highlight the strengths against weaknesses,
and then lift out the success stories. I saw that we had to play up the rental
income stream of Harbour City and how that would be substantially
increased in the forthcoming years as a result of the redevelopment of
the residential blocks into commercial and retail. These elements formed
the foundation upon which to raise expectations. People were attracted
to equity on future potential of the group rather than past history. This
was the line to take.

My career really started to move with this job that fitted me like a
glove. It was good news all round. My son was born on 11th January
1991. We named him Sean and he also carried the names of Walter and
Francis after his two grandfathers. After 27 years since Lesley and a total
of five daughters, I finally had a son. The few years after Sean came into
the world were the most gratifying period of my life. One good thing

followed another as if I was unstoppable. It made Gail and I feel, with some justification, that Sean was perhaps our lucky mascot!

I delved deep into the world of securities analysts and fund managers. A close rapport was established with them. They knew they could get straight answers from me. I began to court members of the business media, particularly the leading business editors of major newspapers and journals in both the English and Chinese languages. High-quality PR consultants were hired to tap investor feedback and we made improvements in our operations in response. It was in this process that I became very close to the seasoned investor relations (IR) professional Anne Forrest who was to be my confidante and sounding board for years to come.

It entailed extreme hard work and dedication. I had to be prepared for long hours wining and dining people in the evenings and at times over weekends. In all these sessions, honesty and transparency were the expected demands and the upshot was the establishment of deep trust which would stand me in good stead towards the enhancement of my IR efforts. There was no gain without pain.

We saw tangible evidence that these efforts were beginning to pay dividends. The share price began to rise.

Katish started boarding school soon after Sean was born. She was put into Geelong Grammar in Australia. Gail and I decided to take a holiday that summer to the United States and to use that opportunity to see Phoebe who was then residing with my brother Michael in Seattle. We were bothered by the need to leave Sean behind as he was far too young to endure a trip that would involve frequent city-hopping in a faraway land. However, there was really no other sensible choice.

We flew to Los Angeles with Natasha in tow. We were to wait for Katish to join us from Melbourne the following day.

I sat on the floor with my back leaning against the bed in our hotel room. Gail and Natasha were resting on the bed. We were on the 18th floor of the Sheraton LAX near the airport and we were all watching the movie *The Prince of Tides*. I always hated to be disturbed when watching a film and commented, "Tasha, can you please stop shaking the bed!" A few seconds later, I repeated, "Stop shaking will you, please."

"I didn't shake the bed, Dad," she protested. The tremors grew in intensity. "John, don't blame her! It's a bloody earthquake!" Gail shouted. We ran together and stood arm in arm under the doorway to the bathroom. The tremors seemed to last an eternity and I tried to calm the girls. The shaking finally stopped. What felt like five to six minutes to me was later reported to have lasted only 55 seconds! The shake recorded 6.9 on the Richter scale from the epicentre at a place called Joshua Tree, quite a distance from us but located near Orange County or Disneyland.

We obeyed the hotel PA announcement to move to the ground floor lobby. It was incredible to observe what people would bring with them under emergency conditions. The only things I took with me were our passports, the credit cards and our money. It amused me that some old ladies came down with fur coats on even though it was July. The Japanese men all carried their numerous cameras, and most of the American locals came down with only their car keys, ready to make a quick drive away from the threat of disaster.

After returning to the room, an aftershock of almost the same severity hit us. We tried to stand together again under the doorway, but by then Gail had already sneaked under the vanity counter in the bathroom, exactly where she should not be. I could not suppress a giggle, but then I heard a voice – "Please God, protect us. I have my baby son in Hong Kong." The voice came from under the vanity counter.

Katish arrived the next day. The original itinerary was San Francisco after LA, but Gail was certainly not keeping that schedule. She would not go deeper into the seismic fault with the reputation of San Francisco. We re-worked our itinerary and made for Seattle instead, then to Denver, down to Texas and would then make our way back to San Francisco. The re-schedule meant that our well-planned holiday had been comprehensively thrown out of sync. What followed was catch-up all the way.

We were not about to allow something like an earthquake to diminish our enjoyment of the trip as a whole. Phoebe was in good spirits and Michael showed me Seattle with its huge brands of Boeing, Starbucks and Microsoft. Denver was superb where we stayed with my good friend Bill Johnson, CEO of Scientific Atlanta, in his beautiful house on Red Mountain. Then we went down to Texas to see our friend Barbara in Decatur where she had her equine ranch before bringing the girls to Disneyland.

Orange County was absolutely overbooked. We were lucky to secure two double rooms at the Pan Pacific. After we were shown to our rooms, Katish remarked "Dad. Is this all we are getting? These rooms are so simple and ordinary." As one involved in hotels, I was nearly always upgraded to top suites and the girls took that as the expected norm. Not this time, I'm afraid!

When we eventually got into San Francisco, we had the chance to meet up with my father Walter's sister, Auntie Phyllis and her husband Albert. It was nice that Gail could meet her. At Fisherman's Wharf, I bought a keyring that I could not resist as it had a message on it which read "Why can't I be rich instead of being well hung?" How could I possibly pass up such a purchase with a surname like mine? The keyring is still with me.

Some years after retiring from active cricket, I was invited to assume the presidency of the Hong Kong Cricket Association, the national body that governed the game in Hong Kong. For the love of the game, I agreed to the challenge. Once installed as President, amongst the first things I did was to support the promotion of the International Cricket Sixes Tournament as a unique showpiece for cricket annually. The idea was untried and anyone backing it would have to be willing to take a short-term financial risk. I did however witness the tremendous success of the

Hong Kong Rugby Sevens and thought that if rugby could do it, why not cricket?

What we needed were two cricket fanatics who also had clout in leading corporations to come up with the sponsorship money and each take a financial gamble. It was not a huge amount of money involved, but whatever the sum, it could all be lost. I tracked down Rod Eddington, Managing Director of Cathay Pacific Airways, and twisted his arm. The Cathay Pacific/Wharf Holdings International Cricket Sixes was thus inaugurated and staged for the first time in 1992. Today, the annual event is acknowledged to be the best of its kind in the world; perhaps not in terms of financial success, but the Sixes has at least emulated the Rugby Sevens in becoming the top tournament of its kind in the international tour circuit. For this, Hong Kong should be proud of the two sports of rugby and cricket.

We also accelerated local participation by introducing cricket to Chinese schools through the use of plastic bats and tennis balls. A school cricket gala was sponsored by the HKCA in 1993 which saw the inclusion of cricket as an adapted sport by 61 local schools. This was certainly a breakthrough. Two New Zealand professionals were employed by the HKCA, and one of those was David Trist who later became the New Zealand coach for their national team.

When one's reputation grows, opportunities will come without the need for looking. I was asked by the Hong Kong Government to succeed David Gledhill as the Chairman of the Hong Kong Sports Development Board, a body similar in nature to the sports council in other countries. The SDB was a quasi-government body started originally by the former chairman of the Hongkong Bank, Willie Purves, who became the first Chairman of the SDB.

My acceptance of the SDB role meant that I had to step down as the President of the HKCA to avoid a conflict of interest since cricket was a constituent sport under the SDB umbrella. Just at that time, my good friend Terry Smith was preparing to stand down as the President of the Hong Kong Cricket Club after many years of service. I thought that Terry would be the perfect replacement for me at the HKCA. Terry thought otherwise as he had set his mind on putting his feet up and relaxing instead. I had been known to be an effective arm-twister and I directed this skill to the full at Terry. It worked, but not before he had his pound of flesh. At the end of the day, we traded places. Terry took on the HKCA and I became President of the HKCC in addition to the SDB. Scores even!

By the end of 1992, with constant exposure in the business press, my name and face began to be widely recognized in Hong Kong. This was significantly enhanced by news on the widely publicized Cricket Sixes and the appointment to the SDB chair. Almost unavoidably, this momentum carried me like a stampede into the corridors of power wherein politicians, senior civil servants and the consular corps reside.

"I sure as hell want to make certain that the people like you continue to be running the company. If you guys leave, I'll find another share to buy"

22

INVESTOR RELATIONS

When the development of the Wharf story became familiar to people, the investor relations initiative evolved into an art form in its own right. Marketing principles had to be applied in full understanding of the product, in essence the company itself. "Knowing the customer" was the call of the day. Investor feedback was essential, yet the management could not compromise its long-term strategy just to appease the shorter-term views of the shareholders. A balance had to be struck but this was more often than not an extremely tricky choice, often demanding sensitive consideration with the application of a high degree of brainwork.

In telling a story, one must never make promises which could not be delivered. It was hard enough to win trust, but once trust was lost, it would take years to win it back, if at all. Trust was the byword in IR, and this trust was a valuable commodity that must be jealously protected. Strategies and targets expressed by directors may be changed or refined to meet changes in the political, economic and geographical arena, and therefore statements made one day might not be applicable say a year on.

Indeed, one could not blame a board for change because a management without the courage to change would be a poor management.

What on earth could an investor lean on then?

Obviously, an investor must first look at a company's quality of assets, the trend on recurrent earnings, the overall debt level and so on. These are givens. In equity dealings however, we must also look at future potentials and trends can tell you so much, but the true intentions of the board and management must be read and in a sense gambled upon. Strategies expounded by the board are useful but these can change. Therefore at the end of the day, an investor can only believe in the people running the company, their expertise, experience and sometimes the depth of their pockets because nothing else could be perpetually dependable.

On one of my trips to the US, I was invited by a substantial private investor of high net worth to his ranch in Texas to "have a chat". My schedule did not include Texas, so he agreed to come to Denver, one of my pit-stops. He asked me, "Who is this Peter Woo then?" I answered that Peter was the de facto majority shareholder. He then pressed on and asked whether the directors held share options and he hoped that we did. Another question: "You guys have golden parachutes?" When I replied in the negative, he looked relieved. He then remarked, "I'm very impressed by your company as I've made a lot of money from your shares. I don't give a damn about glorified words on strategy and mission statements and such like, nor do I care too much about accounting details. But I sure as hell want to make certain that people like you continue to be there running the company. If you guys leave, I'll find another share to buy. Hope you see my logic." I saw his logic alright!

Every time the group moved the goalpost in any direction, the IR man must immediately explain it clearly and create positive messages or sound bites to support the new direction. In any presentation, I would not even attempt to give more than about six messages at most. That was all the audience could realistically be expected to absorb and retain. People's attention span was very short and messages often had to be repeated. It was when we got almost bored and tired of saying the same thing over and over that an audience might recognize the message for the first time; it was extremely testing on one's patience.

Investor relations as a discipline had to be kept "alive". A top class exponent of IR would "live it and feel it to be alive". That would be the only way to be totally sensitive to the issues at hand. The ability to sway listeners depended on saying what the listener wanted to hear. This was only possible if we were utterly conscious of the mood of the meeting or the leaning of the listener to any particular issue. I learned how to watch the body languages of the audience and respond to that as it was always possible to explain one message in a number of different ways. The most effective trick was to make veiled suggestions softly and somehow sway the listener to leave the meeting believing that the arguments he had heard were made through his own deduction rather than that he was convinced. We had to play on people's egos.

Simon Murray at Hutchison and I were the first exponents in Hong Kong to seriously practise investor relations. We were in effect the pioneers of the game. Both of us achieved tangible results and we were regarded by many as the IR "gurus" at that time. Neither of us were financial accountants. Both of us were good marketing men. Is that food for thought?

The media branded me with many names, some highly complementary such as the "Great Communicator", "Approachable Director" or similar descriptions. Others which I did not care much for included "Hype Merchant" and "Spin Doctor". However one wished to be branded, an effective IR drive would probably be enhanced by a degree of "evangelistic preaching" which I admit to having practised. Regardless how the media saw me, success was the real testament. Within just two years, the Wharf share price rose from $6.95 to $43.50, a staggering 625%, an all-time high at that time.

In the first years of assuming the IR role, I won the Wharf Group Marketing Award for three years on the trot. I was one of the two nominees for Hong Kong's Communicator of the Year, an award previously won by the likes of people such as Chris Patten when he was Governor. The award for that year however went to Christine Loh who beat me by two votes. I said in my speech, "If I had to lose, then losing to someone as good as Christine is no shame at all."

Investor relations as a corporate discipline became more fashionable as time went on. What Simon and I had pioneered had become a central "must have" portfolio within every forward-looking listed company by the turn of the millennium. Those companies which understood the value and importance of keeping their shareholders regularly informed reaped the reward of having the support of their shareholders.

"Hong Kong was in fact the principal beneficiary of the combined strengths of South China and Hong Kong as a seamless cross-border trading powerhouse"

24

HONG KONG PLUS

The early 1990s was an intense period at work. One event led to another, and there was an irresistible momentum in play. There was never enough time in a day, but the thirst for quicker and wider coverage of investors drove us forward. This thirst felt unquenchable. Personally, my own keenness was driven by adrenalin. There was almost an obsession in the air, yet I did not feel weary at all.

It was an exciting time. The Chairman and I pushed each other forward. At the outset we decided to undertake a roadshow to visit our equity investors, tell them our story and aspirations with clear messages on the potential growth of recurrent and dependable revenue flow. There was no hidden agenda such as fundraising. The planning was jointly done by us and the London equity house Baring Brothers who would guide us through the trip. Peter and I would go together but the presentations would be split. Peter would concentrate on policies and I would explain the core businesses of the Group and highlight the numbers on asset value and earnings potential.

As that was our very first roadshow, Barings rightly decided to keep the itinerary relatively light. We would only do one large presentation each in London and New York coupled with one-on-ones or small meetings in all the cities including Glasgow and Boston. In all, we probably did no more than 20 meetings. That was enough for Peter, but it just whetted my appetite for more.

Although we were there to tell a story, it was equally important for us to listen to investors' views. We could see the effect even though our investor coverage was limited. Turnover of our stock in the market increased as a consequence and the share price appreciated visibly. We felt that our reputation had already been enhanced and people began to recognize the strength of our assets and the quality of our earnings. In retrospect, it was a case of simply arousing the attention of the market that Wharf, so long forgotten, was really a force to be reckoned with.

It was perhaps the right time to have Wharf rated by international rating agencies. After a protracted series of meetings and fact feeding to them, Wharf then became the first listed corporation in Hong Kong to be rated by Standard & Poor's and by Moody's. That was an important breakthrough as it meant that we could henceforth access the global capital market should the need arise.

As Peter Woo's right arm in the corporate world and ever in his shadow, I had to be in close touch with the consular corps in Hong Kong, and at the same time in contact with the movers and shakers at Westminster and in Washington DC. Within the private sector, the commercial circle was tightly knit and everyone knew everybody else. Some were just held on a friendly basis with others operating in virtual "cartels". In this environment, not only did we have to concern ourselves with the commercial success of our own group, we also owed a responsibility to the larger macro stability of Hong Kong as a whole. There was without doubt a political dimension to my job.

It was an uncertain time politically. There existed genuine nervousness in Hong Kong pending the handover to China in 1997. International investors were reluctant to make commitments. Peter therefore considered it desirable to dispel the fears by forwarding a logical argument that with the help of the Pearl River Delta, Hong Kong was in fact the principal beneficiary of the combined strengths of South China and Hong Kong as a seamless cross-border trading powerhouse, backed by an aggregate population of some 70 million with their considerable consumer muscle in attendance.

The concept needed to be clearly articulated and I set about writing a booklet with illustrative graphics later titled *The Challenge of Hong Kong Plus*. This was widely distributed to the media, business leaders, senior government officials, the consular corps and all financial analysts. It became a great hit. To capitalize on this, we commissioned the making of a high-quality video with its own music score and professional voice-over and we had this video available on request.

Hong Kong Plus was to portray to the business world that we were a group with a vision. The share price bounced a little more. The video became very sought after. Country managers of Hong Kong branches wanted it to convince their headquarters of the long-term attraction of Hong Kong. Others used it to support the stability of their local business in Hong Kong even to well beyond 1997.

I recall that Willie Purves' office called mine requesting some 24 copies of the video at a time when Hongkong Bank was aiming to acquire Midland Bank in the United Kingdom. Some Midland shareholders had shown resistance to the proposed merger. I understood that Willie had intended to use *Hong Kong Plus* to convince the large Midland shareholders on the long-term value of Hong Kong beyond 1997. Such was the power of the story.

Peter was not about to just sit back. He then developed a strong sequel to *Hong Kong Plus*. He was always full of amazing theories, and many were highly logical and visionary. This was yet another. He argued for the strategic location of the city of Wuhan in central China. This was because Wuhan was right at the centre of the North-South axis between

Beijing and Hong Kong; and the West-East axis between Chengdu/
Chongqing to the West and the seaport of Shanghai to the East, joined
by the Yangtse River for water access and egress. This was Peter's idea on
how the extension of Hong Kong's commercial influence could spread
further inland to China beyond the Pearl River Delta. Shanghai would
play a complementary role similar to Hong Kong in this equation.

Cheap land and labour in the Pearl River Delta were the fundamental
attractions of *Hong Kong Plus*. As economic development spread across
the border and prices there rose as a consequence, we needed to find
another region with economical land and labour further inland, hence
the true potential of Wuhan to act as the engine to open up China's
trading with the outside world. This was to become another booklet and
a second video called just *Hong Kong Plus Plus*. To push this argument
even further, we hinted strongly that China was such a huge country with
a population of over 1.3 billion, labour would never run out as it did in
Japan.

Together, these two concepts offered great insight and the market saw
the strong and credible dynamics of the arguments. Analysts and fund
managers gave favourable commentaries. They saw Wharf as the group
which understood China as much as anyone else and were thus prepared
to back us in their investments, especially where Wharf entered joint
ventures in China with local partners.

The Wharf share price soared. The stock was re-rated following bullish
analysts' reports. From a market laggard just two years back, it had
become the darling of investors.

That might have been my finest hour!

"On one such roadshow trip, I actually went round the globe, covered 28 cities with full presentations in each and did it all in 23 days"

25

ROADSHOWS

We could no longer cope with the heavy demand on our time and attention. We had difficulty finding enough hours to accommodate the calls of analysts and journalists. This dictated the need to employ a high-quality executive on board to take some pressure off. We lured the Business Editor of the *South China Morning Post*, Nick Thompson, to join our ranks in the capacity of Chief Manager – Corporate Communication.

Those of us directly involved in the process of driving the share price were exhilarated. The enhanced popularity of our stock was a shot in the arm for the majority of our senior management, many of whom rode on the bandwagon and made handsome profits themselves. Their pride in the group further encouraged greater efforts. Success breeds success and this was certainly the case then.

I struck while the iron was hot. Regular investor relations meetings were scheduled once a fortnight. This forum gave a chance for the heads of business divisions to exchange views with the IR unit. They also understood from IR how best they could streamline their individual operations so that the parts of the group could help to enhance the overall image of the whole. A new dimension was thus added to business management. Everyone had to be aware of IR and its inherent value to the entire staff complement in the group.

Nick Thompson was extremely capable and more was delegated to him. He took charge of editing the quarterly Wharf magazine *Horizon* and handled a good percentage of company visits. With his journalistic background, he was naturally a good writer. However, "once an editor, always an editor" as they say. Nick had this irritating habit of leaving work till the last minute although he always produced high-quality work. "Why rush when all you need is to catch the editorial deadline?" I used to tear my hair out but what could I say?

We pressed on. Roadshows became a regular affair and we went on the road at least twice a year. On these trips, I would normally be accompanied by IR executives or heads of business divisions as were appropriate. Some of those included Nick Thompson, Gary Shing, Penelope Hill, Doreen Lee, and Lawrence Lee. To capitalize on these extensive road trips, geographical coverage was expanded, with regular stops in London, Glasgow, Paris, New York, Boston and either San Francisco or Los Angeles. Additional cities chosen would depend on the purpose of the specific roadshow. These included Edinburgh, Dublin, Milan, Frankfurt, Dusseldorf, Hamburg, Munich, Geneva, Zurich, Milwaukee, Denver, Fort Lauderdale, Tokyo, Singapore and Melbourne/Sydney.

Wharf was very much the Hong Kong pioneer in a long list of innovative financial milestones. We were the first listed Hong Kong company to be rated by international credit agencies; the first to raise a Yankee Bond, a Hybrid Equity/Debt issue, a Samurai Bond in Tokyo, a Floating Rate Note, and inter alia, the first to raise a Mortgage Backed Property Bond. To attract US pension and mutual funds and over-the-counter (OTR) retail investors in the US, Wharf was also the first Hong Kong-listed company to list American Depositary Receipts (ADR) to be traded in the US stock market. We did this through the Bank of New York.

I must have been on at least a dozen of these roadshows in the three years after 1992, followed by many more in the subsequent years. All of these were extremely intense, repetitive and tiring. It was only adrenalin that kept me going. I recall having to physically slap myself across the face to drive away boredom and to remind myself of the need to look and act sharp. One had to remain alert and enthusiastic at all times. If we looked bored or tired, it would show in our body language. Audiences fed on keenness and spark in presentations. I was fully aware of this and constantly reminded my colleagues of the need for similar commitment. My legal training might have helped my public speaking, but it was IR practice that gave me the confidence.

These trips became second nature and I no longer had to depend on extensive preparation nor written scripts. In fact, it was preferable to present impromptu without the assistance of a prepared draft because I could then make eye contact with the audience, thus making it possible to adapt my talk to suit the mood of the listeners.

Nowadays, I no longer have the energy or stamina to undertake such gruelling trips, but when I recall what happened then, I just wonder how on earth I managed to take such punishment and yet come away with good results. Consider that on one such trip, I actually went round the globe, covered 28 cities with presentations in each and did it all in 23 days! That was not so long ago either, as I was already 56.

The satisfaction of having achieved this degree of success with Wharf encouraged the Chairman to consider another bold move and for me to take on an even more complicated challenge. However, before that was to start, I was given a bit of a breather in the form of time to clear the backlog of accumulated paperwork at the office. In the years of running and jet-setting around, I did not have enough time in Hong Kong for sustained periods. It was time that I remained on terra firma for a while and spent some of the time taking care of my family.

I had taken Katish to her boarding school at Geelong Grammar in Australia. The school prided itself on offering a year of basic "outward bound" type of self-subsistent education at Timbertop, a course that Prince Charles had undertaken. Katish left home only a month after Sean was born in 1991, hence Sean grew closer to Natasha in Katish's absence. The boy only got to know Katish better when he turned a teenager, which coincided with Katish's graduation from Georgetown University in Washington DC years later.

Sean was an absolute delight to us. He was always a big lad and had a happy and gentle disposition. We could even foretell then that he would grow up with a relaxed personality and would never harm a fly unless he was provoked. Physically, he was destined to be an extraordinarily tall and big man.

"We would proceed carefully by thinking through all the issues instead of going off half-cooked... It was to be a massive metamorphosis"

26

REVIVAL OF THE BRITISH HONG

Wheelock Marden was one of the big four British trading houses or *hongs* in Hong Kong, the other three being Jardines, Swires and Hutchisons. All of these had histories almost as long as the Colony's. Wheelock was however unique as it started business in Shanghai and moved its headquarters to Hong Kong in 1949 after the Communist regime took control of China.

The wide portfolio of assets and business of Wheelock Marden included ship-owning, insurance, property, manufacturing, trading, infrastructure in the form of the Cross Harbour Tunnel, and retail in the shape of the leading store chain Lane Crawford. In 1985, Sir YK Pao fended off a challenge from Singaporean suitor Khoo Teck Puat to successfully acquire Wheelock Marden in a hotly publicized takeover battle. Wharf was used as the vehicle for the acquisition.

The absorption process of Wheelock Marden by Wharf entailed the retention of the core businesses which were compatible with the vision of the Group and the selling off of non-core or fringe companies or assets. What took place over a period was a vast reduction from over 300 companies within Wheelock Marden to just 30 or so, with the rest sold, amalgamated or just left dormant. It had to be a ruthless exercise. The main companies retained were Lane Crawford, the Cross Harbour Tunnel, and COL (the IT specialists). Certain companies were sold by Wharf to Sir YK's lead company, World International Holdings. To all intents and purposes, Wheelock Marden had been stripped clean. The result meant that the longer-term investment companies from Wheelock Marden were vested in Wharf whilst all the worthwhile trading elements had been moved to World International.

World International shares were not actively traded in the stock market. The challenge that Peter considered was whether we could, with our proven IR ability, exploit the brand name of Wheelock through a revival of that company, and if so, how best to do it? Various different formulae were knocked around. At the end of the day, it seemed obvious to me that the name World International was so generic that probably hundreds of companies around the globe would bear the same name in English or in other languages. On the other hand, not only did the name Wheelock have heritage and pedigree in China and Hong Kong, the name was also unique and it was highly unlikely for it to be replicated elsewhere. It was already a brand, and all that was needed was to re-market that.

It was so blatantly obvious that once identified, a decision was taken to prepare for a name change through the backing of World International into the revised name of Wheelock & Company Limited, dropping the name Marden in the process. However, such an exercise was not so simple. It needed a clever plan to catch media attention through some creative foreplay before the actual launch. The forerunning strategy was as important as the main event if we were to get more than one bite at the media cherry.

Creative planning in tight liaison with Peter involved many brainstorming sessions. A step-by-step block building sequence was to take place, recognizing that the process could not be rushed. We would proceed carefully by thinking through all the issues instead of going off half-cooked – "less haste and more speed." It was to be a massive metamorphosis.

A number of strategic prerequisite developments were earmarked. These were prioritized. Executives with appropriate expertise would be put in place. I was appointed Managing Director to drive the entire project. The preliminary structure would include a number of vital new ingredients. First and foremost, we established a trading arm called Wheelock Pacific to restore the trading element that was the hallmark of a *hong*, and a former Jardines friend Robert Tatlow was appointed Executive Director. Wheelock Capital was revitalized and made active again with the thought of acquiring a bank. We felt that once these two meaningful businesses were established, the rest should fall into place.

The announcement on the formation of Wheelock Pacific and its management team of Hung, Tatlow and Peter Pao (Sir YK's nephew) drew some interest from a wide spectrum of observers. It also attracted would-be partners. Quite a few of those were signed up for joint ventures, and these included some big global names. Richard Branson brought the Virgin music brand to us, creating Wheelock/Virgin to bring Virgin Records to Hong Kong and China. An exciting partnership with Foster's of Australia formed Wheelock/Fosters to upgrade a brewery in Tientsin in northern China. A potential partnership was in place with Allders of the United Kingdom to bid for the duty-free franchise at the new Chek Lap Kok International Airport. These types of activities were reminiscent of the old trading pattern of the traditional British trading houses and totally compatible with the image of a large *hong*. The jigsaw was coming together nicely.

Wheelock Capital had always been a part of the group, although used only sparingly in the financial field. In the scheme of things that faced us then, it was the perfect vehicle for the acquisition of a bank when the opportunity presented itself. Banking was of course a pet business to both Sir YK and Peter since both of them began their careers in that field, Sir

YK in Shanghai and Peter with Chase Manhattan before he joined his father-in-law Sir YK's business.

Although I had already discussed the question of partnership with a number of global banking names and short-listed a few potential candidates, it was felt that we needed an in-house professional banker to lead the initiative. Nick Sibley, a legend with Jardine Fleming before retirement, was believed to be just treading water with a Singaporean outfit in Hong Kong, and we felt that an all-out attempt to lure him across might just succeed provided Nick saw his role as interesting and challenging. It took a great deal of persuasion and arm-twisting but Nick eventually accepted the offer. I vacated my role of Managing Director of Wheelock Capital for Nick as I was already the MD of the parent. To have Nick in the team was a real coup, and his appointment was great PR for us. Nick was to follow up all my early leads but he took the negotiations and analysis to another level, culminating in the establishment of Wheelock/Natwest in a partnership with Natwest Markets in London. Both parties undertook to commit all their funds to the JV and refrain from unilateral or direct fund management. It looked like a marriage made in heaven.

The official launch of the JV was celebrated at the impressive new office in Natwest House at Times Square in Causeway Bay, officiated by the last Governor of Hong Kong, Chris Patten. The future looked very bright indeed.

"Reincarnation had taken place. Wheelock was born again in the corporate body of World International"

27

WHEELOCK AND AFTERMATH

With Wheelock Pacific and Wheelock Capital in place, we were ready to move towards the launch of the Wheelock name. This involved a massive exercise encompassing a myriad of issues that needed to be tackled and surmounted. Forerunning prerequisites which had to be resolved included the passage through company registrars, auditors, and the stock exchange. In addition, the headquarters had to be re-named from Pao House to Wheelock House, thus the agreement of all the tenants had to be secured and all printed materials had to be reprinted. The list seemed endless and would involve heavy cost.

A new company logo had to be designed and adopted as would all PR materials and collaterals ready for the launch. A date was set and we carefully prepared the main messages to drive for maximum advantage. These were drafted, critiqued, discussed and then refined through the same process again. The Wharf IR unit was seconded virtually full time to assist in this project.

A specialist American professional, Kathy Travis, was charged with the task of creating the logo and preparing the design for the press kit. Anne Forrest kept a watching brief throughout and gave us the benefit of her insight into the matter. Brainstorming sessions were regular affairs, led and monitored by Anne. We all had a hand in contribution, but sparks of inspiration would come from anyone, and when least expected, even from the most junior person in the room.

From keen observation and research feedback, it became clear that logos with a modern design ironically aged faster and went out of date relatively quickly. On the contrary, older or more classical designs, so often mistaken as passé, in fact survived longer and might even gain prominence with time. Examples were the logos of Coca Cola, GE, or even the simple "flag" logos of HSBC, Swires or Wharf. Since the choice of the Wheelock name was inspired by heritage and pedigree earned over decades as a Far Eastern trading *hong*, we felt the logo should adopt a traditional look with a flavour akin to perhaps the turn of the 19th century. I also recognized that the logo alone per se, no matter how well designed, would not be well known to start with. Prominence of the logo would only gain recognition through long-term and consistent exposure. It was therefore important that the design should have lasting power.

Kathy reverted to us with numerous samples and we were quite taken by the look of the logo of the Raffles Hotel in Singapore. We viewed that logo as having the type of imagery that would help to reflect Wheelock's long-lasting Far Eastern heritage. It gave us a reference point to work from. Kathy eventually created a slanted map of Southeast and North Asia with China holding dominant central position. The colours chosen were a dark or khaki shaded green on a beige hue background, very typical of the soft and subdued look of pre-World War I fashion. The central theme of the map worked well with the name and image of Wheelock Pacific. It had a solid and non-pretentious look. It was the logo that a revived *hong* would have wanted.

As we approached D-Day, the market wondered what all the rumours meant. What were all the snippets of news all leading to? What was the big story? Speculative articles appeared frequently in newspapers and financial journals. It was humming. I jumped on the bandwagon to feed more appetizers to the press before the main course. Our phones never stopped ringing.

The Wheelock share price which had remained comatose for so long began to show some signs of life. It started as a snowball and soon turned into an avalanche. By the time of the official launch party held at the Mandarin Hotel, the name change was hailed as a master stroke. The revival of the Wheelock name hit the nerves of many seasoned and veteran investors who could recall the past glory of the big hongs. The Wheelock stock traded as though it was a new issue. In some ways, it was just that. Reincarnation had taken place. Wheelock was born again in the corporate body of World International.

The popularity of the Wheelock stock in the days that followed was astounding. Media debates discussed the underlying strengths of the company. Most were concentrating on the future rather than the present. Investors just chose to believe in us. Our joint venture partners were household names and this gave the further impression that they would not have partnered us unless they found us to be people of substance and vision. Embarrassing though it sounded, a large broker was quoted in the *South China Morning Post* that not only were the fundamentals of the partnerships strong, Wheelock also benefited from the "Hung Factor"!

When we started the exercise, the share price stood at $8.95. After the name change, the price had risen to $23.75 all within seven months, a price increase of almost 300% in a half year.

I was on a roll. Things were at an all-time high on all fronts in my life.

It had been my intention for a long time to start a diary. A diary, to me, cannot merely connote a chronicle of daily events on engagements — I shall leave such work to Government Officials and Social & Philanthropic dignitaries. My diary is one which contains my thoughts and observations; in it I shall, from time to time, such impressions of persons, as may to me. There may be terms of praise or condemnation. There will be no indifferent judgements, because in matters of moral conduct, with which I intend to deal chiefly, I believe that one should not arbitrate. I shall also be most critical on my own acts and shall not hesitate to introspect with absolute candidness. All which makes me believe that I am extremely vain, for what is the writing down of ones thoughts but a manifestation of ones vanity — vanity in the sense that ones own ideas are of such importance that they should be perpetuated by making visible that which is invisible, even though it may be but to my own eyes?

The first page of the unfinished rough manuscript crafted by the author's father Walter in the 1930s

The wedding of Walter and Phoebe, circa 1934 (opposite);
The Hunt family in the 1920s – the author's grandfather is seated extreme left (above);
The author's father-in-law Francis Arlidge with large marlin on his boat the "Alma G"
(below)

The author with his sister Wendy just before the war in 1940 (above); Author's stepfather MC Hung just after the war, 1947 (right)

A sports feature in the *China Mail* in Hong Kong, 1957

Captain of the Singapore Cricket Club, 1979 (above left);
At the Hong Kong International Sixes during its inaugural year, 1992 (below left);
Rod Eddington, CEO of Cathay Pacific, and the author representing Wharf, promoting
the first Sixes which were co-sponsored by the two groups (above)

Watching the Sixes with Chris Patten, last Governor of Hong Kong (above);
The author with Pakistani cricket great Wasim Akram (below)

Receiving the trophy for Sirocco winning the prestigious Kwangtung Handicap (above);
With Sir Geoff Hurst, English World Cup winner & hat-trick scorer in 1966 and Lee
Lai-shan, Hong Kong's first ever Olympic gold medal winner (below)

The author seen with Prince Charles (above left); at Hong Kong Jockey Club paddock where Gail made the presentation to the best turned out horse in the Lane Crawford Cup (below left); with Gail at Government House after receiving the Silver Bauhinia Star (above); with Richard Branson and Peter Woo (below)

At Geelong Grammar School, Australia, with Gail and daughters Samantha, Katish and Natasha (above left); Sean with his proud catch of large snapper in Russell, Bay of Islands, New Zealand (above right); Sean with author's mother Phoebe (below)

"The boy appears to have potential but you must not coach him yourself. Hand him to a pro"

28

FRUITS OF SUCCESS

The success of the Wheelock launch was a good reason for us to enjoy the fruits that it brought. Yet I felt some things were missing. Whilst matters were still clear in my mind, I wanted to remind myself how these events came about, and what improvements could still be achieved. I was not about to just sit on my laurels and allow complacency to set in.

My first target was to make clear in my own mind how best to exploit the equity market as against the capital market, consider in depth the sensitivities between the two and draw up a strategy on the best way for the Wharf Group to raise substantial funds through both avenues to build our war chest in anticipation of the group's impending funding requirements. As we already had the advantage of being internationally rated, these options were decidedly available.

The tremendous performance of both the Wharf and Wheelock shares had provided a healthy platform for growth in future potential revenue but the raising of debt from the capital market would require demonstration of the group's discipline in the protection of the downside. In many ways, the two were diametrically opposed in terms of basic management strategies. The attraction to the equity market required investments in an attacking mode with some risks for high rewards, but tapping the capital market for debt required the group to be more defensive in its outlook and needed the exercise of great care to guard against loss. Balancing the two approaches required deft handling with a high degree of sensitivity. Within the period of relative quiet available to me, I was to devote time and effort to hone our craft in this direction. I would spend my inspirational hours on this issue.

Personal acknowledgements from the market came almost without trying. I was featured in numerous financial columns. Internally within the corporate, I was asked to help various business divisions with marketing through short-term involvements in an advisory role. The Chairman decided to extend my retirement for a further five years. It was an appropriate time to savour the taste of success.

I was urged to join the prestigious Shek O Golf & Country Club and my membership came through relatively quickly. Then came my appointment as a Justice of the Peace, followed thereafter by the award of the Silver Bauhinia Star by the Chief Executive of the HKSAR.

My mother Phoebe called from London to congratulate me, but she had no idea what a Silver Bauhinia Star was. Not many people did so soon after the handover. I explained that the SBS was perhaps the equivalent of an OBE conferred by the British Government prior to the handover. In her innocence, Phoebe asked "Is it real sterling silver or is it made of a lesser metal?" My reply was "I don't know yet, mother. I'll tell you after I've been to Government House next month. I hope it is silver!" It was.

All those accolades that were heaped upon me made me somewhat embarrassed, yet I was obviously pleased. It was inevitable then that I would be recognized in the commercial world, in the leading echelons in sport and in the general social scene.

Radio Television Hong Kong (RTHK) was keen to run a live radio programme on me on a Sunday morning. The programme was professionally conducted by the interviewer Martin Evan-Jones who made me very comfortable. He managed it so well that the profile of my life was expertly compressed into just about 50 minutes. I was asked to select four songs to be played to reflect different aspects of my persona. In a light-hearted mood combined with harmless mischief, I selected *Cigarettes, Whisky and Wild Wild Women* for a laugh; *Po Karekare Ana* as a tribute to Gail's Maori heritage; *Mr. Sandman* to recall how I was always daydreaming in my youth; and *Goldfinger* on the Midas touch which I hoped to acquire.

On a more serious note, Martin noted that I had decided to stay with Wharf after it was taken over by Sir YK and then asked if I felt I had as it were "crossed the floor"? My response was quick and simple: "Martin, it was the same floor really. It was just that a new broom came our way to sweep it clean!"

Sean was growing up into a lovable and active young lad and I bought him his first miniature cricket bat when he was only three. By the time he was four, he could already play a straight bat. Natasha took a series of action photographs of Sean batting and it showed a classic off-drive. At the International Cricket Sixes that year, I showed these photographs to Greg Chappell. Greg studied these with interest and then gave me two pieces of advice. Firstly he said "The boy appears to have potential, but you must not coach him yourself. Hand him to a pro." Greg then added "Boys like your son with natural talent have a tendency to fiddle with too many sports, and end up being a master of none. I suggest you watch that, John." That reminded me of myself. Chip off the old block? I hoped not.

Sean was also introduced to mini-rugby at the Hong Kong Football Club. The weekends gave us no rest at all. Saturday mornings were devoted to Junior Gapper cricket at the Hong Kong Cricket Club, and early Sunday mornings were for mini-rugby at the Hong Kong Football Club. Sean enjoyed both but these sessions tired us out. When he turned five years old, we also started him on golf, normally on Sunday afternoons at Fanling, coached by Joanna Hardwicke. Nobody could suggest that Sean was not given a sporting start!

Natasha was also sent to Geelong to join her elder sister as a boarder, and at the same time Sean was in playschool. The children were all settled in an orderly fashion to the relief of Gail and I. My career had reached its pinnacle and I held a reasonable portfolio of blue chip stocks, a few up-market apartments in Hong Kong and a nice property in the idyllic Bay of Islands in New Zealand. Towards the end of 1995, we had nothing very much to worry about. We were a happy family.

*"Your husband can write a book about fishing, Gail. But he
would do well to remain on land..."*

29

BAY OF ISLANDS

It had become almost a yearly pilgrimage that we would spend every
Christmas and New Year in our home in Russell, on the Bay of Islands
in New Zealand. Russell was Gail's place of birth and her family has been
there for generations. The moment I set foot there to meet Gail's father,
I fell in love with the place. There was nowhere else I would rather be,
especially during the New Zealand summer.

Gail's heritage is half European or *Pakeha* and half Maori. Her mother
was from the Ngapuhi tribe or *iwi* who were the occupiers of Hokianga
and the Bay of Islands. At around 1810, under the leadership of Ruatara,
the Ngapuhi was New Zealand's largest *iwi*. Ruatara was responsible for
bringing the first European Christian mission to New Zealand at the Bay
of Islands. He introduced trading with the *Pakeha* and gained valuable
access to European knowledge, plants, technology and weapons including
muskets. The Bay of Islands became one of the most prominent shipping
ports in New Zealand, and the Ngapuhi chiefs were all signatories of the
Waitangi Treaty.

Kororareka (since renamed Russell) then became the first capital of
New Zealand. In the 1840s, the Maoris were engaged in a series of land
wars with the British. The Ngapuhi forces were led by the fearsome Hone

Heke. The story went that many bloody battles were fought all because of the symbolism of the Union Jack. The Maoris were bent on taking down the flag, but the British would fly it again. This was to repeat itself regularly with every tussle and lives were lost on both sides. That was to be known as the Flagstaff War, the landmark of which is in fact on Flagstaff Hill in Russell.

The Maoris are a proud race and their traditions are preciously preserved. They are also very spiritual in their beliefs. The Ngapuhis now have their *iwi* administration in Kaikohe in the Bay of Islands and their motto is *"Kie tu tika ai te whare tapu o Ngapuhi"* or "May the sacred house of Ngapuhi always stand firm".

Russell became a European settlement for whalers and had a reputation for unruly drinking, fornicating, and wholesale debauchery, particularly amongst the whalers and their minions. In a novel by Richard Wolfe which described that period, Kororareka was referred to as the hell-hole of the Pacific and a town that harboured 'a greater number of rogues than any other spot of equal size in the universe'! On the exterior wall of the gift shop next to our house on the Strand waterfront, a bronze plaque is mounted which states "On this site stood the old whorehouse and the grog house. These trades are no longer practised here today." Our house actually stands on part of the site, which made me ask the question whether our house sat on the site of the brothel or the grog house. I can however confirm that those kinds of establishments no longer exist there!

Unlike its historical buccaneering reputation, Russell is nowadays a sleepy and quaint town with a population of only around 1,000. All the residents are known by first names to one another. It is an extremely friendly place unaffected by modern technological pursuits. The preservation of this conservative and almost old-fashioned way of life is caused simply by the strip of water in the bay that separates this tip of the peninsula from the mainland on the other side, occupied by the larger township of

Paihia. Russell's isolation probably arose because access requires a ferry ride of about seven minutes. This is inconvenience in the eyes of New Zealanders. In my eyes, it is this very isolation that has provided Russell's charm. Russell has been and remains the best kept secret in the land.

By absolute contrast, sitting just seven minutes across the bay, Paihia has developed a completely different personality. Tourism's demands have dictated that the town should evolve into a waterfront strip akin to a Californian beachfront, infested by endless motels, hamburger and hotdog stands, bars and fast food restaurants. It is highly popular amongst young tourists and backpackers. We are grateful that Russell has preserved its more sedate and quaint ambience and atmosphere. This is precisely what we love.

Deep sea fishing had always been Russell's main attraction. My father-in-law, Francis Arlidge, was widely regarded as one of New Zealand's best professional game fishermen post-war, having taken luminaries out on his famous boat the Alma G. His clients included the likes of Lord Mountbatten, Sir Anthony Eden, and the famous American author Zane Grey.

Francis never needed GPS or any of the modern gadgets. He could smell fish and knew exactly where to find them. On one of the earlier occasions when Francis took me out, I observed that he picked up one fish after another in quick succession. On the other side of the boat, I just waited with my line and bait dangling off the side for long periods. Francis asked whether I had felt any bites. My answers were shakes of the head. Then suddenly I felt a strong pull and immediately informed Francis. He instructed me to dip and wind, dip and wind, and I did that repeatedly as instructed. When finally the catch appeared on the surface, it turned out to be our anchor!

After one such fishing trip, we went home and Francis remarked, "Your husband can write a book about fishing, Gail. But he will do well to remain on land while doing so!" What cheek, I thought! Nonetheless,

I did eventually learn the rudiments from Francis and once I knew these basics, Francis and I did enjoy some good times together. I had the best teacher, but the ability of the apprentice remained questionable.

Today, I can safely say that deep sea fishing is on par with my favourite sports for enjoyment. On a nice summer day, I would go a long way to be out on a boat, hopefully picking up a few large red snappers. Sean has inherited this love of fishing from Francis. It must be in his blood as he has an excellent feel for a bite. In fact, even from a tender age, Sean was already able to net some very big snappers.

Gail and I bought the house on the waterfront originally owned by Francis' brother Mervyn. After Mervyn passed away, his children, or Gail's first cousins Merna and Max, wanted to sell and we purchased the property from them. There was an old single-storey house resting on their land. When we redeveloped the property, to save demolition cost, we sold the structure "as is, where is". The buyers' contractors managed to move the entire house onto a flatbed and then onto a barge. Now the old house sits on a hilltop at Orongo Bay, not too far away from Russell. In its place, we constructed a double-storey house, preserving the exterior heritage look of an "A" frame structure, but with all the modern conveniences in the interior. The house was completed in 1995 at a time when I was riding high in the world. It became a perfect "getaway" for us from Hong Kong.

Every New Zealand summer, Russell became the perfect gathering place for members of the family from various parts of the globe, particularly during the festive season of Christmas and New Year. It was the one time of the year that we could all relax, away from the pressures encountered in city living, and enjoy instead the simpler pleasures of good weather, idyllic surrounds, casual pastimes and the company of close friends and family. It was the perfect spot to recharge our batteries.

The high-powered corporate career in the pressure cooker of Hong Kong, whilst exciting to me, entailed a heavy stress level. It often took me two to three days to unwind as I began every holiday. The tranquillity of Russell, and indeed New Zealand as a whole, provided the perfect tonic I needed. The Russell house has been our usual destination for our annual vacation, away from the hustle and bustle of Hong Kong. We moved between two extremes.

"I also accept the reality of cultural and social divides, but clearly I have a free choice on the variety I personally prefer"

30

RACING CIRCLES

It was in New Zealand that I first resumed ownership of racehorses since owning a leg of a horse a long time ago elsewhere. It was a partnership formed with some friends that introduced me to the New Zealand thoroughbred scene. Similar to other Western racing centres, New Zealand race meetings had a great atmosphere which was aimed predominantly at horses and horse lovers, not sidetracked by other forms of superfluous activities like fashion shows and pop concerts. I loved that flavour just as I did in England. Race meetings were conducted for the knowledgeable racing public and everyone there had the same common interest.

Unlike Europe or New Zealand, in Asia, Hong Kong in particular, racecourses and race meetings are not only for horse racing but have the addition of facilities for up-market social interaction. People from the upper echelons of society go racing in Hong Kong not only for racing, but also "to see and to be seen" and to enjoy fine dining in a semi-formal atmosphere where decorum has to be kept. Seating arrangements are by separate tables with excellent food, beverage and service at five-star hotel standards. Contrast this with say the Piccolo Bar at Ellerslie in Auckland which provides all that racing needs without any overdose of up-market pretentiousness. To me, that is what racing is all about.

Located close to the mounting paddock, or 'birdcage' as New Zealanders call it, the Piccolo Bar is by no means fancy, but a highly practical facility with tall small round cocktail tables spread throughout the large area. People mill around, engaged in lively conversation whenever they meet a friend. On race days, the bar is packed, filled by owners, trainers, racing journalists, TV commentators, race callers, their friends, wives and partners. Conversations centre on racing or associated topics. The majority would be knowledgeable in racing. The bar is complete with champagne, spirits, wines, beers, mixers and soft drinks. Basic snacks are available from sandwiches, pies, burgers and fish & chips to desserts and cheeses to go with coffee or tea. Even though the ambience is casual, the bar takings would be substantial from high consumption which, I surmise, would bring a race day turnover to a level which would compare very well with any food & beverage outlet at any Asian racecourse.

In Hong Kong, the facilities are separated in the members stand by floors. It seems that the VIPs are on the top floors and as we move to the lower floors, we find the less important. There is no single facility where stewards, voting members, trainers, media, and general owners can readily meet and mingle. The up-market facilities have beautiful décor, but this to me is different from racing ambience. It is almost more like a country club. Waiters stand by and serve with high efficiency but the environment tends to be perhaps a little contrived.

The stark difference between the privileged and the ordinary permeates Hong Kong society in more ways than one, far beyond racing to many walks of life. This phenomenon is certainly noticeable to anyone acquainted with Hong Kong racing first-hand, especially if he has also felt the more relaxed atmosphere in Western racing facilities. The social gaps that exist among the different echelons of Hong Kong society can be more pronounced and acute than even the English class system.

In the New Zealand racing milieu, I befriended Graham Allen and
Haigan Murray, one being the husband and the other the son of Gail's
interior designer friend Rhonda. Rhonda is a woman of great charm
with a wicked sense of humour, not to mention exquisite taste in design.
Graham had long been engaged in the New Zealand racing scene and was
well known there. It was however Haigan who established a long-standing
relationship with me. Having worked in upper levels of management in
Africa, Haigan understood internationalism and thus was not confined
to the parochial behaviour found so commonly in New Zealand. I found
Haigan's outlook so refreshing.

It was through these two that I got to know Cherie Archer who
was to develop with me a close-knit friendship. Cherie helped me in
the purchase of thoroughbreds in the Karaka Yearling Sale as my agent
and this association grew into one where Cherie managed all my racing
interests in New Zealand. In actual fact, Sirocco is now standing in stud
at Archer Park at Drury, near the thoroughbred centre of Karaka. Cherie
is a straightforward woman who just loves her horses. She is to me totally
reliable and I trust her without reservation. She is more to me than just a
business partner in the racing world. She has been and remains my very
good friend.

".... and I did not even charge an appearance fee?"

31

TAKING STOCK

Euromoney magazine published an in-depth article on Wheelock/ Natwest. It was intended as a positive commentary on the joint venture and it must have appeared to be so to the general readership. However, whether it was noticed or not, the newly appointed Managing Director of Natwest Markets in London was quoted as saying that their mindset was in Europe rather than in Asia. Further on in the same article, I was quoted in my capacity as the Managing Director of Wheelock that we were delighted with the joint venture and that Wheelock was in it for the long haul. Those were distinctly conflicting comments but I did hope that most of the readers would not have noticed the two glaringly conflicting statements from the two top men of the JV partners. It was embarrassing.

I did not however believe that the comment from Natwest London was a slip of the tongue, and thought there was no smoke without fire. The fact that their MD had only just joined Natwest might have accounted for that statement since he was not there when the joint venture was formed and was not a party to the initial discussions and negotiations. His comment was nevertheless highly disturbing. However, to do nothing might still have been the wisest move as there would be no sense in us fanning the situation any more than had already been done. We therefore played it down as best we could. When the joint venture began to gain momentum by winning new accounts and the AUM started to increase, the outlook somehow appeared brighter. The article seemingly faded from market memory.

Then one day we read in the financial press that Natwest had acquired the large fund management firm of Gartmore in London, only to receive confirmation of the deal from them after it was done. There was no prior consultation with us or even prior notice given. Things did not appear to be as they should be and we sat up and considered our position. Nick Sibley started to put questions to our partners.

The situation looked bleak and we saw ourselves in an untenable position since Natwest had acted unilaterally against the spirit of the joint venture. In reality, once they had acquired Gartmore, it became blatantly clear that their funds would flow to Gartmore rather than to Wheelock/ Natwest, which was contrary to the spirit of our agreement. The writing was on the wall. What had taken place should not have happened. It began to haunt us. It was just a case of what we would do about it.

The relationship had been strained already when we heard that our partners were looking at re-opening their operations in Japan, a business they had earlier abandoned when it operated under the name of County Natwest. This led us to question their true intentions as it became clear that they were actively engaged in business areas directly in conflict with Wheelock/Natwest, and the future of the joint venture was to all intents and purposes destroyed. All that remained was to negotiate the best terms for our exit. Nick Sibley handled this process with Kevin Westley of HSBC Markets acting as our advisor.

The once promising partnership came to an end when we were bought out. It gave rise to deeply felt disappointment for something that we had worked so hard to establish. Had we adhered to the original spirit of the JV agreement, Wheelock/Natwest had all the fundamentals and credentials for a highly successful business to develop with time. It was a great pity.

The collapse of Wheelock/Natwest caused a noticeable setback in market sentiment towards Wheelock and the share price receded. However, I felt it was something that would pale into relative insignificance with the passage of time. There was no reason to overreact since the group's other core operations remained on course.

I took a bird's eye view of the Group and reminded myself that I should redirect my main attention to Wharf since it was after all a much bigger company than its parent Wheelock in terms of the size and quality of assets, recurrent earnings stream or sheer potential for growth. There was work to be done there.

The call on my attention by the media increased even more. Regular interviews resulted in wider exposure. I was invited to address industry conferences, and to accompany the Stock Exchange of Hong Kong as a panellist in Tokyo with Paul Chow, the CEO of SEHK. The electronics media did not miss out either. Radio and television approached me to participate in programmes with a leaning to the human area of my persona rather than concentrating only on the corporate aspects. The preference was to reflect the complete lifestyle and history of the featured personality. The producers believed that this way, they could capture more of an interesting portrayal of a person and what made him tick.

One of the free-to-air TV stations had a series on corporate leaders and they filmed a one-hour programme on me. The scenes were not restricted to the office as the producers wanted casual backdrops on sports fields, at home, at the swimming pool or just walking along scenic paths. The filming took a great deal of time and ingenuity. I did as I was directed. The result was, to me at least, a good study of my personality, caught at a time when I was clearly at peace with myself and comfortable with the environment and the people around me. The programme was seen by many who made complimentary remarks to me about it.

Auntie Bobbie, a younger sister of my mother and the headmistress of St. Paul's Co-educational College, thought that the programme was an interesting reflection of my life. She especially mentioned that she had not realized that I had such wisdom and she was clearly impressed. She referred to some remarks I had made on film and singled out a clip where I mused over my children's varied education and their chosen careers. I had commented in the programme: "They decide for themselves what they want to do. We don't own our children. We just guide and educate them as best we can, and support them in whatever career they choose. We can't dictate."

In many ways, I thoroughly enjoyed doing these programmes as I found these free-flowing conversations invigorating. Often I found my memory jolted during filming which aided my power of recall. It was perfectly natural and totally unrehearsed. Curiously, I found that I learned something new about myself each time I participated in such filming. It also gave me the chance to show off my little boy Sean as he was often with me especially during the shooting of outdoor scenes or at home.

Television wanted me in another series, but this time on a Chinese channel. The series featured eight leading salaried executives, each in a separate individual programme of 30 minutes. The substance was mainly on corporate success and thus focused purely on commercial activities. One of the eight programmes would be aired each week and the entire series was covered in two months.

One more television appearance was done on a dare. Cable TV, of which I was Deputy Chairman, dared me to appear as their guest in a one-hour programme called 女人心 or Woman's Heart. The programme would be conducted in Cantonese and was essentially a free-for-all with no holds barred. It was to be conducted by its anchor, Crystal Kwok. She could pick any subject that she liked and there would also be a period for call-in questions from viewers. I thought it might be a bit of fun.

Senior executives of large groups would not do such programmes, but why should I not?

It went out live. I found that Crystal's command of spoken Chinese was not much better than mine and she punctuated her sentences with words in English as she was probably Western-educated. I was relieved as that suited me too. I relaxed completely and thoroughly enjoyed the light-hearted chat. Before I knew it, the hour was up. We talked about anything and everything including my two wives, to which I had to quickly assert that I was married to one of them at a time! She asked how I had the time for corporate work as it seemed to her that I had such a wide variety of outside interests. I quipped that I had the Jekyll and Hyde in me, thus I had nocturnal hours as well. There were serious comments mingled with a great deal of good-humoured outlandish remarks or wisecracks. The programme was meant to be fun and I certainly gave that to the audience.

People like my mother, Peter Woo's wife Bessie, and a host of my friends and colleagues all watched the programme and the consensus was that it was hilarious and entertaining... and I did not even charge an appearance fee?

About then, Katish started looking at tertiary education. As she was in Australia, whether she went to the United Kingdom or United States, she would have to obtain additional qualifications in addition to her Australian examination passes. She opted for the US, as a consequence of which she needed to get through the American SAT test which she passed without too much trouble.

Admission into a top university in the US was by no means so simple. After the submission of her applications, she received a few conditional acceptances. I took Katish then to see all those so that we could assess the institutions on the spot. It came down to a straight choice between Northwestern University in Chicago and Georgetown University in Washington DC. As we had better ties through our relatives the Hotung family in their alumni, Katish decided on Georgetown to read Chinese as her major.

Arising from Katish's move to the northern hemisphere, and Sean being at the Peak School in Hong Kong, we put it to Natasha that she could either remain at Geelong in Australia and miss out on long summer holidays with the family in July/August or transfer to an English boarding school. It did not take her long to favour the England option. We applied to a few boarding schools and saw a number of them.

One English headmistress was particularly harsh on Natasha. She criticized her Australian school results and held the superior air that her school was much more advanced than what Natasha had experienced in Australia, and suggested that Natasha's mathematics was "dire" – all said sternly in front of the girl. Her attitude and demeanour irked Gail and I, and undermined Natasha's confidence. None of us was keen.

The moment she set foot in Malvern Girls' College and talked to the registrar and senior mistresses, Natasha did not want to visit another school. She had made up her mind. She loved the atmosphere and friendly disposition of the people in Malvern. Gail and I agreed at once.

By the end of the year, everything was settled but it did mean that Natasha would lose a term as she could only start in January instead of September. We decided to put her back a year as she was still young and this would reduce the pressure of the change for her. It was the correct decision as was proven in her later years.

The family was in good shape. In Hong Kong, Gail and I relaxed as we watched Sean developing into a wholesome boy. We noticed he was slow in learning, but surely this would pass with time? However, Sean went about his preferred pursuits happily. As for our concern over his academic standard, Sean was just oblivious to it all!

"Perhaps the introduction of the International Cricket Sixes may help to take cricket into Communist China and turn them into capitalists"

32

THE HANDOVER

The economy was hot in late 1996 and the Hong Kong property market was even hotter. Some thought it was overheated. Transaction prices on all sectors went through the roof and record highs were set almost every passing week. There was a buying frenzy. Property units were changing hands almost daily. Big money came across the border from the Mainland. This phenomenon carried over to 1997, the year of the handover whereby sovereignty over Hong Kong would be transferred from Britain to China. Property trading at record highs was seen by some observers as the last hurrah before the end of British rule, or was it the beginning of another regime where the locals saw it as the return to the motherland?

By the end of 1996, Tung Chee-hwa had already been elected by the Election Committee of 400, of which I was a member, as the first Chief Executive Designate of the Hong Kong Special Administrative Region of the People's Republic of China, or the HKSAR. This would come into effect on 1st July 1997. The HKSAR was to be governed on the principle of "One Country, Two Systems".

The handover was to be a momentous event in history. It was to be the first time that a former British colony would not turn independent, but rather come under the sovereignty of another master. The "One Country, Two Systems" concept of government was unique and untried in the world. There were regular commentaries, debates and speculations on how this would really work out.

The sceptics were dominated by the non-Chinese residents and foreigners. Many expatriates elected to leave Hong Kong, but some long-term Hong Kong belongers made peace with the imminent change and decided once and for all to commit to Hong Kong as their long-term home. One thing was for certain. The handover did force decisions on people which they would not have taken were it not for its imminence.

As we ran into 1997, Hong Kong became the focus of international attention. Nations began to prepare for attendance at the handover celebrations and named the representatives they would send for the ceremony. Some global leaders would use the opportunity for political networking. Locally, a high-powered task force was assembled, charged with the responsibility of organizing all the proceedings and main events. More importantly, because of the political impasse which existed between China and Britain, the arrangements and identities of the dignitaries from these central players remained undefined.

Peter Woo tried his hand in politics by entering the race for Chief Executive of the HKSAR. After surviving the first round shake-out, he eventually lost out in the final round to Tung. Nevertheless, Peter satisfied himself for making his mark in politics in Hong Kong. His very well thought out "manifesto" presented a political platform which was widely regarded as the most professionally put-together political message put forward by the candidates. He therefore rightly considered that the effort was worth it as the process no doubt raised his profile.

Because of his entry into the political field, Peter's exposure became more pronounced internationally. During the run-up to the handover, numerous commercial and political leaders sought to make personal visits to Peter. Amongst them was the late Richard Holbrooke, the much respected and reliable envoy who served various presidents of the United States, and I found him an engaging person. Inevitably, I was roped in to assist in arrangements or to hold forerunning meetings with those visitors. I did as directed, but in reality, these exposures also raised my own profile, albeit at a lower level. Regardless, many of the friends made over that period became valuable networking connections for the times ahead.

In the handover week, senior executives from most of the large commercial firms were invited to celebration events, hosted separately either by the British or by the Chinese. Many were invited by both sides and this created logistical problems as the dress codes were often different, yet there was inadequate time between the parties to run home to change. Appropriate apparel thus had to be brought to a midway location in a central hotel in close proximity to the party venues to allow us to change conveniently. It was a nightmare, but made even more awkward by the closure of vital roads for security reasons. Any attempt to drive home would have been futile.

Closer to the day, many senior executives and officials were running around frantically, particularly those involved with any part of the organizing which had to be precisely coordinated. It was complicated. It was revealed at a late stage that Prince Charles would represent Her Majesty and the Prime Minister Tony Blair would be here with Governor Patten to form the official delegation from Britain. President Jiang Zemin would lead the official delegation for China.

The population was still kept guessing whether the People's Liberation Army or the PLA would cross the border in numbers with tanks and heavy armour in a show of military might or otherwise. Although a PLA presence to replace the British Forces would have been completely logical, there were those who were apprehensive, particularly people from abroad. I recall friends from England calling me to ask daft questions like "Are you about to be occupied by those people from across the border?" Such misguided thoughts might have been fanned by the international media, including some 24-hour news channels.

We felt no such apprehension. Gossip and rumours always start from afar and generally get vastly exaggerated. Those of us on the spot knew better.

The handover came and went with the celebration events taking place in the midst of a heavy downpour. We did not know whether this could be read as some sort of omen. The Union Jack was lowered and handed to Chris Patten to the beautiful bagpipes sound of *Highland Cathedral,* later to be carried to the Royal Yacht *Britannia* which would sail away after midnight in a final farewell. China's flag was officially hoisted as the sovereign standard with pomp and ceremony for the first time in Hong Kong.

A new era had begun. I was consumed by mixed emotions. There was every reason to welcome in the future, as China's economic might would support Hong Kong commercially for a long time if we played our cards right. Yet I could not help feeling there would be aspects of social life that I would miss. I realized once again how British I was in my habits and how much I loved cricket, dry humour and time spent with my good friends over a few wee drams of single malt.

I recall an article written by my friend Gerry Delilkhan in 1992 which seemed relevant in a warped way. Gerry wrote in appreciation of the inaugural International Cricket Sixes these lines: "I have long held a theory that no cricket-playing country will ever go communist. Some have come close to it, but none so far have fallen. Is the converse possible? If one teaches Marxist ideologues cricket, will they abandon Marx?" He followed on: "Cricketers are a strange breed of evangelists. Witness how the British succeeded in lodging the game in far-flung parts of their empire. They did such a good job, perhaps to their eternal regret, that teams from Australia, the West Indies, Pakistan, India and New Zealand now routinely beat the English at their national sport. So will the last remnant of the empire – Hong Kong – take cricket to the Chinese and eventually China?" Whilst no doubt written with tongue in cheek, Gerry's message somehow looks more appropriate now than in 1992 or even at the advent of the Hong Kong handover.

Today, there are more millionaires in China than in most other places. Their businessmen are all practising capitalism disguised in the politically more correct description as market economy. As for cricket, many Chinese on the Mainland are now learning to play the game. In fact China would send a team to participate in the latest Sixes to be held in November 2010, and China's ladies cricket team competes regularly against our ladies in Hong Kong.

Like many others, I was utterly exhausted after burning the candle at both ends over a sustained period of time. I needed some peace and quiet to recuperate. The family had planned for a month's break at our home in Russell starting mid-July, and I was looking forward to that in anticipation. It was the rest that I needed.

"This is not a garage. You don't have to show me the parts that have been removed..."

33

LUCKY ESCAPE

The unexpected again happened. One evening, I accidentally stepped on a bar of soap in the shower and fell awkwardly. I heard my ribs crack and went to the doctor the next morning. Two cracked ribs were confirmed after an X-ray. They strapped my body and gave me some painkillers and that was that.

After a few days, I complained of a headache and the doctor gave me some Panadols. The headache became more acute and on the third visit, I was prescribed a stronger painkiller, Feldene. I was still the macho man and was certain that the problem probably arose because of the abnormal pressure I had been under during the months before the handover. I told Gail there was no problem. "Surely a few days of relaxation in Russell will clear that. What is the fuss?"

Gail thought otherwise. One evening she confronted me. "John, in all these years, you've never been prone to headaches. I'm worried because this is abnormal." I tried to calm her down. A couple of days later, she asked me to take Thursday off, and I enquired what might be the occasion. She then disclosed that she had made an appointment at the Adventist Hospital for me to have a CT scan on my head and an MRI. I still thought it was much ado about nothing, but agreed to go in response to Gail's care and concern for me.

After the scans, the doctors told Gail that I probably did not feel the whiplash when I fell, but I must have bashed the back of my head against the shower wall because they had detected acute subdural haematoma or a big haemorrhage in my skull, the probable cause of my headaches. One could just envisage what a large blood clot would do to fill up the empty space in one's skull and the pressure this would create. No wonder there were headaches! They informed Gail that the haemorrhage had to be removed as the blood clot was threatening my life. They suggested an immediate operation.

I was told a bare minimum and Gail had to take charge. I later learned that she had consulted Uncle George Choa, one of Hong Kong's leading neurosurgeons. Uncle George came to the hospital and spoke with the other doctors and then advised Gail that although there were famous surgeons and top hospitals overseas, there was really no time to move me as the operation had to be performed at once. He however comforted Gail and told her she was not to worry as I was under the expert care of a strong team of five highly competent and professional specialists.

Thinking back, poor Gail must have been worried sick because I would have thought that no degree of consoling could have assuaged her anxiety. She did however maintain her strength and control. I did what I was told. It was a combination of accepting the need and my total belief in Gail. I agreed to subject myself to the operation. In reality I did not appreciate the danger I was in and just placed my entire faith and trust in my loving wife.

The operation took over seven hours, and the procedure must have been extremely complicated. I woke the following morning in the ICU and felt hungry and surprisingly well. I looked around to the back of my bed and saw a sealed glass jar on the sideboard and enquired what it was. The nurse brought it across and showed me the blood clot that had been removed from my head. It looked disgusting as it was the size of a cricket ball. Apparently, it was hospital regulations that this had to be shown to me. I requested the nurse to please remove it at once and said to her: "I'm not a car in repair, and this is not a garage. You don't have to show me the parts that have been removed!" She grinned.

The doctors were convinced that I survived such a testing operation only because I was a sportsman with a high degree of physical fitness. I was on the mend but had to remain in convalescence for a further three weeks. My hospitalization had completely spoilt the children's summer holidays or at least the first month thereof. They visited me daily with Gail, mostly to bring me meals prepared outside. They rightly thought that I was difficult and demanding because I just dreaded the hospital food. The two girls were fantastic and they took turns to visit, alternating between lunch and dinner. Curry in a Hurry, an Indian cuisine delivery service, was regularly patronized.

Most people encounter a crisis or two in their lifetimes. For some reason, these happened to me more frequently. Perhaps that was because I lived more recklessly or dangerously than most. However, even admitting the regularity of my mishaps, this episode was truly life-threatening. I was operated upon just in the nick of time. A couple of days' delay and I would be somewhere else now and would not be writing this book. Gail had in fact saved my life, but that was not the only occasion that she had helped me through thick and thin. I owe my wife more than I could possibly describe.

At the time of my discharge from hospital, I looked at the total hospital bill for settlement. It was only then that the seriousness of my operation sank in. As a businessman, I had grown accustomed to measuring value against the cost of services and facilities provided. My bill was well in excess of HK$1 million.

After discharge, I had to undergo weekly check-ups by Dr. Edmund Woo, the neurologist involved in my operation. Edmund and I became good friends and he was to later become my Deputy Chairman in a charity known as Enlighten – Action for Epilepsy. Edmund is in fact the husband of the charming and highly capable Audrey Eu, a leader of the Civic Party and a legislative councillor in Hong Kong.

I suffered from a bout of depression thereafter, probably the delayed reaction of the high pressure built up from before the handover, and possibly exacerbated by post-operation syndrome. My doctors cleared me for flying and I took the family on a one-stop trip to New York. This would compensate Katish and Natasha for their boring July when they spent so much time taking care of me in hospital.

New York as a destination was excellent. We could see Tracey and her husband Robin. It was convenient for Katish too as she could return to Georgetown with just a short hop, and Natasha and Sean would have a chance to see the Big Apple for the first time. New York was a tonic for all of us. Sean had a good time and we all went to take in "The Lion King" on Broadway; nice horse and carriage rides in Central Park; a visit to the aircraft carrier, the USS Intrepid; all of which pleased us. This was all capped by Sean's visit to the famous toy shop FAO Schwarz where it was a delight to watch him marvelling wide-eyed at the choice of toys available.

New York, as a great metropolitan city, was of course a gourmet's paradise in terms of variety of international cuisine. Being people who had widely travelled the world, we took full advantage of the wide choice of culinary delights. Our visit also coincided with the US Tennis Open which I very much enjoyed on live television.

Although I tried my utmost to shut it out of my mind, I was fully aware of the Asian economic crisis back home. In fact, I had seen first-hand television news of this even when I was in hospital although I had deliberately put it out of my mind for as long as possible. From New York, these troubles were compartmentalized as being remote, but I knew that big problems would await my return to Hong Kong.

"We took a good look over the horizon, but land seemed a very long way off"

34

ASIAN ECONOMIC MELTDOWN (1997/8)

The severity of the crisis hit us smack in the face upon our return to Hong Kong. The economic contagion, which had started in Thailand, swept through Asia like a swarm of locusts. No country in Asia was spared, but that was nothing compared to what was coming down the line.

The stock and property markets had risen to record highs prior to the handover. Most people were heavily invested. Some expatriates sold and cashed in. They were the lucky ones, but their actions were, I suspect, not due to their educated reading of the market nor their ability to foretell accurately the future trends, but rather driven by their inclination to exit their investments in Hong Kong at the end of the colonial era, probably wary of Hong Kong under Chinese sovereignty.

By my limited standards, I was deeply invested in Hong Kong stocks and residential apartments. Some had been acquired in the early 1990s but a few were purchased in 1995/6 when hindsight would tell us that prices were near their peak. Stocks had also hit a high point. I can recall that Chris Patten had left Hong Kong in a strong economic position with the Hang Seng Index standing above 16,000 points.

When I was still in hospital, an offer was received by Gail for one of our apartments at a price almost double the purchase price. I was out of commission in hospital and Gail had thought seriously about acceptance but did not want to bother me because of my operation and in any case the economy was still unclear at that time. The offer lapsed. Just bad luck I suppose but by August, coinciding with our time in New York, the market slipped further as the contagion deepened.

It is always easy to be wise after the event. When things were happening around you, it was hard to read when the markets would reach the bottom. The puzzle was there and the irritation was our inability to gauge the future. Those were dreadful months, but little did we know that the years that followed were to be far worse. By absolute coincidence, 1997 was also the year the Queen had dubbed her "annus horribilis"!

23rd October 1997 was a day that not many in Hong Kong would forget. The market crashed throughout Asia. On that very day, Wharf received notice that we had been awarded the Kowloon West development of the mega MTR property project in Kowloon involving huge capital. It was perhaps the only occasion in my memory when, at that moment in time, we probably wished the award had gone to someone else! It was not that we did not have deep enough pockets or strong assets to back the development. The problem we faced was one of cash flow as a deposit of a considerable amount had to be paid within a tight deadline.

The local financial market had effectively been bombed out. There was not a bank in town that would fund property projects since the Monetary Authority had imposed stringent limits on banks for lending by sector or to single borrowers. The crisis had by then escalated and the term "Asian Economic Meltdown" reflected it.

Without wasting any time, and with the Chairman's endorsement, I immediately set off on a fundraising trip to Europe and the USA to call on our senior banking friends at their headquarters. Wharf had strong assets and recurrent earnings. We were after project financing support, and I thought that provided I could convince the banks that loans to us carried virtually no risk, I might just be able to raise a good portion of what we needed. I also thought that if we could not get the full amount from a single bank, perhaps I could at least pick up a bit here and there from several banks and then "club" the transaction ourselves. Unorthodox definitely, but desperate times demanded desperate measures.

I made my way through the US first, stopping only in San Francisco and New York, and then continued my trek through the United Kingdom, France and Germany. After a frantic nine days, we had secured six separate commitments from six different banks which aggregated the equivalent of about 75% of what we required. We still needed a lead bank in Hong Kong to write the documents and were lucky to convince my good friend Mervyn Davies (now Lord Davies of Abersoch), the CEO of Standard Chartered Bank, to act in that capacity. We did exactly what I had set out to do, namely to virtually "club" a deal ourselves with the final step helped by Standard Chartered.

We had to secure the 25% shortfall with just a week to go. I went to Chris Langley at the HSBC. Chris knew me well from his days in Kuala Lumpur when I was in that part of the world. Basically, Chris did me a huge favour to the best of his ability by granting us a short-term loan to cover the amount we needed. Our requirement was fully met in time to meet the deadline, and not surprisingly the finishing touches were once again covered by the two reliable Hong Kong institutions of HSBC and Standard Chartered.

When I was travelling for this deal, I was so intensely driven by the focus of the mission that I had totally forgotten about my operation in hospital which had taken place only five weeks earlier. The trip was in a way probably therapeutic. When the fundraising was over, we all breathed a sigh of relief. I could then take things a little slower and perhaps pay some attention to my own personal affairs.

The stock market had lost 50% and the property market likewise. Suddenly, my personal net worth had been halved. Paper profits had to all intents and purposes been wiped out and faded away as a dream that had passed. Monthly mortgage payments calculated against the original purchase prices suddenly looked very expensive as rentals could no longer cover mortgage payments. We did not have much choice but to simply mark time.

The sensible thing to do was to cut losses and reduce recurrent cash outflow even if this would hurt. The bitter pill had to be swallowed. I sought to divest certain holdings. This meant the sale of stocks because at least there was a visible market and trades could be done with just a call to the brokers. As for properties, it was more difficult as there were very few transactions. Potential buyers were bottom fishing, causing prices to dive further. Banks were also dumping foreclosed properties in the market which aggravated the poor sentiments already in existence. Sellers were made to wait without much alternative and there was not much point holding even a bated breath as a recovery was certainly not something we could expect for the foreseeable future.

We took a look over the horizon, but land seemed a very long way off.

Taking into consideration the history of Hong Kong's ability to recover and the resilience of the market economy, I hoped perhaps some rebound could come in less than a year. That never came. In retrospect, we had not considered two important elements which might have made this crisis different from those past. Firstly, there had been a change of sovereignty, and we had to belatedly ask whether the new sovereign would be able to help as effectively as the former one? Secondly, this time around, there was a serious attack against the Hong Kong currency, the severity of which had not happened before.

Corporations felt the threat too, perhaps more so because of their responsibilities to their shareholders. For Wheelock, it was to be safety first. One by one, the business partnerships under Wheelock Pacific were dismantled. Having built these up with blood and sweat, I found this heartbreaking. Yet I acknowledged that it took courage and conviction to accept the overall scheme of things. It was more important to support the core business units than to spread resources to new partnerships which would take time to mature.

Wheelock/Natwest had already died an unnatural death. Wheelock Virgin was just marking time as entry into China had to be deferred because of inadequacies in the intellectual property laws in China. This would leave foreign companies exposed to infringements of copyright protection. We decided to withdraw personnel from the JV and leave things in abeyance for the time being. Virgin also saw the light and agreed.

Risks attached to the duty-free bid at the airport escalated as tourism and retail both suffered in the wake of the meltdown. This proposed joint venture with Allders never materialized.

Our partners from outside Asia might not have seen things our way. The circumstances were however so difficult within the region that they did not favour decisions to sink more capital into ventures to nurse what were to us peripheral lines of business. Wheelock/Fosters required big capital for the upgrading of the plant in Tientsin, but meaningful income would only come after the venture was given time to "brew" into maturity. Fosters would be happy to share the funding for this development of what was their main line of business, but not for us. To cut to the chase, it eventuated in the reluctant agreement that we should seek a buyer after Fosters declined to take over our 50% equity. The business was finally off-loaded to South African Brewery as they had a strategy of concentrating on the Northeast region of China.

Wheelock Pacific and Wheelock Capital had by then become virtual non-entities. Wharf was once again the giant within the wider group in the eyes of the market makers. No one had to tell me that my place should logically be back at Wharf corporate.

I took a deep breath and wondered what surprise might await me next.

"What's so great about seeing a sunrise anyway? There's one every morning!"

35

MILLENNIUM

It was a time for consolidation rather than bravado!

We called for a complete analysis across the group. The object was to identify the non-core businesses and grade those by strategic importance, cash injection dependency, synergy with other cores and so on. The idea was to weed out non-essential activities that might drain group financial and manpower resources while being off-balance with potential expected returns.

The result showed that we must play the conservative game by concentrating on organic growth within the cores of property and communications, with spare capacity given to transport and hotels. China business requiring large capital would be put on hold. All these would be reviewed at frequent intervals. The emphasis across the group was on marketing, to push for increases in market share.

Activities were naturally in a comparative lull. As far as I was personally concerned, this was a welcome change as it meant I would have time to take stock of my own priorities. I also formed my own discipline whether applied to the group or to myself – "Focus on immediate requirements. Avoid being sidetracked by distractions presented by so-called opportunities. Engage in fewer selected projects but do these well." This became my mantra.

There was a happy event within the family. Samantha was getting married. Under her unassuming and casual appearance she hid an extraordinary intellect. Samantha had achieved straight As in eight O-levels, which I suspected was a fluke. When she repeated straight As in her Australian High School Certificate (the equivalent of A-levels), I began to think she had something special. She never had an air of supcriority and always behaved like everyone else. She did as she pleased and rarely bothered to dress fashionably. While those around her showed visible agitation when confronted by problems, she would retain an air of insouciance. She never studied hard either, yet she regularly achieved the highest grades. Samantha just had a photographic memory and a highly developed academic brain.

She declined opportunities to study at universities in England and the United States, and gave preference to Melbourne University instead to read a double degree in Commerce and Law over five years. Samantha had never been one to look for financial rewards. She is of the breed that wants to do things for the good of humankind. She turned her back on the options of law practice and investment banking, and joined UNICEF as a volunteer in Hanoi, Vietnam. When she finished her first contract, she returned to Melbourne and took a position with Legal Aid in Victoria, Australia. UNICEF Vietnam was happy with her contribution and offered her another crack in Hanoi, this time as a staff member with a proper contract and benefits. Her career in international development has since kept her mobile and has taken her across many countries in the Asia Pacific region.

She was to marry a Vietnamese young man she had met at the Hanoi Press Club. They both enjoyed running on weekends with the Hash House Harriers. The wedding coincided with Vietnam's 25th Anniversary of Independence and we all descended on Hanoi amidst their national celebrations. As usual, the weather was piping hot as we checked into the old French charm and ambience of the famous Metropole Hotel where Gail and I had stayed before.

The wedding reception was held in a leading local hotel. There were hundreds of guests, half being expatriates and the other locals. Speeches had to be delivered in English and Vietnamese. Just to be gracious to Samantha's Vietnamese in-laws and guests, I made a remark that it was indeed fortuitous that my daughter was getting married in the same year as the 25th anniversary of their country's independence and I hoped their marriage would grow in unison with the development of their country. This drew a big ovation from the Vietnamese half of the large dining ballroom where the banquet was held. I guess I had drawn approval from the locals.

It was in the corridor outside the ballroom that Sean ran into my first wife Gloria. She said almost immediately to the boy, "I know you! You're Sean, aren't you? You look just like your dad." A nice way to break the ice! Gail and Gloria met formally for the first time. Samantha was the last of my first three girls to be married. The couple was to have children in succession virtually one after another, a boy followed by two girls. They are the youngest of my six grandchildren so far.

Times at Wheelock and Wharf remained uneventful. We had not done any significant new business since we acquired a telephone franchise in 1995. Without any new developments, things were quiet in the IR unit. We acted when good news arose or when damage control was called for. To my specialist eyes, there was a need to maintain regular roadshows whether or not there was any intention to raise funds. This was simply good practice for a large listed group if only to keep investors interested from time to time. Unfortunately, not much support was forthcoming from my fellow directors who believed we should play low profile. We withdrew back into our shell and lost all the momentum gained in the peak years of 1992 to 1997.

To save costs, roadshows were suspended. PR and advertising also took a back seat as budgets were cut. I found myself often as the lone voice pushing for at least a semblance of IR initiatives if only to keep our image in the public domain. My voice was not heard. This was decidedly contrary to the principles of image preservation or brand integrity which needed constant protection. One just could not turn off the tap and turn it back on again at will. Consistency had to be there. To those who fully understood the value of public relations and advertising, such activities should in fact be increased in weak market conditions, not the other way around.

The decision to suspend these activities was *plain wrong, and I took it seriously.* It had always been my nature to make my sentiments known forcefully even though my opinions might not have matched the appetites of my colleagues. Those measures did not achieve much. The group was operating ostensibly in a consolidation mode, but in reality we went on the defensive and avoided all risks. Wheelock Capital and Wheelock Pacific had come and gone. The last big deal was in 1995 when Wharf T&T came into being and there had been no other meaningful new initiatives, yet we were already on the cusp of the 21st century. We depended solely on organic growth in the redevelopment of our property portfolio.

This state of affairs pleased credit rating agencies because they generally loved companies that did not take risks. However, such an environment would not excite equity investors, particularly when the competition engaged in new joint ventures and acquisitions of new lines of business. Investor relations work became spasmodic and there was not much point for me to bash my head against the corporate wall until the economy improved. It was wiser to toe the line, keep opinions to myself and cease rocking the boat!

Corporations and governments across the planet were all worried about the speculated threats of the "Millennium Bug". All kinds of theories were forwarded by all and sundry. People talked themselves into fear and apprehension that things could go radically wrong from midnight on 31st December 1999. Clocks and computers would all stop and records and archives maintained for 100 years would be obliterated. I somehow suspected that not many knew what they were talking about!

It had been a virtual annual ritual that we would spend Christmas and New Year in New Zealand. For the millennium, many people from around the world chose New Zealand as a popular tourist destination because Gisborne would be the first city in the civilized world to see the first sunrise of the new millennium. Russell was not far from the extreme east coast and would thus see the sunrise only a tick after Gisborne. We had the perfect spot, I thought.

Typically, Gail had to be contrarian. This was the one year she did not want New Zealand. She might have had a point because she wanted to avoid the mad scramble of tourists visiting New Zealand for the millennium and reasoned that as domestic flights were not efficient, roads would be packed bumper to bumper with traffic jams. Her words were "What's so great about seeing a sunrise anyway? There's one every morning!" So when the whole world went East, we would go West to South Africa. The decision was enthusiastically supported by the children. Just thinking of going on safari got them all excited.

Planning for the South African tour needed precision. To do that wrong would waste time and incur needless expense. It was an expensive holiday. Our South African friends Hans and Karen Hawinkel put us in touch with some travel agents in Johannesburg. They did all the bookings for us under close consultation. It worked like a dream.

We arrived in Johannesburg scared stiff by the rumours of carjacking, robbery, GBH and homicide. This caused us to choose the relative safety of Sandton City, something that resembled our Harbour City. We flew the next day to Harare in Zimbabwe and could sense then that the exodus of the white population had already begun. We stayed at the massive

Elephant Hills Resort and knew at once that we had made a mistake. The resort was highly popular with the nouveau riche Africans and the atmosphere was not our cup of tea. Katish actually pleaded with me: "Promise me Dad! We should never stay in a hotel or resort with casinos in it again. It brings all sorts of funny and scary people and I don't feel good here. OK?" I agreed with her and gave her that promise.

Instead of spending that day in the resort, we had wonderful afternoon tea outdoors at the famous and more sedate Victoria Falls Hotel and soaked in the superb ambience. We should have chosen that hotel in the first place. When we returned to South Africa from Zimbabwe, Sean was happy to visit Sun City because he had seen the movie of Jackie Chan at that venue. To me, even Sun City looked ostentatious and not really to our taste apart from the pristine golf courses of typical Gary Player design as we had experienced when playing the magnificent Bintang course in Indonesia, another Player-designed course.

The Sabi Sabi safari camp in the famous big game centre Kruger Park was undoubtedly the highlight of the entire holiday. We had a ranger and a tracker all to ourselves over four days and the family was kept together throughout. The food was magnificent, normally broiled on an open fire. The meat served included ostrich, venison and such like, but my favourite was warthog. The ambience was typical safari. On a "boma" outing in the middle of a jungle, we took dinner on a white cloth laid table with roasts and fine wines from Stellenbosch. It felt as though we were indeed "Out of Africa" with more than a hint of adventure and romance.

We saw all the Big Five and when we tracked a leopard across the jungle on our vehicle, I understood the true meaning of the phrase "the chase is better than the kill". We did not kill, but only shot the leopard with the camera.

Our time in Cape Town was to coincide with the turn of the century. We saw in the millennium from a waterfront restaurant. There was a fireworks display echoed by the cheers of the revellers who were there to see in the new century. To our eyes, however, the fireworks were puny compared with the usual fireworks displays in Hong Kong. We then spent a memorable day of wine tasting through the Stellenbosch wine region. There were so many excellent vineyards that by the time we reached the end of the day, the excessive tasting had taken its toll.

On the following day, we took a drive from Cape Town via the most breathtakingly beautiful scenic route via Chapmans Bay to Hout Bay. The dramatic coastline route took us through some of the most amazing cliffs and bays we had ever seen. We have some magnificent photographs and film footage to remind us of that wonderful journey.

South Africa is a beautiful country unmatched in terms of its unique and dramatic scenery and its sheer size. Were it not for security concerns, it would be a country in which I could happily settle. It was by far the best holiday we had as a family, and the diversity of attractions offered in South Africa could not be matched anywhere.

But then, there is New Zealand, a land mass known by many as "a world in miniature". It does not have the size of South Africa and there is no Big Five, but New Zealand is also a land of rare beauty where the scenery changes by the hour as one drives from Cape Reinga at the extreme northern tip to Invercargill in the extreme south. Wild New Zealand offers a myriad of incredible attractions from geysers to lakes to snow-topped mountains, the most unique features of which are the sub-tropical sand and sea up north, and the fjords down south at Milford Sound... and the residents do not have to worry about security issues.

"What do you mean? That's golf. Learn to play the rub properly"

36

NEXT GENERATION

The so-called Millennium Bug was a non-event as we moved into the new 21st century. All the fuss around the world came to nothing!

After the most incredible trip to South Africa, we came back down to earth in Hong Kong. By September that year, Natasha had entered the Law Faculty of Nottingham University, and at the same time Sean started boarding at age nine in a friendly prep school in East Essex called Ashdown House. Both of them were in England and we felt a touch relaxed that Natasha could keep an eye on Sean from time to time.

Realistically however, Gail had to spend a considerable amount of time on multiple trips to England during the first months of Sean's stay at Ashdown. Gail's regular visits did give Sean a sense of comfort. I felt it did the same for Gail in relation to her feelings towards Sean's wellbeing. This was very much a "mother nature" thing. It was only in time that this pattern eased.

In her school life at Malvern Girls, Natasha was a good athlete in lacrosse, field hockey and track & field. She was highly popular and was elected head of house, but narrowly missed out on being head girl after a close vote. In all, those were excellent achievements for one who was ridiculed at an interview by another school in England she had applied to, and eventually declined in disgust.

In all those years since the late 1980s, I had been fortunate to have the most efficient and loyal personal assistant in the person of Amy Kwok. Her standard of English and shorthand proficiency made my job so much easier. Her loyalty was unfailing and even after my retirement in 2002, she remained happy to help. Regrettably, in these days of IT and extensive web usage, I am afraid the super-efficient personal or executive secretaries like Amy are fast becoming a dying breed! Shame, but it is a reality. Today, Amy is very much a friend to me and my family.

Reliance on Amy had to give way to self-sufficiency after retirement. I had to get acquainted with the use of the Internet and the web. As the Chinese saying goes, "When the horse dies, one simply has to walk." I learned that one is never too old to try new tricks.

Amy knew me better than anyone. As they say, an executive spends more time with his PA than with his wife. Amy could no doubt attest that I was out of sorts when there was a dearth of problematic puzzles for me to solve at work. There was a definite scarcity of IR challenges for me in the office at that time. I was effectively deprived of the chance of doing what I did best. As I could not find satisfaction at work, I resorted to other pursuits, and my mind subconsciously started to assess places where I could conceivably live away from Hong Kong.

Preferred places had to be separated into one group where one "lives to work" as against those places where one simply "works to live". The former include large cosmopolitan cities where one strives to achieve success. At that stage of my life in the year 2000, I only knew how to get satisfaction from driving myself hard. To my taste, these places would only include London, New York, Tokyo and Hong Kong. Everyone's preferences are different. I suppose Gail's top choice would be Paris. Tokyo could get my top vote had I understood Japanese!

I love London and knew it well from the "Swinging Sixties" when I was there as a law student. That was the time of the Beatles, the Rolling Stones, beatniks, flowers, drugs and wild sex parties. Some decade that was! London also offers world-class sporting events like Wimbledon, Ascot, and of course test cricket at Lord's. I know most of the haunts in the city and where to find them. The city has a charm of its own and I still try to be there as often as I can.

There are many great memories of England that stand out, most of which relate to moments of magic in sports. I can recall clearly a test match when Richie Benaud turned his legbreaks off a footmark and changed a match that looked home and dry for England to Australia's favour. Then there was the Wimbledon Men's Singles Final where Rod Laver demolished Tony Roche in straight sets in an awesome display of dominance, the impressiveness of which I have not seen since. To cap it all, there was that glorious day in 1966 at Wembley when England won the World Cup. I could have sworn that the ball did not cross the goal line. Years later in Hong Kong, Sir Geoff Hurst insisted to me that the goal was legitimate. Geoff was my guest in Hong Kong when I was the Chairman of the Sports Development Board and as I was his host, the matter was not disputed, especially when Geoff was such a gentleman. As a matter of interest, goal line technology is still not used nowadays, almost 50 years since Geoff's "goal".

Ever since Lesley was married to Andrew Tattersall, I have seen too little of them since they live miles away from London in Cheshire. They met when both were attending university in London. Andrew started his career in executive search and Lesley worked for Thai Airways running the Royal Orchid Tours. A few years after their marriage, Andrew's father decided to take early retirement and wanted Andrew and his brother David to take over the business. As most of their operations were up north, it meant that they would have to leave London.

The Tattersalls held the franchise of the French petrol stations of the "TOTAL" brand covering a substantial region in the north of England, and the brothers began in partnership. David was to run the corporate side and Andrew the operations. I was in London when Andrew met me and I asked him how much he knew about the running of petrol stations. Without any hesitation, Andrew gave me a quick reply: "I don't know the slightest about the business at this stage, but it does not seem to matter. All I have to do is get in my car, drive round to check on all the stations and meet the individual station managers. They are all very polite to me whether I know the business or not!" *I thought that was just priceless!* That was years ago, and I guess he is now much more of an expert in his line of business.

The United Kingdom would not be complete without Scotland, the place of my ancestral heritage, and an aspect of significant pride to me. Even young Sean has inherited this. In his prep school at Ashdown House, Sean was the only boy who opted for the bagpipes instead of the more popular instruments like piano, violin or the trumpet. He continued with this throughout secondary school at Milton Abbey, being taught by Scottish pipe majors. He even acquired his bagpipes and kilt with the tartan of turquoise and light blue, consistent with the colours of the Hunts.

Any golfer must experience playing the Scottish links to understand the real meaning of strong wind when the choice of clubs can be a four or five clubs difference depending on whether you are playing against a strong headwind or with it. I can clearly recall being advised to take a three-wood against the wind on a 160 yard par 3, and was still short of the green; yet when we turned for the back nine, I could reach a 460 yard par 4 with a driver and a sand wedge. This is but one of the many features of play at the home of golf in Scotland. It is a privilege to have experienced that.

The Scotsman's knowledge of the game is legendary and I recall an incident which I would not easily forget. I was at the British Open a few decades ago at St. Andrews and standing behind the green when Arnold Palmer played his approach shot. The ball came straight at the flag, landed about 20 yards short but took a cruel bounce to the left and ended up in deep rough. An American voice boomed from the crowd "Jeez! Hard luck Arnie! Bad bounce!" A Scottish voice immediately echoed a reply "What do you mean? Learn to play the rub properly."

I have read Ian Rankin extensively with much enjoyment. I find his prolific Rebus series describe the places so well that I can almost feel and smell Scotland. There has got to be a reason why I have a kinship with friends from north of the border. In fact, when I was in court for my trial, those who attended in my support had names like Jim Mailer, Jock Mackie, Murray Burton etc., all Scotsmen, and to cap that, my defence counsel Ray Pierce was yet another.

The Big Apple is a city you either love or hate. It is perhaps the most cosmopolitan city around, with the greatest diversity of ethnic, cultural and linguistic presence. It is a city chosen by my second daughter Tracey and her husband Robin whose origin is the Philippines.

People from the Philippines seem to have a natural ear for music. Robin is no exception. When he was at the Berkeley College of Music in Boston, he made the five-piece ensemble in his first year, but his love of jazz led him to change course to jam sessions. He soon became an accomplished jazz professional. His forte is the electric guitar and he has featured regularly in recordings, concerts and on the road with big names like Linda Ronstadt, Harry Belafonte, Rihanna, Lizz Wright and many others.

Tracey has adapted to a career of a realtor in New York despite her university degree being in languages. However, I suppose this skill would come in handy in her work in New York where many languages are spoken by the diverse population. Tracey and I always have a great deal to say to one another. She would open her thoughts and aspirations to me and I would suitably respond. Whenever we met, we would exchange views, but in her own career she had the conviction to back her own instincts. When in New York, I always tried to give Tracey as much time as I could simply because I never saw enough of her.

A few years ago, I spoke on the phone with my grandson Ross and I asked the six-year-old where (meaning which school) he was being educated. His answer was "Grandpa John, I am educated by the city of New York of course"! To my way of thinking, those were of course Tracey's views.

I have travelled widely through the United States and have found each place to have its own charm and attraction. I have been fortunate enough to have seen a fair portion of this vast country, but in my own view at least, none of these places measure up to New York City.

"My retirement would mean the end of three generations of continuous service to Wharf by the Hung family"

37

END OF 34 YEARS

Nothing exciting was happening in the group; it plodded along in an ultra-cautious mode, and I marked time by carrying on mainly with routine housekeeping. I was getting bored and restless.

For years, I had longed for more time in New Zealand. It seemed a waste to leave the house in Russell so under-utilized. However, were we to live in New Zealand, there were concerns that I had to resolve. Firstly, I had to be involved in a business in Hong Kong to ensure there would be a steady flow of monthly income after retirement, yet not so intense as to tie me down completely. Secondly, I needed to establish a foothold in the commercial circles in New Zealand so that I could have meaningful work, as I could not see myself as a man of leisure. Resolving these issues would permit my gradual migration physically from Hong Kong if I wanted to.

I took stock and weighed the options and concluded I was getting stale at Wharf, having served 33 years. It was time to make a change and I was already 63. The Chairman was informed that I would work through my contract to 31st January 2002, and then call it a day. The board began to plan for my succession.

My attention then turned quite naturally to the personal front as I had only a year before retirement. There was no great urgency but I should be alert to possible opportunities that might come my way.

I was invited to be a Vice-President of the Hong Kong Rugby Football Union. That opened the door to my involvement in the periphery of a game which I loved but was never able to play seriously because of the handicap of wearing spectacles ever since I was eight years old. This gave me the chance to mingle with the likes of the mighty All Blacks, including the likes of Sean Fitzpatrick and Jonah Lomu, to the envy of my son Sean as my wife's family idolized the All Blacks. Sirocco kept winning or at least finished in the frame in most races. Winning photographs soon filled one entire wall in my office. The horses in New Zealand were also amongst the winners.

My retirement wind-down started midway through 2001. There was no intention on the part of the board to hire a replacement from outside the group. I might not have had the highest IQ nor was I as academically equipped as some others, but I was hard to replace as I was equally comfortable with Westerners and with the Chinese, had the gift of the gab, was socially affable, my connections had international spread and I had special expertise in corporate relations. As the Americans would say, I could talk the talk and walk the walk.

There was to be not one successor, but I was to pass my experience to four different individuals. Investor relations were in good hands as my right arm in the IR unit had been well trained although I wished a director from the main board would lead. Public relations and advertising were taken up by a highly capable lady who had worked with me. Banking relations as a discipline was seamlessly transferred to competent senior finance executives. It was the networking aspect of my role that presented problems, but I was not at all surprised.

We had a self-motivated and highly intelligent executive who ran the Transport Division uplifted to this role. On the surface, he already had good connections with the district boards and some legislative councillors. He was quick on the uptake and had all the appropriate credentials to fit into the job. However, if there was one thing that could not be taught or passed on, it would be the friendships and connections that I had personally nurtured through years of social interaction. These relationships were exclusively mine and could not be passed on like a baton in a relay. I could open doors with people much wealthier or of a higher status than myself, and this coverage did not stop in Hong Kong but extended to other countries. How could this be handed over? I concluded that if the occasion demanded, perhaps Peter might have to handle it himself.

The Chairman rightly decided that apart from handover work, I should be relieved from recurrent duties. Instead I was to concentrate on special tasks or projects as directed by the Chairman himself. This would demand my focus. Peter had always known how to get the best out of his people, and I was to complete a comprehensive analysis of the entire group and present a five-year plan along the following terms of reference:

Where was the group going? What did we want the group to be in five years?

Recommendations were to include how best to restructure the group, the steps that were needed and the timing of each step.

The object was to streamline the group to achieve the realization of maximum shareholder value, the enhancement of profit, the reduction of cost without loss of efficiency, and to preserve cash flow with a specified percentage limit on group gearing.

This looked a tall order, but I felt confident in my ability to tackle the mission. There remained a few months for me to complete this and I went to work at once by reading extensive research, gathering financial data, and speaking to colleagues and investment banking friends. All of these efforts were designed towards assembling a comprehensive knowledge base as the foundation of my analysis and recommendations.

In the meantime, personal planning commenced on what I would do after retirement. I had to be associated with a going concern rather than a start-up to avoid having to face a slow build-up of distributable income. Just at that time, an opportunity came my way.

A private company engaged in graphic design, annual report printing, export of up-market packaging creations, brand name envelopes and stationery etc. was looking to expand. The company was founded six years earlier by the principal shareholder who was the lady CEO. She was smart and motivated and her impressive achievements stood up to scrutiny. She was also involved in charities and was a radio host one evening per week – altogether resourceful with a defined ambition. The list of her overseas buyers with ample orders in hand would bring income to cover at least the rest of the financial year. Recorded turnover and profits had been in a growth mode for the previous few years.

She was looking at a London listing to lift the company to the next platform of growth and needed some funding for pre-listing expenses. Professional advice from London had confirmed the viability of the listing. Due diligence verified these views, and I began to negotiate an entry into the business. Legally drawn agreements were executed. I was to be an executive director, the CEO and a substantial shareholder. My service would commence on 1st April 2002 after a short break of two months.

Hard work never bothered me as I had been a workaholic for years. Gail and the children used to complain at my inability to forget work even over weekends and holidays. With the promise of the new role just negotiated, the possibility of satisfying work demands and more leisure time, the New Zealand proposition seemed more than a remote possibility.

The festive season was abnormally busy since many kind people insisted on having Gail and I for my pre-retirement dinners. Where we could not find an evening slot in our schedule, we made do with lunches instead.

It was not my nature to decline these well-meant invitations. That would not be the way to repay kindness. There were those who mistook my retirement to mean we were leaving Hong Kong. We were to postpone those on the assurance that we would be around for a while yet.

The five-year plan was duly presented to the Chairman in the New Year of 2002. Peter had a quick look, and then put it away. It was a well-considered dossier that would take time to digest and I left him to study it at his own leisure. It was gratifying to note in the years after my retirement, some of my strategic recommendations were acted upon, especially those concerning group restructuring. Nostalgically, I felt that the paper was perhaps a fitting parting gift from a long-serving man.

My career of 34 years with the group came to a close with a retirement banquet given in my honour at the end of January 2002. I was told that it was the biggest bash for a retiring director for a very long time, and was of course flattered. Peter began with a formal welcoming speech which lavished embarrassing accolades on my contributions to the group. This meant the world to me because it was Peter who had given me my big break in Singapore and worked so closely with me throughout my every move upwards. He encouraged me in every aspect of my career, partnered me in golf and tennis, and we had frequently enjoyed social interaction together with our families. I regard Peter as a true friend, more than just my superior. He will always have room in my heart.

Many senior colleagues took turns to speak at the dinner. Good-humoured but often rude remarks were made in jest. Some well considered remarks were made by Stephen Ng, and as I had always been happy to laugh at myself, these utterances fell on my appreciative ears. Gonzaga Li mentioned that my retirement would signal the end of three generations of continual service to Wharf by the Hung family. It was only then that I was somewhat stirred by emotions.

It was all good clean fun. I dutifully replied with suitable decorum, but when urged to continue, I recall that I pulled a tall bar stool on stage, sat there, and then things degenerated into a Johnny Carson type of talk show. With the encouragement of the famous single malt from Scotland, I spoke with relaxed eloquence to entertain the audience for another 40 minutes. I enjoyed myself thoroughly but was not sure whether the audience found it amusing or otherwise. I would never know. On second thought, perhaps it was OK as one of them was kind enough to take me home that night!

*"The government franchise system in Hong Kong introduced so
successfully by the colonial administration was the envy of most
Asian countries, yet we seem to be bent on destroying it"*

38

Post-"Handovers"

This was a time for reflection as two "handovers" had taken place as
far as I was personally concerned. Firstly the change of sovereignty
for Hong Kong in 1997, and secondly I had handed over all my portfolios
in Wheelock/Wharf to my successors.

For a time even after my retirement, I held on to a few board positions
in affiliates or subsidiaries within the Wheelock Group. These were
companies such as Realty Development Corporation and Lane Crawford
International, companies which were identified as candidates for
privatization. As I was retired, I could probably handle those in a more
detached manner when the time came. In the circle of my close friends,
a joke went round that wherever I remained on the board of directors of
a group subsidiary, that company would be privatized soon! This actually
came about and these are in fact private companies now.

Over perhaps the last two decades, and accentuated after the handover
in 1997, I have observed some disturbing trends which could permanently
change the political, commercial and financial fabric of how Hong Kong
works as a whole. These have arisen from a combination of anti-business
sentiments, the government's virtual subservience to the legislative

council, "people power" of the masses and the growing influence of the media.

The two areas in which I am most concerned are firstly, how quasi-government statutory bodies or "quangos" are run; and secondly, how people power and anti-business sentiments are affecting the hitherto highly successful government franchise system that has existed in Hong Kong for such a long time. I was deeply involved in both aspects personally, and therefore take an active interest in these issues.

A large number of important quasi-government statutory bodies such as the Airport Authority, the Housing Authority, the Sports Development Board, the Hospital Authority and so on have traditionally been run by boards comprising people from the commercial or professional circles by way of government appointments. These non-government appointed officials accept the appointments in good faith and perform their functions and responsibilities on behalf of the government as their civic contribution, and they are not paid at all for their services. In this way, the government saves a very substantial sum of money which would have to be spent on emoluments if these jobs were held by paid civil servants. Moreover, all these quasi-statutory bodies cover essential areas of Hong Kong's overall administration and their success is dependent on the generous civic-minded citizens of high status who take on these roles. I was one of them.

In days gone by, the board members of these quangos, in particular the chairmen thereof, would receive unreserved support from the government in the process of performing their functions. In recent years however, because of the call for transparency, the work of these quangos has been put constantly under the media microscope. Every purported small malfeasance, minor mistake or alleged error in judgment is exposed in public, with the inevitable witch-hunt that follows. The public and the media are keen to apportion blame, and unpaid board members of these statutory bodies are often crucified by public outcry.

Upon the excuse of accountability, the government leaves these bodies, and the individuals therein, to fend for themselves and little support is given to them. The end result is that most of these appointees become disenchanted. Think about this. I did when I was the Chairman of the SDB: "I spend endless hours in public service for free, at times even encroaching on the time needed for my own central career, and yet when something tiny goes wrong, no one comes to my aid and I am crucified by the press and at times even by official panels. Why the hell should I do this?"

The upshot is the natural reaction of the appointees that it may simply not be worthwhile taking on these positions. If fewer and fewer are prepared to accept such roles, either the appointees in the future would be of a lower standard or government may have to contemplate turning these into paid positions, thus creating a larger and more expensive government.

Hong Kong was very much the envy of other Asian countries when we talk about the franchise system of providing essential infrastructure in Hong Kong. I know this to be so as I was engaged in an Asian conference in which a full session was devoted to this very question.

Firstly, it should be noted that this system has been in force in Hong Kong for a very long time. If we are to include schemes of arrangement, licences as well as franchises, over 70% of Hong Kong's infrastructure is provided by the private sector. This includes all transport services, all utilities for gas and electricity, the entire container port, all the cross-harbour tunnels, all the telephone services whether landline or mobile, all television services whether free-to-air or cable, etc. By handing out what I would term broadly as franchises, the government carries no risks whether financial or operational, as all these are passed to the franchisees.

At one time, franchised business was good business. However, in recent years, each time an application is made for rate or fare increase, no matter how marginal and commercially justifiable, it invariably attracts cries of the public's inability to afford these increases. Approval never comes easily, to the extent that franchised operators are often unable to cover their costs, let alone make meaningful returns. Examples are the ridiculously low fare of the Hong Kong trams in this day and age; and the period of 13 years before the Western Harbour Crossing could break even and declare a genuine dividend. I just ask this simple question: "If you had a pocket of X million dollars, would you invest and wait 13 years for your first dividend (remembering that there are only 12 years remaining before the franchise expires and the tunnel reverts to government ownership) or would you place the money into lucrative financial funds or bonds?"

Government must ensure that franchised operators are given a fair run, and this would be by means of supporting the operators and not turning a blind eye just because there are public objections. Otherwise, I would surmise that franchised projects may no longer attract serious private sector bidders. What then? Well, in my opinion this could lead to a dry-up of private sector interest, eventually requiring that these essential projects are taken up by the government itself. What will be the result of that? It would probably bring higher taxes and less efficient services.

The government franchise system in Hong Kong introduced so successfully long ago by the colonial administration was the envy of most Asian countries, yet we seem to be bent on destroying it.

My mind is not influenced by the opinions of others. Here in Stanley, I can see things clearly. It may not be out of place for me to assess the realities that face us now.

Hong Kong has undergone immense changes in the recent decades, and these have become more pronounced and noticeable since the 1997 handover. It did take a bit of time to sink in, but one cannot help but try to discern the difference between colonial rule under the British and the so-called "self rule" that we are said to have under the guise of "one country, two systems".

Hong Kong is not a country, but a special administrative region of China. In practice, when it comes to matters of importance, the ultimate decisions are invariably influenced by Beijing. Whilst Hong Kong continues to function well in international commerce, we are in effect politically driven by China. In that sense, it is more "one country" than "two systems". We do have "self rule" but there are limits in its degree as many vital issues require China's approval and Beijing's directions cannot be ignored.

What has changed, then? Unlike other former British colonies, Hong Kong has not become independent. Rather, in a practical sense, we now have a different sovereign. Our sovereignty no longer rests in Britain, but with the People's Republic of China. Yet we are a special administrative region of China, not under the direct rule of China itself. The Basic Law defines this special arrangement. In a bizarre way, are we not in essence like a colony of the PRC? Simply put, is it not true that instead of London, we now look to Beijing as our sovereign?

The energy that Hong Kong exudes is second to no other city, especially in terms of international business. It is a great place in which to make money. Realistically, we do not match up to other major Asian capital cities in terms of culture, whether in the arts, heritage, conservation or sports. Somehow, we do not show the same commitment to these values as they do from the point of view of national pride. We tend to leave this to the motherland. However, we are second to none in relation to economic strength, infrastructural development, financial success and our position in world trade. What is Hong Kong really then? Are we not simply a marketplace of mammoth proportions?

It is after all a place where living is relatively safe, with a reasonable degree of freedom for us to get on with our daily lives, and where commerce is conducted with due regard to market forces most of the time. Are these elements not the basic demands for most of us? We have most of these to permit our marketplace to thrive, so long as we do not expect dramatic political and social changes in the short term.

But is this good enough for some of the people living here? That is the question.

"Hey, look at those legs! Is that what good money can buy?"

39

PURE NEW ZEALAND

Some things were just not meant to be!

In January 2002, I tried to contact the lady CEO of the company I was to join after my retirement. She could not be reached. I thought she might have been travelling. When she remained not contactable after a week, I began to wonder. After a fortnight, suspicion turned to alarm. I wrote to her but the letter was returned to sender. I had my messenger hand-deliver the letter but the messenger returned and told me that the office was locked. Delivery to her home was attempted, but I was told that she had left the apartment. A friend who had worked with her could not enlighten me either. From scattered information gathered in the following days, I deduced that she had probably done a bunk as nobody seemed to know where she was.

What I had discovered subsequently would confirm that my visceral fear was probably true. From one of the company's stranded staff members, I was given to understand that the company held many orders for goods to be supplied, and most of those were placed by large buyers from the United States.

At that time, a political row had been brewing between China and the United States on trade imbalance and alleged unethical trade practices.

The US administration thus imposed anti-dumping regulatory bans on Chinese exports and all US buyers had to comply in response. The products of the lady's company were manufactured at factories in China, thus the orders which the company had relied on for cash flow suddenly fizzled out. The lady probably did not have as deep pockets as suggested by the impression she gave, and had nowhere to turn. The deduction which I had formed was the best that I could make in the absence of any confirmation of the actual truth and the lady's whereabouts.

Having known and worked with her for years, I was obviously disappointed and angered by her lack of courtesy, but was nevertheless thankful that I had at least not yet paid for my shares. I no longer had the job that I had counted on, and had wasted all my time and effort in that process. I was left high and dry.

It was a hell of a way to start a retirement!

Incidentally, Gail did say to me months before that she did not have a good feeling about the lady, citing reasons of the lady's open display of intemperance and extravagance. Gail's sixth sense would never be dismissed again.

We all suffer from economic and political variations and we are sometimes affected by other people's lack of sincerity or dishonesty. In everyone's lifetime, there are ups and downs. I had gone through many economic and market cycles and seen tough and frustrating setbacks. My motto has always been to avoid moping and get on with the next phase. This was such a situation.

Since I had already planned to "land" in New Zealand business circles, why not set off without delay, as there was no longer anything to keep me in Hong Kong in the short term? I put the disappointment aside and made ready for New Zealand.

I had for some years been preaching the gospel on the attraction of cross-border trade between China and the outside world through the use of Hong Kong as a bridge. That was essentially "Hong Kong Plus". My personal ties with New Zealand gave me a vested interest to promote cross-border trade. With the help of my good friend Frank Wilson, the New Zealand Consul-General in Hong Kong, we lined up a series of meetings and speaking engagements in Auckland and Wellington. The theme of my speeches were adaptations of the "Hong Kong Plus" messages.

The sessions went exceedingly well and these drew much interest from the audience and the news media in New Zealand. To be honest, my motive was not altogether altruistic. I had hoped that my talks would provide the foundation upon which I could build a consultancy practice. Unfortunately, I had not yet fully understood the psyche of the resident New Zealanders.

Without wishing to be disparaging, apart from the expatriate New Zealanders who live abroad, the majority of resident New Zealanders would not wish to pay for advice and experience if there was a way they could obtain it free of charge. I say this with reason because after my return to Hong Kong, I was bombarded by numerous letters and emails, seeking information, advice and even favours such as introductions etc. The moment I broached the question of fees, these people just disappeared into oblivion.

I was in retirement and no longer remunerated by a corporation. It was quite legitimate for me to ask for a consultancy fee if people wanted my service or advice. If they wanted to live in Hong Kong, gather their own experience and local knowledge and set up a Hong Kong office, staff up and cover all operational costs, then that would be their privilege. However, if they elected to remain in the comfort of their own homes in New Zealand, yet wanted advice from me to further their market development, then it would be logical that they should pay for my professional services. Could this curious phenomenon be the effect of the remote geographical location of New Zealand from the rest of the developed world?

I had been a dedicated member of the select Asian Business Advisory Board of New Zealand, and had frustratingly tried my absolute utmost to promote and encourage cross-border trade. These efforts came to nothing because of the New Zealanders' reluctance to leave their shores and physically visit the marketplace at work in China.

I was asked in an Advisory Board special meeting in Hong Kong by Prime Minister Helen Clark why New Zealand had found it so difficult to penetrate the China market when Australia had done so well? My short answer was "Prime Minister, I hate to say this, but the brutal truth is that New Zealand businessmen have so far refused to get off their butts and come to Hong Kong and China. They expect the business to come to them at home." The PM took note of my remark with a smile, and repeated my words with an "Aha!"

From the very first day I set foot in New Zealand years ago with Gail, I soaked in the breathtaking scenic beauty, the warmness of the people in the small communities, the attraction of the outdoors, the pollution-free environment and the ideal location for sporting pursuits as a participant or a spectator. To make things more complete, throw in the excellent wines and, right there in Russell, the best deep-sea fishing in the South Pacific. It struck me as a place as close to perfection as I could find anywhere.

As a keen spectator or participant, the cricket, golf, horse racing and rugby were all there. With these offered on the cable TV channels, the summers in the Bay of Islands were idyllic – warm sunshine during the day and the slightly cooler evenings to enjoy a BBQ with friends and relatives, always accompanied by a glass of Marlborough Sauvignon Blanc, or better still a Central Otago Pinot Noir.

I was fortunate to have Gail to introduce me to her country. As a native of Russell, she gave me a vicarious sense of belonging in the small town. Within a week, I was to know most of the people in the street, many of whom were Gail's relatives as the Arlidge family had been residents there for generations. A foreigner arriving on his own for the first time would find it difficult to assimilate into the community. As for me, the people were most generous with their welcome and many relatives actually paid special visits to meet me. My father-in-law Francis however suggested that they did not come for the sole purpose of meeting me, they were rather there to "view the curiosity" to fill the day. As it turned out, this "curiosity" was probably more curious about them than the other way around.

My growing love of fishing dominated my time in Russell. I would go out on a boat at every opportunity. After the passing of Francis in 1988, not only did I miss his presence, but there was a need to find new fishing companions. This normally came in the form of professionals who hired out their fishing boats as this was the surest way to get a decent catch. When the opportunity arose, we would go out with Max Arlidge, Gail's first cousin. Max was probably the one who had picked up Francis' tricks on fishing more than anyone else in the family. He was one of the best fishermen other than Francis I had shared a boat with.

Gail is the youngest of six siblings of four girls and two boys. I could see at once that Gail was close to Evlyn, the eldest sister and Johnny, the younger of the two brothers. Both were the kind and undemanding type. Evlyn was always game for a laugh, but Johnny was quiet and introverted. Sadly, they were the first two to pass away. There were the other sisters Fran and Airini and their husbands Allen and Russell, both affable and easygoing characters. They all shared many happy hours with us.

As far as I was concerned personally, I took immediately to the eldest brother Clive and his lovely wife Eileen. This affinity probably emanated from the fact that Clive and I were from the same vintage in terms of age. Clive was to become my trusted brother-in-law and we shared many interesting conversations on rugby, cricket, golf, fishing and a host of other matters of common interest. Eileen, being one of the kindest souls I know, became very attached to our family as we did to theirs.

One of the daughters of Clive and Eileen was Paula who has to be the biggest scream. She oozed hilarity, always ready to entertain with her outlandish remarks, and should have been a comedienne. In our early days in New Zealand, people somehow had the idea that we were quite well-to-do. This was presumably because we bought Uncle Mervyn's house and rebuilt it, then furnished it with tasteful furniture and artifacts shipped in from overseas. We flew in and out of New Zealand, sent our children to boarding schools, and generally lived well albeit without extravagance.

One morning, I was sitting on a deck chair reading a book and wearing just shorts which exposed my long spindly legs. Paula walked out of the kitchen onto the verandah and, quick as a flash, called out "Hey! Look at those legs! Is that what good money can buy?" My self-consciousness evaporated in the face of cracks like that, even though directed rudely at me!

"China Coast was the most appropriate charity for me to chair. It brought home to me who I really was"

40

HOLISTIC APPROACH

JTH & Associates was set up on my return from New Zealand to promote services on consultancy, advisory and investment activities. It was a deliberate decision even though some business friends in New Zealand had suggested that I should set up base there, a move that I resisted.

Anticipating that potential business opportunities would probably be largely on cross-border trade between China/Hong Kong and the outside world, my value was obviously dependent on my knowledge of Asia and my connections in Hong Kong which was my home ground. Were I to live in New Zealand, I would essentially be playing "away", and would soon be out of the loop in Hong Kong and thus lose all my connections. Even my Kiwi friends saw the wisdom of this decision.

The concept was to use JTH & Associates as a catch-all umbrella outfit as I could not at that point in time predict the exact types of business that might come my way. A handful of consultancy roles soon surfaced and those were in the main project- and fee-based with small listed companies or companies eyeing a listing in the near term. These covered a range of completely different businesses all looking for corporate advice. To me, management was management with no rocket science required.

I was invited to join the Advisory Board of CVC Partners Asia, a global private equity house of substantial size. The advisory board consisted of experienced business hands from major Asian cities like Tokyo, Singapore, Kuala Lumpur and Taipei, and I was the Hong Kong link. CVC deployed their considerable funds selectively and would only invest if the opportunity fitted all their stringent criteria. They would step in, take control, enhance profit through a well defined strategy and then exit after a few years when the business matured. These transactions were generally so large that they would be happy with just three or four deals per year.

I found this involvement invigorating. The lively exchanges in their annual retreats were both educational and thought-provoking as we heard each other's presentations on a wide variety of macro subjects on political and economic trends. It was a role that I thoroughly enjoyed.

As far as my consultancy was concerned, it was no surprise that what people wanted from me was not my management expertise. They looked to me for business ideas and corporate structuring but most of all my network of valuable connections. I knew then that my biggest asset was my business leads.

Out of the blue, I ran into Robert Ng, Chairman of South China Holdings, a listed group engaged in stock broking, corporate finance, manufacturing, credit loans, publishing and China ventures. Robert had heard about my retirement from Wharf and thought I might be of help to them. I was then offered the role of advisor to their board. They provided an office for me but did not tie me down to South China only. I was free to continue other work so long as this did not come into conflict with their business.

It was then that I marvelled at the power and flexibility of modern communications, without which I would not have been able to conduct multiple roles for various companies at different geographical locations. I had become holistic in my pursuits. The laptop was virtually my office.

This permitted total mobility and I could operate whenever and wherever I was, save for important face-to-face meetings. So many advances had been made in the virtual world that even retired people like me had to be honed in the use of these web tools. More were to come in the forms of the blog, Facebook, Twitter etc. There was no hiding. We had to become part of this world if we were not to be marginalized from modern commerce.

I had discovered the power of persuasion early on when I managed to talk myself into the sixth form in school and into Hong Kong University. This ability had stayed with me throughout my career and was practised extensively in my investor relations initiatives. With emphasis on the web, the usage of persuasion is no longer limited to physical audience coverage. It is now possible to exploit the web as a medium to make one's voice heard by many. In the past, the world was dominated by military, economic and industrial might. But now, the power of persuasion can be exploited more and more with devastating effect. This is now widely known as *soft power* and nobody can afford to ignore its effect and reach. How I wish the ability to use this soft power had been available so readily when I was at the height of my career in the early 1990s. My success could have been even more pronounced.

It was then that Sean was about to complete his prep schooling at Ashdown House. His academic achievements were passable but he was weak in mathematics. I was not surprised, as it must have been in his genes! Indeed, Sean seemed to have inherited many of my traits, be these good or bad, and weakness in mathematics was but one of them. He was a good cricketer, a reasonable lock in rugby and possessed a glorious swing in golf.

Somehow, he managed to get past Common Entrance and chose to board at Milton Abbey in Dorset for his secondary years. He grew to love that school which enhanced his confidence in both academic and sporting pursuits. He came into his own on the cricket field, excelling in his new ball opening spells and pulling his weight with the bat. His golf improved as he learnt the value of practice around and on the green. He represented the school in both sports. He was already 6'3" tall.

At about the same time, an old friend David Davies (now Sir David) invited me to join the board of EFG Private Bank in London. David had been the Managing Director of Hongkong Land, which was under the Jardines group (as Wharf was at the time). We were thus sister companies. After he retired from Hongkong Land, we invited David onto the Wharf board and we became colleagues. It was his turn to bring me into EFG of which he was the Chairman. David saw my role as their Asian link as he regarded Asia as too robust a market for the bank to ignore.

I was excited by the prospect and the challenge of the mission. It was also fortuitous as the EFG position in London meant that the director's fees would virtually pay for Sean's education in England, and the quarterly board meetings in London would enable me to visit Sean more frequently.

To join the board, I had to satisfy the stringent requirements of the Financial Services Authority (FSA) which included their acceptance that I was a "fit and proper" person to hold office. My credentials were more than adequate and no problems were encountered. One aspect that did astound me however was the extreme rigidity that bordered on absurdity in the FSA. As I worked in Asia, I needed my contact printed on my EFG business card, otherwise people would never know how to reach me. I agreed with the EFG compliance group that my card should be identical to everyone else's, including the London address, email, telephone etc., but with only a single specific request for the inclusion of my Hong Kong mobile number. That seemed a simple thing, but did it get caught up in the FSA bureaucracy? Endless questions and endless answers were exchanged hither and yon! It took over four months to clear this. Unbelievable!

The consultancy, advisory and board positions were coming together nicely. New Zealand was not going badly either with the racing partnerships and a good potential being explored with Haigan Murray to market New Zealand-based financial instruments in Asia.

It also appeared that my profile was still there. RTHK had a series on leading businessmen titled "View from the Top" comprising eight separate programmes of 30 minutes each conducted by Phil Whelan. Despite my initial hesitation, Phil twisted my arm and I eventually succumbed. The interview was recorded in the casual atmosphere of the Cricket Club, and this was my first radio exposure after the Wharf retirement. I recall a slip of the tongue when I referred to the 1997 change of sovereignty as the "hangover"!

My attention was then severely distracted by the issue of sports administration. A few media reports appeared on the purported confusion between the roles of the Sports Development Board (SDB) and the Sports Federation & Olympic Committee (SF&OC). There was an incongruous partnership in Hong Kong between the Sports Federation, a body that just grew from the grass roots, and the Olympic Committee. In everyday working, individual sports associations representing different sports would take their grievances to the SF&OC, and on certain occasions the SF&OC would take these cases to the SDB.

The SDB was established by the Hong Kong Government and their principal role, inter alia, was the distribution of annual funding to over 70 sports associations on behalf of the Government. Thus it was the body that held the purse strings. However, the Government had never given sufficient subvention of funds to sports and the SDB could only appease some 12 elite sports with adequate funding. The others would receive only a little or nothing. The under-funded associations were understandably aggrieved, but there was nothing the SDB could do. There was nothing left in the kitty. As Chairman of the SDB, I had to balance the impossible year after year.

The overall structure of sports management in Hong Kong was all wrong. The SDB was a government-established statutory body, thus responsible and accountable only to the Government for the management and finance of sports. Technically, the OC was independent from Government and only answerable to the International Olympic Committee (IOC). In the logical scheme of things, the SF was really not in the equation for sports funding, and yet they would take on the role of advocate with the SDB on funding matters by leaning on the OC as their twin association. All this left the structure of sports management muddled and almost impossible to understand.

I found the SDB's role under this cloud almost untenable. Without adequate knowledge of the true position, there was speculation in the media that a feud was in existence between myself and Tim Fok, the President of the SF&OC, as though we were both power-grabbing. This could not be further from the truth as Tim and I had been good friends for a long time, way before I was the SDB Chairman.

Things came to such a head that the Chief Executive of the SAR, Tung Chee-hwa, had to intervene. Tung called Tim and me for a three-way meeting to try to stop the escalation of the problem which had turned public. Having served the SDB for over seven years in one of the most harrowing and thankless jobs I had ever held outside my central career, the Government later decided to let me stand down, and allowed someone else to carry the mantle. I was extremely relieved. I had given sweat and tears to the job, which at times even encroached on my attention to my main job at Wharf. The exit from the SDB also saved me embarrassment when the SDB was disbanded some eight months thereafter.

Back on the commercial front, I was put in touch with a company called the FCP Group, engaged in private equity, corporate and marketing services. They already had two partners and wanted me to join them as the third on the basis that we would all own approximately a one-third share each. I agreed to give the matter thought and left it at that.

A charity aimed at the promotion of awareness of epilepsy had been in existence in Edinburgh for some years. Hong Kong was picked for the establishment of its first overseas chapter. A forerunning party was sent out to Hong Kong and their main representative Karen Barclay consulted with various leaders. I was later told that the people consulted all came up with my name as the ideal person to be the first chairman of their charity in Hong Kong. This was because I was seen firstly as a good fundraiser with adequate status; secondly, I could react well with the Scots in Edinburgh; and finally, my involvement with rugby was seen as a good fit because the person who championed the epilepsy cause in Scotland was Tom Smith, the Scotland and British Lions prop forward. The inspiration was that if Tom could reach such heights in rugby despite being an epileptic, others could emulate his success, and Tom was prepared to stand up and champion the cause.

The charity was to become known as Enlighten – Action for Epilepsy. As Chairman, I assembled a strong board. I managed to persuade Anson Chan, Hong Kong's former Chief Secretary, to be Honorary Patron and this was our biggest coup. The entertainment celebrity Karen Mok came in as our Ambassador. The General Manager was a charming lady called Joanna Perez who loved her job and was popular with her staff, the board and the medical fraternity in which she worked. When Joanna had to leave our shores, we hired Orla Gilroy, a lady with immense energy and devotion, as Executive Director. We were well on our way. I was to serve for five years until the constitution demanded that I must retire. I reached that step at the end of 2008.

Enlighten was in fact the second charity that I had chaired. My first boss at Wharf in 1967 was Gerry Forsgate. Gerry had always kept an eye on me and gave me every chance in my early days. He was a good sportsman, having played rugby for the Colony, and in later years was very keen on golf. When I was selected to represent the Colony in cricket, Gerry was amongst the first to pat me on the back and had no hesitation in granting compassionate leave of three weeks to permit me to tour with the Hong Kong team to Ceylon (as Sri Lanka was then), Singapore and Sabah.

Gerry had been the President of the Hong Kong Rugby Football Union for years, and never missed a single Rugby Sevens until his illness in the last year of his life. When I visited him in hospital, he was obviously not well, but he still insisted with the nurse that he must receive me. In our casual chat, he made me promise that I would agree to succeed him as Chairman of the China Coast Community, a charity designed for the aged with Western habits. There was simply no way I could refuse his request. He passed away a few days later.

That was how and why I became Chairman of the China Coast Community. Out of respect for Gerry, the board voted to welcome me to their fold. There was a degree of wariness when I took on that role. I did not really know what to expect. It was in December and China Coast would have their annual Christmas party at the charity's home itself. The board members, patrons, volunteers and donors were invited, but the most important attendees were the residents themselves. The party would be the most opportune event to introduce me as the new Chairman.

For me, what had started with some apprehension soon turned to a sense of emotional belonging. When I began to mingle with the old folks, to my utter surprise, many of them asked me to pass their best wishes to my mother Phoebe. A few even mentioned my father Walter, whom they had known before the War. Those special senior citizens were really the old Hong Kong hands, just as my parents were. I knew then that China Coast was the most appropriate charity for me to lead. *It brought home to me who I really was!*

"Don't bother to do business in China unless you are prepared to accept the Chinese ways and their culture"

41

BEIJING

I agreed to take 25% equity in FCP on the proviso that apart from some networking contribution, I could not spend too much time thereon. That was how the collaboration started. Six months on, I was asked to do more on fundraising for the FCP private equity funds. I needed an assistant. We advertised and Frances Fong applied.

Frances had a degree in civil engineering and another in financial engineering, both from North American universities. She was fluent in English, Cantonese and Mandarin and had a pleasant personality. She was a bit shy to start with. However, once I drew out her true personality, she displayed her confidence, a clear sense of humour and a broad smile. I could see the qualities she would bring at once. Her home address in a prime area on Hong Kong Island gave away the fact that she was from a good family and had the obvious breeding that would equip her with the social graces to be comfortable in dealings with senior executives. These attributes clearly differentiated her from the other applicants. On the belief that I was a good judge of people, I decided to hire her after a single interview. There was no mistake and this was vindicated when I found that Frances could tackle any project placed before her, always willing to walk that extra mile as the jobs demanded. The lady was to follow me through various companies and this has prevailed to this day. She is an absolute gem and has now become my very good friend.

For a prolonged period at the beginning of the new century, global stock markets were plagued by volatility. Cycles became much shorter. Sharp rises were often followed by big declines. Markets were no longer "local". Modern real-time communication had turned all major markets global. If some bad news arose in New York or London, this would almost certainly affect the Hong Kong market; the same thing would happen vice versa. The markets were driven by the actions of large investment banks and the large funds. Retail investors who were in essence only "followers" were often caught and many ran scared and shied away from listed stocks. Alternative forms of investments were sought. It was in this climate that I encountered the emergence of private equity as an alternative avenue for investments.

I found myself involved in private equity work at the two extremes of the spectrum. With CVC, the emphasis was on large transactions on buyouts of mature companies. At the opposite end, FCP ran small funds targeting small companies just past the incubation or start-up stage. This was a clear choice between high cost and low risk, as against low cost, higher risk and high rewards. I appreciated then that private equity funds could be tailored in many different ways to the taste of the issuer provided there was a solid business base there.

Private equity funds were not then shackled by regulatory restrictions anywhere near the same extent as the stock market. Yet the degree of transparency in private equity was high by virtue of the requirements of self-regulation which, by necessity, existed between the issuers and the investors. Governance was largely voluntarily observed within a controllable universe of participants. To me, private equity provided a viable alternative for investments outside the world of listed stocks. I was to delve deeper into this field in a variety of ways.

Out of the blue, two close friends called me to discuss "some extraordinary opportunity". It seemed that a big powerful group from Jersey in the Channel Islands wanted to establish an Asian branch, and they wanted me to be a player in it. Needless to say, I wanted to meet the principal and was told he was on the way out to Hong Kong. He duly arrived and met us over a drink at the Island Shangri-la.

They had great plans for developing business in Asia in areas of fund management, IT and telephony, sports management, property and infrastructure and a host of peripheral but compatible lines. We heard their success stories and track record. They looked impressive and full of potential. With Jersey's undertaking to fully fund a Hong Kong branch company, we saw no good reason against participation, especially when shares would be allocated to us free of subscription payment.

A limited company was formed in Hong Kong as the Asian base. Six directors were appointed to the board, three each from Jersey and Hong Kong. Before the Hong Kong branch was even fully established, we were requested to meet in Beijing for discussions with the mainland's China Youth League, this being the training ground for the elite youths of the country, the best of whom could eventually graduate to the Communist Party.

Incredibly, within only three days of meetings in Beijing, we agreed on the development in principle of a number of mega projects on the basis of joint ventures. A Memorandum of Understanding (MOU) was signed to include defined projects on media and entertainment, mass telecommunication, development and promotion of a football academy, and a mega theme park near Beijing. It was obvious that a great deal of resources and work were on the cards.

We recognized that the emphasis had already shifted. The original mission of pan-Asia coverage had already given way to a focus on China only, at least for the immediate term.

Albert Kan, the entrepreneur who made the introduction, and I would have to lead the initiatives since we were both Hong Kong residents and more significantly, the only two Chinese speakers in the group.

We were thrown into the roles by circumstances but we understood that we would be supported by professional and technical teams to be sent out by Jersey for the different disciplines as and when required. Albert was at one time a senior executive in Jardine Fleming with control over the China desk. He was therefore a China specialist. These attributes were invaluable and his close connection with Mr. Li Zhong of the China Youth League was vital to our ambitions.

Under the pressure of urgency, I flew to Dubai for meetings with the principals from Jersey. Although Jersey was the headquarters of the group, it had extensive business in Dubai; in fact it was so deeply immersed that it was about to shift the operational base there. This was sensible because the geographical location of Dubai was smack in the middle in terms of distance between London and Hong Kong. In the meetings, we made plans for every China project and agreed on the major issues to be tackled in order of priority. A casual approach would no longer suffice.

The question was whether I could tear myself away from my everyday commitments and dedicate myself full time as the Executive Chairman. It was early December, and I needed time to consider their proposition carefully, not so much whether to take on the challenge, but rather how I was to adjust my other commitments. We agreed to maintain contact through Christmas and New Year by long distance even though I was to be in New Zealand.

We maintained contact and eventually agreed on the basic terms. A draft was prepared and agreed. I was to be engaged by the head company in Jersey and my role was as Chairman of the incorporated Hong Kong branch responsible for Asia. My emoluments would be paid by Jersey as would all the expenses incurred in Hong Kong and China for the furtherance of business. Jersey would remit funds on a monthly basis to Hong Kong.

After the New Year, I met the principals again in Dubai and the agreement was signed. Appropriate board resolutions were prepared at the same time to authorize all the moves to reflect the true intentions of the parties. The Hong Kong branch was thus in full operation with a small complement of nucleus staff.

By April, it became apparent that if the China Youth League and the Central Government were to have faith in our sincerity, we would need to establish an office in Beijing, especially since the four major projects would logically require a permanent physical presence to be demonstrated. Jersey agreed and a small representative office was set up with Albert as the CEO. We recruited an experienced lady executive originally from Hong Kong as the General Manager.

Albert and I had to be in Beijing regularly to move the projects along. Specialist technical teams did come out from Europe and detailed planning progressed after meetings with the Chinese counterparts. Progress was slow, deliberate and painstaking as there were obviously gaps between the different cultures. Our thinking had to adjust to the omnipresence of issues associated with Chinese philosophy, design and even political sway. Funds were remitted monthly from Jersey from February onwards.

The work was extremely intense, under trying and at times frustrating circumstances, but this was expected with the Chinese public sector at a high level. Albert and I had fully understood and foreseen this. We just had to drive on. We noted that Mr. Li had his own problems as he had to appease and take instructions from his superiors. The bigger the project in China, the more stringent these controls would be.

In the case of the theme park project which required a land grant of a huge plot of land in a select location, the majority of the land marked for alienation belonged to the Central Government, with a small adjoining plot held by the Beijing Municipal Government. A process of amalgamation first had to take place, requiring the approval of the Municipality before it could be merged with the larger plot. When this was done, the painful process would start again for Central Government approval. All this red tape took time.

These were accepted procedures embedded in the bureaucracy of Communist China and those of us who understood China from years of dealings would not raise questions. However, the Jersey group saw this red tape as cumbersome, over-testing and the delays hard to accept.

To placate Jersey, I had to write long letters to virtually give lessons on Chinese culture and how the Chinese system of control was exerted by the government, even to the extent of explaining why the Chinese practices were different from those of the Soviet Union, for example, due to the existence of ancient philosophies that still prevailed in China. Further, the Chinese had not been embroiled in communism for as long as the Soviets before their "Open Door" policy and thus still retained much of their ancient practices. For people dealing with the market economy in China, most adopt the motto: "Don't bother to do business in China unless you are prepared to accept the Chinese ways and their culture."

Jersey had submitted the feasibility studies with fully illustrated recommendations. These were then passed up the ladder within the Chinese hierarchy by Mr. Li. Clarifications were sought and we were to send for the technical team to come out again to answer the numerous questions. Jersey was reluctant to dispatch teams again until acceptances in principle were received. The Chinese would not offer acceptances in any form until their questions were answered. There was a total Mexican stand-off.

Albert and I knew the rising star Mr. Li was breaking his back trying to move things along within his own hierarchy, but he also had to follow party rules. Although progress seemed slow to Jersey, Albert and I had no doubt that Mr. Li was doing his best, but even he had obstacles to surmount.

I was caught in the crossroads of two extreme cultures and felt the pressure mounting. It was a conundrum that I could not solve on my own. I flew to London to meet the principals around late April and prior arrangements were made for meetings to discuss how to break this impasse with the Chinese.

"I saw in Sean the exact problem that I had at the same stage of my schooling"

42

Sean

I arrived at Heathrow early in the morning and immediately called the London office of the company. I was informed apologetically that the Jersey principals were engaged in emergency meetings that day and could not meet me. These things happened in business and I said I would call again the next day. In the meantime, I thought I would use the time to attend to other matters.

When I called again the next day, they were still in those meetings and I was told it was unlikely that they could meet me until the following Monday. Naturally I was irritated as firm arrangements had been made and I had come a long way from Hong Kong for the meetings. It meant that I would waste almost a week just waiting. I called Sean at Milton Abbey and made arrangements to see him that weekend. I then told the secretary of my principals that in view of the circumstances, I would go out of London and return to meet them the following Monday.

I then secured an appointment to see the headmaster of Milton Abbey before seeing Sean. It was Sean's penultimate year before sitting GCSE 'O' levels and thought it would be useful to assess his progress in school. I hired a car close to my hotel in Mayfair and drove to Dorset. I checked into the only hotel in the village and saw the headmaster, Jonathan

Hughes-D'Aeth, the next morning. I was concerned about Sean's weakness in mathematics which needed to be addressed. Jonathan was quick to advise that Sean was held in high regard as he was considered one of the most polite boys and very much a gentle giant. He was one of their better cricketers and was already in the school team for golf. Most of the teaching staff found him friendly and helpful. His academic achievements were improving markedly but he remained weak in maths. I thanked Jonathan and was generally pleased by what I had heard.

Quietly however, I was worried because if Sean did not pass mathematics, he would not get certificated at GCSE even if he did well in all his other subjects. I saw in Sean the exact problem that I had faced at the same stage of my schooling, and I was determined to find a way out for him although I did not know what that might be. I decided to put the matter at the back of my mind. Instead, I just wanted to enjoy my weekend with Sean, especially the cricket match on Saturday afternoon in which Sean would play for the school.

I had also the opportunity of meeting some of Sean's close friends on the Saturday morning. He seemed highly popular and they were all very much at peace with the school environment. I discovered that Sean also played some good golf in school where they have their own course. He had obviously improved as he was already in the school golf team even though he was the youngest and only in the fourth form. His length off the tee and accuracy with his irons had always been his strengths, but the painstaking practice around the green was also paying off. All he needed was to improve his mental approach and maturity in course management. These would however come with age and more experience.

It was a beautiful sunny afternoon in late spring when I travelled with Sean's team by coach to the "away" ground. They had regarded that as a "blood match" against regular opponents from a rival school. I could recall the sensation of nervous anticipation before the battle that I had experienced in a similar situation in my youth. Sean's heart must have been pounding and his nerves jangling! After eight overs when the opposition was 15 for 0, Sean had bowled 4 overs for no runs, beating the bat consistently. His outswingers, bowled from a great height, had produced such bounce that the batsmen could not even get an edge. The skipper rightly took him off.

I walked across to fine leg where he was fielding and he seemed pleased with himself. It was an aggressive opening spell. On the other hand, I thought he should have used his head a bit more and told him that if he was brought on again, he should bowl a fuller length and make them play! The batting side went to about 130 for 4 when Sean was brought on again. He did what I had told him, found a line and length and finished the innings with figures of 7.4-4-13-4 with three of his wickets going to full pitched deliveries. I guessed Sean had learnt something that day.

They won the match comfortably with the captain batting out with an anchor knock. Sean did his bit with a well-made 25 or so. Everyone in the team was happy. With the headmaster's permission, I could have Sean for the weekend in London. I took him for dinner where I could talk calmly to him about his academic comfort zone but would touch gently on his frustration with mathematics.

Sean and I also talked about the family, especially about Natasha who had graduated with a law degree from Nottingham University and was seeking a job. The global economic climate remained weak and apart from the high flyers with top honours degrees, fresh graduates found jobs hard to come by. Natasha tried to work in England, but failed to find a suitable position. She weighed her options and decided against law practice in Hong Kong. After 1997, the inability to read and write Chinese had become a big disadvantage. With the emergence of China as a major world power in the market economy, most jobs in Hong Kong, including solicitors and bankers, had a Chinese language requirement. As an example, most of the large investment banks would have 90% of their younger executives committed to Mainland Chinese business, leaving only a handful for international work.

Without the knowledge of Chinese as a language, it was impossible for Natasha to secure a decent job in Hong Kong. The reality struck and we decided the best and most sensible course of action for Natasha was to follow her sister's footsteps and spend a year at a university in Beijing to study Mandarin. This was later arranged and Natasha was to take that step and defer the question of a job until the year in Beijing was completed.

Sean and I enjoyed our time together talking about home, his sisters, his mother, and his friends back home. Boys at that age in boarding schools often found that type of conversation therapeutic and he of course liked to spend time with me every now and again. It was a good weekend.

43

PEARL HARBOUR

It was Monday afternoon when we finally met, but their minds did not appear to be with me. The Jersey men looked far away in deep thought. I sensed they only met me because I had gone all the way to London. I did not want to waste their time nor mine and asked them point blank what was troubling them. Amidst a predominance of garrulous utterances, they gave me an answer of sorts but the meaning was not at all clear.

What I could sense from the general conversation was that the European arm of the group (nothing to do with our Asian operation) had acquired one of Norway's largest telecom companies. There appeared to be quite a few areas which needed restructuring if the acquired company was to fall seamlessly into the group. What made it awkward was the need to send a highly professional team of specialists into Norway for a prolonged period to get the task done. There would be significant cost and human resource commitments involved. I surmised that it would be difficult for HQ to send an IT and telecoms team to China at that point in time.

It dawned on me then that it was probably not the best time to press them on China issues. However, having gone all the way to London, I had to remind them of our contractual commitments to the China Youth League and the urgency attached to our need to answer the questions posed by the Chinese if the projects were to proceed. It was not an option to sit and do nothing. They did give me time to explain the status on each and every project and they had to agree that apart from IT and telecoms, technical teams from other disciplines must be assembled and sent to China. The meeting closed with their verbal promise that technical teams would be in China "within the next few weeks". They gave me that assurance and I hoped they would live up to that.

On return to Hong Kong, I gave Albert a full rundown of what had taken place in London. Albert remained silent and apprehensive, worried that we might let Mr. Li down. Albert's concern was understandable as his personal credibility was on the line with Mr. Li since he was the one who brokered the relationship.

April came to an end, and as in the previous two months, we received funds from Jersey to cover all April expenses as expected. Word was received to my surprise that an IT & telecoms team was scheduled to be out in Hong Kong en route to Beijing in a fortnight. Our earlier concerns seemed groundless. We alerted Mr. Li and all concerned looked forward to the arrival of the IT & telecoms people.

Just two days before the team's arrival, Jersey emailed to say that the visit had to be put off because of another "emergency" need for them to be in Europe, but a re-scheduled date would be advised as soon as they were in a position to do so. Despite our soft protest, Jersey stood firm. Mr. Li was not pleased as he had already held out to his masters in the Central Government that progress would be made. Albert was furious.

When our May expenses were not paid, I began to have concerns although I was told by the Jersey office that the principals were out of town and there were no bank signatories in the office. They however assured me that remittances would be forthcoming once the travelling stopped. The position was made worse as no team came in May and similar excuses were made regarding the unpaid expenses. We started to be embroiled in protracted correspondence. As we had a serious responsibility to the China Youth League by contractual agreement, I continued to fund the group personally under utmost good faith. We just could not afford to see the collapse of the company at that stage. Albert helped along the way by covering some incidental expenses in Beijing. By mid-June, things felt distinctly uncomfortable.

In July, instead of sending a team out as promised, Jersey dispatched a newly appointed senior "envoy", armed with full authority to discuss matters with Mr. Li. In meetings held in Hong Kong prior to flying to Beijing, we had the distinct impression that there had been a paradigm shift in Jersey's attitude. The keenness to work with the Chinese was no longer there, and the demeanour seemed more inclined to a strategy best described as "attack being the best form of defence". I felt in my gut that it was best to let the envoy take the lead in Beijing and keep myself clear from disputes as much as I could. U-turns were not in my vocabulary in business.

Albert and I tried to deduce the real cause behind this change. We had no evidence, but suspected that perhaps Jersey's due diligence work on the Norwegian telecoms company might not have been as thorough as it should have been, thus the absorption process facing them demanded more resources than first thought. If that was the case, then it would have triggered a domino effect on the group where an "honourable withdrawal" from China with an excuse would have been convenient. We shivered and hoped that our speculation was not true because if it was, we would be heading for dire embarrassment.

The "summit" held in Beijing was a pantomime. Outward appearances of courtesy disguised true intentions. Flattery mingled with toughness. The drama left little to the imagination. Basically, it amounted to a "take it or leave it" showdown. Before we left Beijing, Mr. Li called for a meeting with Albert and I so that he could understand the position better. We could not help him much because even we ourselves were uncertain. It could be said that the meetings had succeeded in a warped way because the revised agenda had disturbed Mr. Li so much that he no longer pushed for speed or the technical teams' arrival.

Suddenly, instead of paying the expenses owing to me from May to July or apologizing for the delay, Jersey went on the offensive. They demanded that my claims must be subjected to audit by the "envoy" although no audit was requested from February to April and yet the expenses were paid. To expedite matters, all the papers in support were sent to Jersey. Questions came and were comprehensively answered. Further elaborations were demanded and these were also satisfied. It was quite obvious these were all stalling tactics since they had paid all expenses for February to April, thereby giving tacit admission that such monthly funding was due as clearly stipulated in the signed agreements. Further, their earlier promise of funding us in advance was never fulfilled. In fact, the bank account of the Hong Kong company had not been credited with a single deposit other than the original HK$5,000 required for account opening paid by the Hong Kong directors. After their questions were exhausted, the audit was completed with no disputes outstanding. The expenses were all legitimate and we waited for their settlement. Jersey was unable to challenge the audited accounts any longer.

The entire situation was bizarre. Jersey was essentially taking on the Beijing Central Government. Yet, instead of buying the loyalty of Albert and I, their non-payment of our legitimate expenses of a sizeable sum had the effect of alienating us. For Mr. Li, it was time to "show hand". He simply could not compromise his political future by continuing to play games with the "foreigners". Albert and I were summoned to Beijing again. It was a call that we could not ignore. We went north at once.

Mr. Li was a troubled man. His life was under severe pressure within his own political domain as he was highly regarded as a leader of the future. He did not need Jersey to add to his problems. He was earlier led to believe that Jersey had men who were trustworthy and honourable as demonstrated when Li had been invited as a guest to Dubai in May by the Jersey principals with all expenses paid. He was then made to feel like a king and an important partner. So why the sudden change? He felt threatened.

Sitting where he was, Mr. Li was not accustomed to be subservient to people other than his political superiors, yet suddenly he felt cornered by his reliance on Jersey to deliver the projects which now looked unlikely. He felt more and more vulnerable by the day. He was also offended by being lectured by the "envoy" the week before. After some deliberation, Mr. Li was not about to accept these things lying down. Not surprisingly, he decided to call Jersey's bluff!

Whilst we sympathized with Mr. Li's sentiments and his anger, the position of Albert and I had become untenable. We were caught betwixt and between two parties with diametrically opposed values. With full knowledge of Mr. Li's mindset, I made a last-ditch effort to talk sense with Jersey by suggesting diplomatically that walking the extra mile for Beijing should not be regarded as weakness, but to cross them could in reality mean the end of Jersey's ambitions in China.

My suggestion for reconciliation was summarily dismissed. Jersey decided their patience had been tested enough even though in truth the delay in approvals of the projects was equally caused by the absence of technical teams on site. Jersey considered they had reached their "defining moment". It seemed a lame excuse, but Jersey went ahead and delivered an ultimatum threatening the collapse of the MOU unless approvals for the proposed projects were received within a matter of days. Mr. Li was left with no option but to accept the collapse of all agreements under protest and accused the counterparty of insincerity. There could be little doubt that the behaviour of the Jersey group and their subsidiaries would be 'placed on record' in China.

I could feel that doomsday might be just around the corner even though I could not predict exactly what was to come even at that stage. I just felt that if the relationship was to break down, it would be a huge pity because developments on the projects had in reality already reached advanced stages, some of which were at the 11th hour. Control was however no longer in our hands.

On 31st August, without any forewarning, I received an email from Jersey which stated they would no longer provide funding to Hong Kong, with immediate effect. To me, it was my "Pearl Harbour", yet the substance of the email would suggest there was an implied admission of debt owing to me for the period from 1st May to 31st August.

I reluctantly concluded that protests would fall on deaf ears, and got on with the onerous task of having to close two offices in Hong Kong and Beijing literally overnight and paying off all the staff for premature termination. I was then holding a total of unpaid bills by Jersey, including my own salaries, expenses and operating costs for both offices, travelling and hotel bills for the months of May, June, July and August to an amount in excess of HK$2.5 million.

My calls for immediate settlement were met by total silence. It was disconcerting but I could not help but remember what Dudley Moore had said to Peter Cook on television years ago: "I would not accept 'no reply' for an answer!" I used to laugh my head off hearing that. I did not laugh this time, yet I thought how appropriate that humorous remark was in the context of my frustration.

By absolute necessity, I arranged for a well documented and well reasoned solicitor's letter to be sent to Jersey demanding full payment of the amount owing to me. This was resisted by veiled counter-threats. Those people were incorrigible. After seriously weighing my options, I reluctantly accepted that pursuing the legal route would entail spending time in London, and engaging lawyers to bring a legal action there if it was to have any chance of success. I saw difficulties especially when technical legal issues could cause a protracted process. I was not prepared to be embroiled in something which would consume my financial resources and which could go on for years without any guarantee of success. Instead,

I just put this aside and got on with planning an alternative future, rather than seeking legal mitigation of my loss just because I felt cheated. Serious damage had been caused by unscrupulous people – people that I would not care to meet again.

In retrospect, the aborted deal in China, the loss of more than HK$2.5 million and a year of my life, had delivered such a devastating blow to my equilibrium and financial position that I was knocked off balance. This episode could arguably have been the root of the problems that beset me in a series of difficulties, culminating in my time here in Stanley.

Bastards!

"It gave me a new lease of life and a much needed renewal of confidence after the recent debacle"

44

REAL ESTATE INVESTMENT TRUST

With the demise of the Beijing projects and the practical collapse of the Hong Kong branch of the Jersey group, Albert and I felt dreadful that Mr. Li had been badly let down. It might not have mattered to the people in Jersey, but our relationship with Mr. Li and the China Youth League was of importance to those living in Hong Kong, an integral part of China, as our commercial future was tightly linked to the Mainland. With this in mind, Albert and I advised Mr. Li that we would like to visit him in Beijing. It was to be our personal peace offering.

Mr. Li did not blame us at all for the parting of ways. In fact, he made it clear that he and his colleagues regarded us as their good friends. We had salvaged our personal relationship with Beijing. It was an encouragement Albert and I needed to firm up our idea to establish a partnership company with a 50:50 share split. That was to be known as Inroads Company Limited. We set up an office at the Convention Centre complex and I brought in Frances Fong to assist us in the build-up of the company. We offered a small percentage of free equity to Frances as an incentive.

With the substantial loss suffered from the Jersey episode, we managed Inroads conservatively. We had to attract consultancy or advisory accounts quickly to provide bread-and-butter cash flow. Larger projects would be considered, but not regarded as priority. P&L was not expected to look good for a while but cash flow was important. After the setback with the Beijing ventures, we simply had to look forward.

We were lucky that Albert had his connections and I had mine. Within a relatively short time, Mr. Li called and indicated he had a few projects in Beijing and Dalian which needed our assistance. He introduced us to his associate Mr. Zhang from Dalian who had two property projects and the development rights for the fifth largest island in China, namely Changqing Island just off the coast of Dalian. All these looked interesting, but the island development was to me an over-ambitious project which would take years to bring to fruition. After a physical inspection and a preliminary assessment, we concluded it was too large a project for us to undertake but we would act as promoters for the two property projects for commission. This was a good start in the revival of cooperation between Beijing and we at Inroads.

After seeing Sean in England, I had expressed my concern over his weakness in mathematics to Gail. Unknown to me, Gail had since then been doing her homework. In December, she told me that she had learnt from her Australian friends that mathematics was not a compulsory subject in the state of Victoria and perhaps we should consider transferring Sean there. Melbourne was familiar to us as we had been there many times since Katish and Natasha went to Geelong and of course Samantha had been to the Presbyterian Ladies College and Melbourne University. We were however advised that Scotch College was perhaps the best school for boys. I went to work on that at once and made enquiries with the Admissions Officer.

The response was immediate. I was informed we were lucky because the school had a single vacancy and that could be given to Sean provided we accepted within three days. We were also told that Sean would have to enter Year 11 as it was the school's policy not to accept new students for the final Year 12. In other words, Sean had one chance. If not taken, the opportunity would be gone. This presented a headache as Sean was due to sit his GCSE 'O' level examinations in May, just six months away.

Acceptance of Scotch would mean Sean would have to forego the GCSE in England and go direct to Melbourne immediately after the New Year holidays. Sean was already in mid-air on the way home from England. I could not wait as Scotch would not hold the place any longer and thus I accepted the offer. Sean was registered as a new entry for the term starting in February.

Sean arrived in Hong Kong and was happy to be home for Christmas. Once he had settled, we told him that he would have to transfer to Australia almost right away after the New Year and the move was to his own benefit since he could drop his weakest subject. He did appreciate that the rationale behind the decision was sound, but understandably his mind was in a state of confusion. He resisted, saying that he would miss Milton Abbey and his good friends there. We did not press the issue and allowed time for the decision to sink in. It did, as he slowly saw the inevitability of the move. I made it easier by suggesting that I would fly to England with him and visit Milton Abbey so that he could have a proper closure and a chance to bid farewell to his teachers and friends. He seemed happier.

We landed at Heathrow, hired a large car and drove direct to Dorset. When we saw the headmaster, we were surprised that Jonathan fully understood our decision and actually concurred that Scotch was an excellent school. He even mentioned it was the correct move and Sean would enjoy himself in Melbourne. We then discovered that Jonathan had taught at Melbourne Grammar School for two years before taking the job as headmaster of Milton Abbey. This helped tremendously in turning Sean's sentiments around. Jonathan's words did much to dispel uncertainties and misgivings in Sean's mind.

I obtained permission to take 10 of Sean's best friends to a pub dinner for a farewell party. The boys all had a pint or two and the pub kept one eye closed on the boys' young age. They all gave Sean farewell presents such as a can of beer, an old rugby shirt and a packet of condoms, etc., all great fun for them and that made Sean's day. He had accepted the transfer to Australia, yet he remained morose on the flight home to Hong Kong. I felt for him but was confident that once he settled in Scotch, much of his negative sentiments would pale into relative insignificance. His fond memory of Milton Abbey would however remain with him for a long time if not forever. That experience was part of his growing pain!

My former colleague from Wharf, Stephen Ng, called suddenly and wanted an urgent lunch with me. Knowing Stephen, he would not call unless he had something important to discuss. I re-scheduled another lunch and met Stephen at Grissini's in the Grand Hyatt. Stephen advised that Wharf was seriously considering the launch of a huge Real Estate Investment Trust (REIT) to raise a target of HK$12 billion. They wanted me to lead the initiative as the CEO of the REIT to be known as Harriman Asset Management Limited (HAML). The promoter of the REIT issue and the property assets to be sold to HAML would be Wharf Holdings.

This call for me was obviously in recognition of my experience in the capital market and my fundraising ability in presentations and roadshows, all of which were essential ingredients for a successful REIT launch. My first reaction was of pleasant surprise. I could not recall that a retired executive director had ever been asked to help Wharf corporate in a major project on a committed basis before. I was clearly interested.

It was however a major move for me because I would need to resign from all the boards of companies which had the remotest conflict with Wharf or HAML in finance or property business. I would also have to suspend my involvement in my private companies as the Securities and Futures Commission (SFC) demanded that the CEO of a REIT must be on full-time and totally committed. I would additionally have to "go back to school" and pass the SFC examinations to qualify as an accredited Type 4 licensed practitioner in asset management. My loyalty to Wharf had not waned and I still referred to Wharf as "we" after retirement and not "they". Admittedly, I was also tickled by my ego. This type of challenge had always motivated me and frankly I did miss it after retirement. It gave me a new lease of life and a much needed renewal of confidence after the recent debacle.

Approval for the launch of a REIT had to be cleared essentially by the SFC although the Stock Exchange also had to endorse it. The SFC's requirements were extremely onerous. The demands comprised a myriad of compliance issues. Because REITs were a relatively new form of financial issue in the Hong Kong market, practitioners as well as the SFC were all on a learning curve. Consequently, with each new REIT coming to the market, the regulator became more draconian. We were the fourth or fifth proposed issue to come to the market, and were thus subjected to extremely harsh requirements. Some of these demands became absurd to the point that the SFC was virtually micro-managing our planning process. It was administratively frustrating, and financially wasteful in terms of cost incurred for lawyers, bankers and executives at a time when the team was really only engaged in the appeasement of the SFC on planning for an issue which might or might not be approved. It was madness!

We were to witness how this painful process was to drag on for close to a year, at the end of which we would miss the window of opportunity in the market. To a large extent, this arose from over-regulation. Some potential issuers of REITs were beginning to hold the view that it might be preferable to raise a REIT in say Australia or Singapore where the REIT markets were more mature and the regulators more friendly.

Leaving the matter of corporate frustrations aside, a REIT in Hong Kong needed to have at least two qualified Responsible Officers, one of whom would be the Executive Officer who would normally carry the role of CEO. These two officials must be people accredited by the SFC. Thus the existence of the REIT itself would be dependent on the presence of these two qualified officers who would have passed the SFC examinations. To put it in a nutshell, an individual could not practice asset management under the SFC rules unless accredited under an approved company. Conversely, the company would be granted approval to operate a REIT only if it had two qualified Responsible Officers. The two requirements were therefore inter-dependent in this web of complications. Timing became a thoroughly intriguing test resembling a punt with only a small element of certainty.

From my personal point of view, it was imperative for me to pass the SFC examinations and the "fit and proper" test if I was to qualify for the CEO post. Had I failed, the REIT would simply be disapproved unless HAML could somehow recruit a qualified replacement on an urgent basis. These people were not easy to come by. The pressure of responsibility weighed heavily on my shoulders, and I simply had to ease that by passing the exams.

There were two papers and I sailed through the first without problem. The other had 40 multiple choice questions requiring 29 correct answers to pass. I had not been in examinations for over 40 years and had never faced the multiple choice format before. I felt out of place as the majority of people in the examination hall were not much older than 30 and I was double that age.

I missed the pass by one mark and when I sat it again, I was not about to take chances. I did nothing else but memorize the facts and surprised even myself by getting 37 answers correct. I was there, but what of the approval of the REIT itself?

Without exaggeration, the total questions we had to answer for the SFC numbered over 3,000, the time spent back and forth spanned over 15 months and we were still not there yet. The delay had caused us to miss the window of opportunity as the market had gone sour in the midst of it all. A successful launch looked unlikely unless Wharf was prepared to discount the issue price by reducing the valuation of the properties. Wharf did not regard this proposition as attractive. We were frustrated as we believed this could have been avoided had the regulators been more accommodating. In my mind, I felt that was not the way to promote the attractions of a city which prided itself on being a leading international finance centre.

"Bridges had been burnt and it would be very difficult to claw back"

45

DEAFENING SILENCE

There was nothing we could do about the REIT but to mark time, hoping the market would improve soon. It would have been a great pity if the issue failed for this reason after all the hard work that had been put in by a dedicated team. HAML had been incorporated, the CEO and the other Responsible Officer had both qualified, hundreds of millions had been incurred on professional fees and 15 months had been spent on this process. Could this make sense to anyone?

From a personal standpoint, I cared an awful lot. I had discarded many business ventures to commit to the REIT and resigned from the boards of listed companies to avoid conflict. All this was done because if I was not found "fit and proper", the REIT could not be approved for want of a qualified executive officer. I did all this in good faith as I was only on a retainer basis until the REIT was successfully launched. At that point, I would be confirmed as the CEO permanently with much enhanced emoluments and a meaningful bonus. I went through the painful process of passing the exams, spent time and effort to plan the REIT management, marshalled the team and had all the manuals completed. We were all set to go except for the condition of the market. I waited in silence but the silence was deafening.

Gail and I were hopeful that the REIT would be launched before the end of the year so that we could have our minds settled prior to our travel to New Zealand for Katish's wedding. This was important to us as we had planned for her wedding to Dan Green on 17th February in the Bay of Islands. It was to be a Maori styled ceremony on the hallowed grounds of the Waitangi Treaty site just off Paihia, the other side of a ferry ride from Russell. We wanted it to be the "wedding of the year" for the joining of the Green/Hung families, especially because Michael and Judy Green had been good friends of Gail and I for some years and all four of us were delighted that Katish was to marry Dan.

Preparations for the wedding had started more than a year earlier. Although Dan and Katish were both residents of Hong Kong, we collectively decided on the choice of a New Zealand wedding, or more specifically, a Maori wedding. We thought this would be unique as the chosen venue of Waitangi held breathtaking scenic beauty as well as the symbol of unity defined by the signing of the Waitangi Treaty between the British and the Maori tribes. The union of Dan and Katish on the site therefore took on additional significance.

We had block-booked hotel rooms in Paihia and Russell, booked the wedding venue with the Waitangi Trust, made preliminary plans for catering, the marquee, transportation and flowers and so on. During the year, Gail and Katish had to travel to New Zealand to complete the finishing touches as most of the supplies had to come from Auckland including a large generator for electric supply. A planner had to be engaged to put it all together since we could not be on hand from Hong Kong. The list of requirements seemed endless. We were lucky that some members of Gail's family were there to lend a helping hand, especially Gail's sister Airini.

Invitations went out from Hong Kong to guests the world over. Replies and acceptances were recorded. Hotel bookings were coordinated and confirmed. Transport links with flight arrivals were arranged. By the time the week of the wedding was upon us, excitement had mounted, and when guests started to trickle in, the carnival had begun. All of us in the family played our parts as hosts. It seemed nothing else in the world mattered, except for the final rehearsal on site.

It was the eve of the wedding when all the players gathered on the lawn at Waitangi. It was early evening and the sun had cleared the rain clouds. We had been concerned because there had been torrential rain the week before, with flooding and landslides reported. All seemed well as we proceeded with the Maori rehearsal which went like clockwork. We were extremely relieved.

A mobile phone rang and it was mine. I signalled to the others that I was on the line with Hong Kong. It was Stephen Ng on the phone and the call had nothing to do with well wishes for the wedding!

The conversation lasted for a good 20 minutes. In essence, Stephen mentioned that the Wharf board had taken the decision to pull the REIT issue from the market and disband my team. They thought there had been too long a delay and the bankers had advised that the market was unlikely to improve in the short or even medium term. Wharf was not prepared to continue putting in good money after bad. They wanted to cut losses.

Stephen had always been a true friend and would only relay the truth to me. Any counter-argument from me would have been futile. I knew in my gut that the decision was correct from the viewpoint of the corporate. Personally, I was devastated as my hopes had been dashed. I had been deprived from earning a big bonus and permanent employment in a CEO role. Monthly income from this source was gone and I had curtailed or suspended my private ventures for the REIT challenge, including my resignations from listed boards. Bridges had been burnt and it would be very difficult to claw back.

My mind was blank and I was consumed by disappointment. I was however sufficiently level-headed to recognize that it was the wrong time to despair. I had to push the wet blanket away from the wedding party. A good mood must remain all round for the wedding day. I gave my own face a soft slap with my hand and snapped out of any negative thoughts about the loss of the REIT and then drove slowly home in silence to Russell.

"One could not help but experience the emotions evoked and the spiritual dominance that was omnipresent"

46

THE WEDDING

Perhaps it was my pink spectacles, but I did not think so. Katish looked ravishingly beautiful on her wedding day. She was complemented by three young ladies in refreshing turquoise dresses, Samantha as the matron-of-honour, Natasha as one bridesmaid and Louise Graham, the daughter of Peter and Annabel, the other.

Dan looked very much the part of the groom and the best men included his brother Josh. Dan's sisters Emily and Kate were radiant as were the mothers Judy and Gail. All the men wore open neck, white long sleeve shirts with Maori motifs and black trousers, very fitting for a glorious summer day outdoors. Michael Green, Sean and I were similarly turned out in these "uniforms". The wedding party looked smashing, collectively in tune with the nature of an open-air Maori wedding held on the hallowed grounds of Waitangi with a salubrious backdrop of the blue sea and the hills on the other side of the bay. It was idyllic.

I sat with Katish impatiently in the limousine. It was imperative that our arrival was precision-timed to synchronize with the Maori choral group from the Bay of Islands College which was waiting for us. The boys and girls in the choral group were attired in traditional Maori costumes. As I walked Katish through the seated guests on the way to the altar,

Gail's brother Clive led the procession with his cries in Te Rua (Maori dialect) and the response echoed from the Maori lady elder. The girls in the choral group raised their voices in harmonious Maori melodies, dancing in rhythm to the music, complemented by the deeper voices of the male singers. The setting, the sound and the overall ambience worked in unison to form a mystical atmosphere befitting the occasion. Even if one did not understand the Maori language or their culture, one could not help but experience the emotions evoked and the spiritual dominance that was omnipresent. Amidst this moving flow of emotive energy, the wedding ceremony was conducted with dignity.

For Gail, who grew up in that very tradition, it brought tears to her eyes!

The choral group continued to perform outside the marquee as the guests gathered for their pre-dinner drinks. The girls sang and danced, showing off their craft with the poi, and the boys punctuated their singing with war-chants in their performance of the famous Haka.

The nicely decorated "dining room" inside the marquee was a reflection of Gail's taste as an interior designer brought to life in the guise of a decorator for the daughter's wedding. The food and wines were all New Zealand specials. The atmosphere was decidedly jovial.

Known as a superb after-dinner speaker, and acting as master-of-ceremony, Peter Graham entertained us throughout the evening as he subtly guided us through the proceedings. I had to earn my drinking rights by first delivering the father-of-the-bride speech. Dan spoke light-heartedly but with sincerity on his appreciation of the parents, his love for his new bride and his thanks to the bridesmaids. Many thought Natasha stole the show with her witty and often wicked humour with almost a no-holds-barred roasting of her sister.

I have attended many weddings, not least two of my own! Yet I can say without any doubt that this had to be the most beautiful and touching wedding I have witnessed. The open-air surroundings, the spiritual

Maori culture and the generosity of the guests all made this unique and memorable. Gail and I were delighted. Katish and Dan went off on their honeymoon and Gail needed a good rest.

With Katish married, we had time to look at Natasha's career. She had by that time been working for Bloomberg for a while and learning an awful lot from them. Her job involved the answering of enquiries from Bloomberg users. As she was posted to Singapore, the people who called were from a variety of nationalities and ethnic backgrounds ranging from Japanese, Koreans, Indonesians, Thais, Malaysians, Chinese of different dialects such as Cantonese, Hokkien, and Mandarin, not to mention the English, French and Spanish. Natasha has an ear for languages and a knack for mimicking. Within a matter of three months, she had managed to acquire sufficient vocabulary in these languages to be able to carry on a conversation for a minute or two, enough to ask the caller the nature of their enquiry so that she could refer them to the appropriate departments. Natasha demonstrated these spoken languages to us in an animated fashion as we were driving back to Auckland from Russell. Gail and I cracked up with laughter and marvelled at her hidden talent, especially on the recollection of Natasha's effective mimicking of animal noises when she was much younger!

Natasha also had an American young man with her. They met in Mongolia when they were both at university in Beijing, and quite naturally they both spoke good Mandarin. This young man, Ben Furneaux, struck me as polite, down to earth and affable in disposition. He looked people in the eye and offered a firm handshake. These attributes mean a lot to traditional men like me. Ben impressed me in that he was made of solid stuff, and his caring nature was a quality that Gail utterly approved of. They are now engaged and we are faced with yet another wedding soon.

Since he went to Scotch College, Sean appeared to have gained confidence. When he went from Melbourne to Russell for the wedding, he had only been in Scotch for a few weeks, yet he already looked more like an adult at an imposing height of 6'6". He was actually a helpful host and chatted with the guests more or less on equal terms. I was pleased with what I saw and thought that was another thing off our worry list. Perhaps it was the change of environment from a secluded village in Dorset to the metropolis of Melbourne that had opened him up. He had become a citizen rather than a student. Whatever it was, it did him good. Scotch (the school) was a good choice.

Sean found the Australians highly competitive in anything they did. He did not have to practise much in Milton Abbey, yet he was already in line for their 1st XI in cricket. In Scotch, he could only just hold onto a place in the 2nd XI. What was more, they practised every evening but instead of batting or bowling, they spent more time on fielding. By the time the match came along at the weekend, Sean found himself already tired out by the daily practice sessions. I told him he would get used to that soon, adding "Perhaps you now see why the Aussies normally give England a hiding in the Ashes."

He took up basketball in the winter months at Scotch as the coaches encouraged him in view of his height. He later grew to love the game and quickly improved to an extent that in addition to playing for the school, he was also roped in to play in the leagues in Melbourne. He trains regularly with devotion and I believe that basketball might in time prove to his best sport.

As I look at Sean grow and mature, I see that the world of sports has changed dramatically. In my younger days, one was a cricketer, a tennis player or a golfer. The emphasis was on the honing of one's skills at that particular discipline to the best of one's ability and that was that. Nowadays, that is not enough. Every sportsman or sportswoman has to be an athlete as well. Fitness has become an absolute requirement, without which one simply cannot reach the top. We used to "practise" in our days. Now they "train"!

Very much like me, Sean's character is given to stretches of obsessions to excess. This drives Gail round the bend and she asks often why she has to live with two males consumed by excesses. It may be an annoying trait, but some may call this enthusiasm or keenness. Whatever it might be, basketball had driven Sean to such dedication that his room was filled with posters of Michael Jordan, LeBron James, Kobe Bryant and other NBA players of repute. The Shane Warnes and Ricky Pontings of the world were temporarily moved off his radar. Tiger Woods however did not lose his place on Sean's wall – at least not at that stage anyway.

"Gail prided herself on her reliability, her eye for detail and quality, and the guaranteed satisfaction of her clients"

47

DOWN TO EARTH

My arrival back in Hong Kong hit me with a thump. Everything went wrong.

Just before I had left for New Zealand, I was questioned by the ICAC. I thought nothing of it, as I did not see I had done anything wrong. However, even though I had not been charged and was released on my own recognizance, I was required to answer bail periodically as the case was under investigation. To ensure that I would be well protected, I engaged solicitors on a retainer basis. They were to accompany me each time I answered bail, for 13 times in all, over a period of well over two years. During that long period, no decision was made whether to release or charge me. It just went on and on. Needless to say, I was constantly under threat and the emotional torture was hard to bear. It upset my power of concentration and distracted me from my business focus.

It was a wonder that I was able to concentrate on the wedding in New Zealand. I had lost my REIT role with Wharf. Income would once again depend on whatever I could muster. Due to a merger of their London and Geneva arms, EFG had no further need for all their non-executive directors. I was thus released from the London board along with all my non-executive colleagues. Sean still needed to be educated. The family still had recurrent expenses. Legal costs were mounting and I was essentially out of a job, and the wedding had drained me financially. I badly needed to find ways of making some money.

With all the pressure facing me and the frequency of my travels, I could not do justice to all the roles I held. Some of these just had to be relinquished because money-making ventures had to take priority. In those circumstances, much as I loved China Coast, I believed the charity could stand on its own without my involvement as Chairman. I gave notice that I wished to stand down and the General Committee was sympathetic. It was a relief in more ways than one. To be chairmen of two charities was awkward anyway as it was difficult to choose between them when it came to fundraising. Which one should I favour? The exit from China Coast meant that I could concentrate my efforts on Enlighten, a younger charity that needed more help.

Meanwhile Gail was well on the way in the development of her interior design company, "Gail Arlidge Design", and she had acquired a good reputation for her tasteful design and dependability. Her forte was on up-market residential houses or large apartments, all individually purpose-designed in accordance with her customers' preferred style, whether European or Oriental, classical or modern, masculine or feminine, or whatever special quirks the customers may have. The customers' preference was all Gail needed to know and she would do the rest. Gail prided herself on her reliability, her eye for detail and quality, and the guaranteed satisfaction of her clients. She shied away from jobs such as show flats or multiple units because she felt that would prevent her from the full exploitation of her best attributes in creativity and self-expression. She has exquisite taste and it showed in her work. I had always admired her for her artistic flair.

After settling down as a married lady, Katish joined Gail's company and became a reliable associate. She picked up tricks from Gail as she went along, and seemed to have inherited good taste. Katish was a shopaholic and loved all the good things in life – a dangerous and expensive habit, but I suppose that was an asset in the design field since she would certainly know where things were in the marketplace!

Dan continued as Managing Director in his family's business Arnhold & Company, a leading building materials supplier in Hong Kong. The pressure of managing this company in the competitive environment placed a heavy burden on him. Huge responsibility and the constant need to travel added to his stress level. Being "Mr. Dependable", Dan had always tried to be a perfectionist, a target not easy within the growing trend where principals could deal direct with manufacturers, and the role of an agency-based business was placed under pressure. Yet Dan appreciated that everyone in that field faced the same dilemma and he just had to deal with it. Dan always managed things well with a head on his shoulders far beyond his years.

At about that time, Natasha was maturing fast as an executive. After serving them for a few years, she resigned from Bloomberg having learnt from them some strong fundamentals associated with the corporate and financial world. She then joined GFI Securities, engaged in market data support, in their Singapore office. She learned quickly and within a short period, she became the Data Support Manager for Asia. From my observation, Natasha works hard and plays hard. She is extroverted and likes partying and a few drinks, yet she is sporty and keeps very fit through regular running, cycling and gym-work. It strikes me that she is the type that does not let a minute go to waste and would fill her day with one thing or another, and she is definitely an achiever. Overall, she is very much like me in character even though she is a girl. I see her resembling my approach so much that she could well be a "female John."

"...Dad, you forget I access the Internet all the time, and my home page is the South China Morning Post"

48

KEEPING FAITH

I was able to derive some meaningful income from offshore earnings in the main. My consultancy firm had a client who was intent on corporate development work overseas, with projects concentrated on various regions in Mainland China. His thoughts were to develop and grow these companies and then list them when ready. I was called upon to act as advisor and make these happen through corporate planning, fundraising to bolster pre-listing equity and to assist in the process of listing. In some cases, I was also invited onto their boards as non-executive director. As most of these projects were outside Hong Kong, fees were mostly paid offshore in the currencies of the companies' domicile. For example, in the case of companies seeking listings in London, I would be paid in Sterling.

Time went by, and Sean had sat his Victoria Certificate of Education or VCE examinations. His results were satisfactory but he did not attain sufficiently high grades to qualify for leading universities such as Melbourne or Monash where places were highly competitive. We were not deterred and looked elsewhere rather than settle for a lesser university or a course that was not of his choice.

It came to us that Sean could do worse than to try and take advantage of his nationality and attempt to seek admission into a New Zealand university in a degree course more akin to his leanings. We had family in New Zealand and a home in Russell. Everything made sense.

We did preliminary searches through the Internet, wrote to leading universities in New Zealand, selected Sean's preferences and earmarked suitable degree courses. Sean and I flew to New Zealand and it was most fortuitous that Samantha was at that time resident in Wellington, working for the New Zealand Government. She was to prove invaluable as the principal link for her brother's application process which was tedious rather than complicated.

Shortlisted preferences were Auckland, Dunedin and Wellington. Of these, Victoria University in Wellington offered the most suitable degree course in Asian Studies. Sean had always been strong in history and Asia was in his blood. It was his decided area of interest and the qualification for the course did not require mathematics. We felt we needed to look no further provided Sean could somehow secure admission.

It was then that the "Maori card" came into play. After the submission of his Maori ancestral lineage to the university, Sean was at once welcomed by that ethnic faction into their fold. Sean's future in tertiary education was settled. He would enter Victoria University in Wellington and was allocated a place in a hall of residence known as Te Pune Village situated very close to the university campus.

By the middle of his second trimester, it was clear that university life suited Sean. He had developed a maturity that was missing in school. More noticeably, there was an air of confidence about him in everything he did. He was comfortable and at ease in his independence. He could be left alone without an overload of guidance from us. His academic and sporting prowess grew in unison. He had reached his optimum height of 6' 7" and begun to fill out. Sean had become a big fellow, and thankfully he held on to his gentle and generous nature.

In anticipation of the worst, I had forewarned all my daughters and my in-laws of the chance that I might be charged by the ICAC even though I considered that possibility to be remote. I just did not want them to read about it in the newspapers without warning. It was a precaution. One thing I had stressed was that it must be kept away from Sean because he was still young and about to sit his university examinations. I did not want to distract him from his studies. Besides, what might happen in Hong Kong was of no interest to the New Zealand media, thus Sean was probably sheltered from such news so long as nobody told him.

The ICAC took their sweet time and advised my solicitors that the matter was out of their hands since the details had already been submitted to the Department of Justice. On that understanding, it became a matter between the ICAC and the DOJ. What irritated me was that I was still kept in the dark, waiting in suspense since the start of the investigation over two years earlier.

By any reasonable measure, this must bring into question whether there could be any moral justification to keep a person in suspense over such an extended period. To me, it represented a blatant disregard for the hardship and disruption caused at a time when I had not even been put on trial, yet I was already being punished. What if it turned out that I was not charged at all and released? Would that have embarrassed anyone? Surely, the case was not so complicated that it would require over two years to come to a decision whether to prosecute or not?

I was finally charged in December 2008, but I had to wait a further seven months before I would stand trial. Due to my high profile in society, the news went on radio and television and the report was splashed all over the newspapers the next morning, a few of those on the front page. There was nowhere to hide although I had no intention of doing so. I did have the presence of mind to know from my media experience that news always turned stale with time, especially if there were bigger stories to push mine into the back pages. The media at that time was concentrating on the contested will of Nina Wang and I had every hope that would dominate the news. It was essential that I should live normally and frequent my usual places. I thought at least Sean would not be exposed to the embarrassment.

How wrong I was! Sean called almost immediately from New Zealand and found me on my mobile. His first words were "Don't worry Dad, I'm behind you and you needn't worry about me. I can handle it." That made my day. Whether he could really handle it or otherwise, I was not sure, but the fact that he said so meant an awful lot to me. I asked him how he knew. "Dad, you forget I access the Internet all the time, and my home page is the *South China Morning Post.*" I should have thought of the power of the Internet. People no longer depended on the print media. We could not keep the news from Sean, but I was relieved that he seemed able to deal with the matter.

When Sean returned for his Christmas holidays, he visited me in prison and that pleased me immensely. So many of his mannerisms that resembled my own younger days drove me to recollect the past, the vividness of my memories thus refreshed. It all helped me to move on with this story, especially what happened when I was young.

Sean appeared to have matured into a man almost overnight. It was my surmise, or was it imagination, that Sean had begun to see things in a different light once he knew I had been convicted. My theory was that he must have decided to take responsibility as the man of the house since Dad was no longer at home. I wished wholeheartedly that life should not have put such a heavy burden on my son, but it was at the same time gratifying to see him rise to the occasion with such adult dignity. I was so very proud of him.

The charges against me were all related to a notion that I had received an "advantage" for proposing a candidate for membership in the Hong Kong Jockey Club, a suggestion that the candidate and I had both denied. Despite all that was said, I maintain that the accusation was ludicrous.

I acknowledge that when people proclaim innocence, others say "the courts will decide" as if to suggest the courts are always right. I know that not to be true. Courts can and do make mistakes; otherwise, why would there be a system of appeal procedures?

Having revisited all aspects of my personal history in this book, the causes and effects of events now appear much clearer. It is apparent that I had been so driven by the demands of corporate and civic responsibilities that I did not always give myself adequate time and attention to keep a clear head. There were times that the work overload might have thrown me off balance in my priorities. If I have to be honest with myself, whilst I had undoubtedly been hit by a series of misfortunes, my optimistic outlook might also have bordered on naivety at times. Gail had always said that I was intelligent, but probably too generous and over-trusting for my own good. Perhaps she was right?

In the final analysis, my retirement from Wharf could not have begun any worse than it did. The unforeseen disappearance of my would-be lady business partner put me on the wrong footing, as this had deprived me of a well planned job. Although I did manage to find alternatives, it effectively placed me in catch-up mode. It was a poor start. It went well for some years in terms of income from directors' fees and actual hard-earned retainers and management fees, although not much from investment returns. The Asian Economic Meltdown came at a bad time. The recurrent slippages in the markets had enforced the sale of stocks and properties. Things were tough but I had no cause for serious complaint since everyone faced the same economic climate. I took the view that so long as I could hold on, the market would eventually return.

What broke the camel's back was the Jersey debacle. If I were polite, I would say that I was badly let down. However, if I put politeness aside, the truth was that the China exit and the non-payment of the debt legitimately owed by Jersey to me had in truth inflicted irreparable damage to my financial position. I was already in my late 60s, and had suffered losses in time, energy, private ventures, and directors' fees earned from listed companies, not to mention the liquidated loss in excess of HK$2.5 million plus interest. I was put on the back foot and it was uphill from then on.

The Wharf REIT opportunity gave me some hope, but permanence did not materialize. In retrospect, it seemed that I had been plagued by a string of bad luck, starting with the disappearance of the lady. Things seemed to have recovered when a number of directorships and advisory board positions such as EFG and CVC were secured. However, these were curtailed by circumstances beyond my control at a time when I needed their perpetuation. The stock and property markets were unfavourable when the Jersey episode happened, followed by the REIT venture which did not happen. In summary, the confluence of all these mishaps caused my world to implode.

My appeal hearing was then pending. I held no speculations for the probable outcome, and self-imposed a defensive expectation that the result could go either way. This frame of mind was adopted not because we did not have strong grounds, but rather that I knew the law does not always dispense true justice. I had by then become much more cynical against the common belief that kindness and generosity would always yield reciprocal rewards.

Having said this, I still hold on to the belief that empathy and charity must remain the principles I would continue to live by.

"The knee-jerk reaction was to throw in the towel and put the matter to bed"

49

THE APPEAL

The appeal hearing was scheduled for 19th May 2010. My team of lawyers was ready for it. In late April, the court selected the three appeal judges, all of whom were members of the Jockey Club. As the Jockey Club was deemed the main complainant in my case, my counsels decided to challenge the selection. We were summoned to a hearing at short notice for the court to consider the objection motion. It appeared bizarre that the judge presiding was in fact one of the three appeal judges we objected against. My counsels strenuously presented our reasons, but in the end, our objection was refused.

My lawyers did not relent as they continued to feel strongly on this issue. They appealed against the dismissal and requested that the motion be heard again by a full complement of three appeal judges. This took place on 14th May and, based on the persuasive arguments presented by my lead counsel, the bench reversed the previous decision and allowed the appeal. They ordered that the actual appeal should be heard by another three appeal judges, all of whom should be non-members of the Jockey Club.

Three replacement appeal judges were selected and a postponed date scheduled. However, Mr. Justice Hartmann later decided to withdraw to avoid possible conflict because he had a friendly relationship with Michael, the father of my son-in-law Dan Green. A replacement appeal judge had to be identified and her diary had to be coordinated with the availabilities of my counsels. This process caused a further postponement of the hearing to 30th June, a delay of 40 days. Having already served a year of my sentence, what was another 40 days, I thought? No big deal!

My day in court duly took place. My legal team and I sincerely believed we had strong grounds to support the appeal. My family members turned up in court in support, including Gail, Katish and Dan, Natasha and Ben plus many close friends including Jim Mailer, Albert Kan, Nick Brown, Richard Zimmern, Harvey Black and Frances Fong amongst others.

The legal arguments consumed almost five hours, but the bench was able to reach a decision after a recess of only about 12 minutes. They dismissed the appeal and said they would deliver the Reasons for Judgment at a later date. Their decision seemed visceral and all too extempore to my way of thinking!

To be honest, I was deflated by the outcome and the manner in which the court made its decision. It had been a long tussle which started in December 2006. I was tired of the protracted legal battles in which I had been embroiled. The knee-jerk reaction was to throw in the towel and put the matter to bed. I had virtually lost faith in the justice of the local legal process.

I recalled then a couple of paragraphs from Ian Rankin's novel *Dead Souls* which seemed to express my sentiments. Detective Inspector Rebus' views of the law courts in Edinburgh were cynical in that he says:

> *"...behind the splendour of the architecture, and the weight of tradition, and high concepts of justice and law, this was a place of immense and continual human pain, where brutal stories were wrenched up, where tortured images were replayed as daily fare. People who thought they'd put the whole thing behind them were*

asked to delve into the most secret and tragic moments of their past. Victims rendered their stories, the professionals laid down cold facts over the emotions of others, the accused wove their own versions… and while it was easy to see it as a game, as some kind of cruel spectator sport, still it could not be dismissed. This was where things sank or swam…

Lawyers speak for both sides. A judgment is made. But the whole thing was a matter of words and interpretation, and facts could be twisted, misrepresented, how some evidence sounded more eloquent than others, how juries decide from the off which way they'd vote, based on manner or styling of the accused. It turned into theatre, and the cleverer the lawyers became, the more arcane became their games with language…"

It seemed that the factual evidence in my support was not permitted to surface in court, thus quite naturally the truth could not emerge. I wondered whether there was any point in taking the case further, to the Court of Final Appeal. My counsels Barrie Barlow SC and Kevin Egan were nevertheless bent on taking my case to the final step. They were not totally surprised by the decision of the appeal court, but regarded the appeal as a necessary step on its way to the CFA. They were convinced that we still had strong grounds to get a fair hearing. My family and friends rallied behind me and insisted that I should not abandon ship without taking the final step. Their encouragement restored my resolve and I agreed to commence the process of applying for leave to appeal to the CFA.

"Once I leave Stanley, the intensity of my current emotions will never be the same again"

50

THE NEXT BUS (MID-2010)

Once the reality sank in, the loss of the appeal was not that hard to bear since I was to be released a few months thereafter, having served the full term of 16 months. Somehow, I found it more purposeful to count my blessings and reflect on what I had ironically learnt from the reluctant time spent in Stanley. I had managed to resist the strong temptation to feel bitter towards people and the system. I did feel cheated by the events and the injustice of it all, but once this thought was compartmented away into the backwaters of my mind, I found it pleasing that I had developed a greater sense of compassion and empathy towards people, a heightened awareness of philosophy towards life and the acceptance that there are inevitable ups and downs. I had almost been moved to the Hindu belief of reincarnation and wondered whether this ordeal was in fact payment for what I might have done wrong in my previous life?

I was much leaner but much fitter. The tasteless diet was admittedly well balanced and as I had not been exposed to excesses, I was in good health. My mental state was one of clarity. I was in pretty good shape overall. I also had a strange sense that I was more alert of what was happening around me rather than what affected just my own self.

I have learned that life is not all about success or the need for recognition by others, albeit that these ambitions are important as the catalyst for the driving force that we all need. Self-disciplined balance and temperance should be the central values of our existence. Prison has taught me that one can exist on basic necessities and whilst we all enjoy luxuries, I am certain that I can do without these even when I return to society. For a start, the deprivation of alcohol has not been a problem to me and I find that I do not miss that at all. This is a surprise since I have been a heavy drinker for the best part of my adult life. I am now determined to keep this habit and refrain from over-indulging again. In any case, I feel better because of the abstinence.

I felt that my mind became more and more settled as my prison term went on. Questions disappeared and I began to find my own answers in most of what was happening to me. Writing this book has been great therapy, and I also found solace in the inordinate amount of letter writing. During this entire period, three great friends helped me to maintain my sanity by corresponding with me regularly no matter how busy they were and regardless of where they travelled. They were Jim Mailer in Hong Kong or Scotland; Toby Heale in New Zealand, England or France; and Daphne Boyce in Hong Kong, London or Melbourne. Throughout the entire period before and after my court case, Jackie Langridge, Terry Smith and Murray Burton stood firm behind me. The attention and support they gave to me never wavered. They visited me in Stanley more than once. I owe a deep sense of gratitude to all of them.

It was at that juncture that I received a letter from Toby who wrote from France. He expressed his sympathy over the appeal outcome but urged me to "wait for the next bus" and perhaps consider the CFA as the next "port of call". This was the exact route of that "next bus" and I left my experienced legal team to steer me there.

As we are on course to proceed to the CFA, I am not at liberty to discuss details at this stage. The process of leave application is highly complicated because it involves a serious point of law of "great and general importance". The leave application will be a time-consuming affair and by our estimation, it is highly unlikely that the CFA hearing would take place any sooner than late 2011, way after my discharge from Stanley in October 2010.

My appeal had never been aimed at a reduction of sentence, but rather against conviction with the view to the clearing of my name and reputation. This is just as well as I will have virtually served my full sentence already. This book is written under the emotions which I have felt throughout my custodial sentence in the surroundings and environment of prison life. I am therefore anxious to complete this manuscript whilst I am in here because once I leave Stanley, the intensity of my current emotions will never be the same again.

I have not had the luxury of access to any of my files, records nor the use of the Internet. Accordingly, this manuscript has been written from memory and straight from the heart, uncontaminated by facts and figures. Other than possibly an epilogue which I may or may not write later, this manuscript is to all intents and purposes now completed, save for a summing-up chapter which follows.

As I approach the end of my stint in Stanley Prison, I very much look forward to being reunited with my beloved Gail. This alone will give me solace and the strength needed to move on regardless of the eventual decision handed down by the CFA. After all, there is really only one "true final court of appeal" and that is the Almighty.

Some may ask why I should continue to bother fighting through the courts when I shall shortly be released from Stanley? Why would I want to continue my fight to reverse my conviction? To answer this, I would borrow what Michael Chamberlain of the "dingo" case in Australia said to enquiring reporters: *"I don't think people realize how important innocence is to innocent people."*

"Perhaps there were times when I might have made some wrong choices for the right reasons, just as some right choices might have been made for the wrong reasons. That is how life often pans out"

51

SOBERING THOUGHTS

In this book, I have tracked all the milestones in my life and commented on the influences that have affected it. I have lived my life a second time through writing this narrative and found the exercise enlightening, therapeutic and highly rewarding.

In examining the circumstances and the forces that had driven me to the peaks of my achievements or to the depths of my adversities, I had to be introspective in my self-critique. As a prerequisite to a realistic assessment of what actually made me tick, I needed to know what I really am, being the product of my heritage, culture, upbringing and perhaps even my birth signs.

I was born in the Year of the Tiger. The Chinese character is 虎, pronounced *foo* in Cantonese. The characteristics of a tiger are mysterious, secretive, a predator that hunts alone, and if unsuccessful, withdraws to try another day.

The Cantonese dialect is rich in descriptive variations. The phonetic of *foo* can also be applied to the word 苦 which sounds the same but can also mean hardship, toil or bitterness. Cantonese people in Hong Kong adopt colloquialisms extensively and when two words sound the same, it is not unusual for them to use both meanings. A person born in the Year of the Tiger is therefore regarded as one who is successful but self-made, and success is achieved only through hard work and toil. Nothing is given to him free.

By a coincidental twist, I was also born on a day of two festivals in 1938. The 31st of October was of course Halloween but it fell also on the ninth day of the ninth month in the Chinese calendar, this being the Chung Yeung Festival, 重陽節, dedicated to one's ancestors and expressed through visiting the cemetery and cleansing the graves. As most Chinese cemeteries are traditionally built on hill slopes, the grave sites can only be reached by a steep climb. Consequently, this gave rise to the theory that a person born on that day would be destined to rise with every step – or 步步高升 – to the top.

By the horoscope, I am a typical Scorpio: generous and loyal, passionate, a great friend but a deadly enemy when provoked.

From all these readings, my fate can perhaps be summarized as one destined to rise to great heights but which would not come easy. Generosity, compassion and loyalty would come naturally with good friends and family. Whilst passionate towards ambition, love, and devotion to career and sporting pursuits, there would however be a tendency towards secretive missions which, if not met with quick success, would lead to probable abandonment, either temporary or permanent.

This summary would appear to be a reasonable reflection of what has in fact taken place in the course of my colourful but volatile life. There were no malicious or vindictive motives in any of the things I have done, but if there was any lack of wisdom in my actions, these were more likely to hurt myself more than others around me. Perhaps there were times when I might have made some wrong decisions for the right reasons, just as some right choices might have been made for the wrong reasons. That is how life often pans out.

I was brought up during wartime when the family had to endure a degree of hardship. We were not to enjoy comfortable living until MC came into our lives when he married mother. Our standard of living did not improve appreciably until my teenage years when I was given the best opportunities in education and all the breaks in my early career. For all of this, I have MC to thank.

My heritage stems from a mixture of Western and Oriental cultures with all the bias and bigotry that went with it. For my father's generation, to be Eurasian was a clear disadvantage. However, by the time I turned adult, a clear choice was in the offing. It was up to me to go for what I wanted. By taking a positive view that I could get the best from both worlds, I strove to become an equal to both the British and the Chinese. In many ways, I succeeded with confidence and flair as indeed I should have. My language proficiency matched both sets of native speakers. My behaviour matched compatibly with either side. I could relax totally in either the Western or Oriental settings. I was at ease and able to connect with both.

I felt that I was well equipped to meet most challenges if I put my mind to them. Optimism was the principal driving force behind my targets for achievement. However, there was at times an inadvertent tendency to overreach or even obsess to excess in the eyes of my critics. People sometimes mistook my enthusiasm as obsession, my munificence as extravagance, and my pertinacity as stubbornness. I found these misinterpretations disturbing because my accommodating gestures were on occasions taken as gullibility. The dividing line between good and bad is frequently only marginal. A person's strengths could straddle his weaknesses depending on how things are assessed.

Hong Kong is my home. My family has been settled here since the 1850s, just a decade or so after it became a colony of Britain. We have survived here for close to 160 years and obviously have a deep sense of pride and belonging. As people from "old" Hong Kong, we have a right to be here, perhaps more so than the majority of the present population who did not arrive until post-1949 on the establishment of the People's Republic of China.

In the first 150 years, Hong Kong was transformed with unquestionable success from a "barren rock" to the world-class city it is now, largely because of the British who were responsible for the administration of the Colony. Putting aside the history prior to the cession of the territory, all those who decry the British for their occupation of Hong Kong should remember that there would have been nothing worthwhile to fight over at the time of the joint declaration had it not been for the British. We owe what we have to the colonial rule.

In the scheme of things after the Handover in 1997, we must recognize there is a marked difference between colonialism and the legacies of the British. Colonialism is a phenomenon of the past and we no longer tolerate discrimination or suppression of the locals. On the other hand, the legacies of the British such as the rule of law, the code of commercial practice and proficiency in the English language are matters of the highest value which must be preserved jealously at all costs.

It makes me angry and frustrated when I see the beauty, serenity, charm and the heritage landmarks and icons of the "Pearl of the Orient" being gradually eroded and destroyed in the name of progress or localization, to the current depraved condition where the fragrant harbour is reduced to a garbage-infested river, the heritage buildings are damaged or demolished, and the polluted air challenges our ability to breathe.

On the flipside of British legacy, Chinese presence has also been a vital ingredient in the evolution of the rich local culture. There is no Chinese dialect as expressive and colourful as the spoken Cantonese used in Hong Kong wherein snippets of English have been injected. This blend has become a vernacular dialect unique to Hong Kong.

The intellectual and philosophical wisdom of the Chinese is not limited to the domain of Confucius and the classics. Words of wisdom expressed in colloquial form are pervasive in the everyday life of the people. The Cantonese are past masters at the extensive use of puns and synonyms, leading to immense richness in the Cantonese dialect. Many sayings are instructive on the paths to purity and achievements. Although some have historical origins, many such idioms are equally applicable to present-day use because true wisdom is ageless.

My children are Western-educated and not exposed to Chinese culture in the same way and extent as I was. I have tried to impart selected Chinese teachings and philosophies to them in the hope that they may gain similar benefits. At times, I do regret that I did not give them the fundamental grounding in Chinese values as that is a part of our heritage too.

It is gratifying to me that many of the children have decided to take up Chinese voluntarily at university, either in their undergraduate years or as post-graduates. Their years spent in Beijing or Shanghai have given them an edge in Chinese language proficiency that they will never regret. It is decidedly the wish of Gail and I that Sean should also spend a year or two in China after his degree in New Zealand.

All said and done, Hong Kong is a blend of the best of the British and the Chinese. As I am of a similar blend in my genetic make-up, Hong Kong will always have a special place in my heart. Regrettably however, we can no longer ignore what Hong Kong has become in recent decades. The natural beauty and tranquillity have given way to heavy pollution and overcrowding. We would do well to remember that just after the war in 1946, Hong Kong's population numbered approximately 400,000, compared to over 7 million now.

For some of us, whether we remain here or move to another land is a question we ask ourselves often. Hong Kong continues to exude a high level of energy for extraordinary opportunities to surface. It remains a dynamic city where smart and resourceful people can achieve unbelievable success, albeit at the expense of huge pressure and stress. It is a place for the younger set. Some in the older generation may prefer a foreign land with less excitement, but where the environment remains clean and a high quality of life is preserved. Tough choices involve trade-offs. Such is the reality of life.

There can be little doubt that I have done my bit in bringing up the children reasonably well. They have all been put through education in the best institutions. They were guided to different schools and universities of their own selections and I gave them absolute freedom of choice every step of the way. Bearing in mind the wide choice of careers in the modern world, none of them have been forced or coerced into adopting professions in medicine, law, accountancy or banking, as people of my generation were traditionally expected to pursue. Things have changed. In fact, all the girls obtained degrees in one discipline and ended up working in something completely different.

Sean is currently reading Asian Studies in Victoria University in Wellington. This should give him a good grounding for a wide variety of career pursuits. However, like his siblings, his eventual career choice remains enticingly unpredictable at this stage.

Almost without exception, the girls have married well to husbands of different nationalities and ethnic origins. The men work in contrasting careers and some are more comfortable than others, but they all seem happy and invigorated in what they do. They are spread all over the world and I can see at least one of them whether I am in England, the United States, Australia, New Zealand, Singapore, Manila or in Hong Kong.

In the hours of my ordeal, the children have rallied behind me in unreserved support. They all write frequently and have visited me in prison even though they had to fly in from afar.

My ultimate blessing comes in the person of my beloved wife Gail. She is completely genuine and would not waste her time lapping up to people of supposed importance. She prefers to spend her time and patience with the young, the aged and the needy. She gives, but expects little in return.

She does not beat about the bush and if she has a point to make, she will just say it without embellishment. She would probably exercise a controlled degree of diplomacy but has no time for politics. You know exactly where you stand with Gail.

Gail's devotion to the family knows no boundaries. Her thoughtfulness is deeply appreciated by us all. She has tolerated my idiosyncrasies for years and has consistently been my strength and inspiration. She often puts on a brave face to hide a soft and caring heart. I am fully aware of all this and know how my present fate has affected her. The strength she has shown in these last years has increased my admiration for her even more.

This period of custodial sentence has given me time alone to take stock of my position with undisturbed clarity. It seems to me that the values I previously held could be challenged. I no longer regard corporate or social status as important so long as I have my family around me and the basic essentials are there to permit comfortable living to a reasonable standard. Excesses are, as the word itself connotes, really surplus to basic needs.

The need for ownership is only a state of mind ingrained in us from the influence of the society in which we live. Ownership is not perpetual, as what we own one day may be lost the next. Perhaps we could be content with the simpler things and avoid entering the rat race. It may be easier to find peace and happiness that way. If contentment is thus found, then there could be some truth in the saying "less is more".

It has been an interesting journey with many twists and turns. There have been dramatic cycles of ups and downs. I have enjoyed the moments of triumph and suffered many setbacks. In both these cases, they never last forever and are in essence just passing phases. We learn to deal with these and live through them. Even as I write now, I can see that with enough fighting spirit, I shall find satisfaction again.

From a young age, I walked with bat in hand to the wicket on a cricket ground, took guard and have occupied the crease ever since. There have been wonderful shots made which yielded good runs. There were also chances given off the bat but I managed to survive through spilled catches in the field. It has been a hard grind throughout, yet this most enjoyable knock continues and my innings remains unbeaten...

EPILOGUE

Haunted House

I have waited six months since my discharge to write this epilogue. I wanted to understand the changes that might have occurred in Hong Kong society since I started my custodial term in June 2009. While I was confident that the majority of my friends and associates would stand by me, I was equally aware that some would inevitably turn away, either because they do not wish to be associated with a convicted person or they are simply embarrassed to be seen with me. I needed time to assess how my network of connections had been reduced in size.

I had a feeling of being in a haunted house. I did not quite know how people would react. Who were my friends and who were not? I had to find out. There was no easy way of determining how many of my connections would remain in support. It was only meeting a wide range of people that would give me some clue. I decided I would not rush into any commitments on work, either on my own or in partnership with others. I needed time to assess how people would behave towards me before I would make decisions. This self-imposed patience proved highly frustrating, but I was equally certain it was the right course to take.

In those early days after my release, I would often look over my shoulders. Many old associates and acquaintances did not call, but thankfully the majority of my true friends came forward in support and I shall always be grateful to them. As time went by, I started to make new friends from all walks of life and no longer only those from the upper echelons of society. I found that my network became, if anything, even larger than before albeit that the types of friends were decidedly more varied. It then came to me that in one's lifetime, friendships evolve anyway whether one has been to prison or not.

On reflection, the prison term gave me 16 months of peace and quiet, away from career and social pressures. It gave me a time to think and read. It gave me the opportunity to consider the things that really mattered to me. It was as if the Almighty had given me a signal that it was time to stop running from pillar to post, and instead stop and think clearly on what I really valued. Ironically, it was in this atmosphere that I was able to write this book. In this sense, I was grateful I was given the time and singularity of mind to do so.

With the passage of time and social interaction with people, my apprehensions began to fade. I then realized there were really no ghosts in the haunted house. It was just a figment of my imagination. I began to sort things out in a patient and orderly fashion. With that, my confidence slowly returned.

I needed to find work to stay busy and had to exploit whatever resources I had to make a new career for myself. Gail then flashed me a riddle: "What are you good at, John?" I did not know what to make of that because all through my career, I had been engaged in management in one form or another and perhaps also in finance. To be engaged in management meant adding to someone's headcount, but who would employ a man of my age? Finance meant investment, but I had no meaningful excess funds to speak of. Recent events had bled me dry.

It then became clear to me what Gail was getting at. She thought that I should use my experience and expertise to find a new career. That meant the exploitation of my knowledge base and creative flair to launch a completely new career unlike anything I had done before. Gail thought that would be the best formula for a new start, unhampered by any baggage from the past. But how was that to be done?

After due thought, I began to piece the jigsaw together. I planned for a change of pursuits by using my mental capital instead of financial capital. I would make a move into a career in consultancy and in academia by lecturing in subjects I knew best. There was little doubt that not many in Hong Kong could say they have led 40 financial roadshows across the world. To have done that, as I did, gave rise to a genuine realization that I possessed deep expertise and experience in investor relations. Indeed, I had given many speeches and presentations on this very subject. I had lived investor relations for longer than a decade and felt that I was more than equipped to impart my knowledge to others as a consultant or a lecturer. In addition, I would offer myself as a moderator or panellist in large conferences.

Encouraging inroads have since been made into these pursuits and I am excited by the prospects these initiatives can offer. It is a significant change of direction but one which gives me excitement and motivation like no other. It is a path that perhaps leads to the unknown, but if one does not go out on a limb, how does one gather fruit? There is a determination to make this a serious and lasting effort, not just an ephemeral pastime, albeit that I would not turn down interesting consultancy assignments in the wide range of fields in which I have gained considerable expertise and experience.

I am a great deal more clear-minded these days compared to my life before my prison term. Apart from giving me the time for reflection, prison life helped me to quit drinking. Since I had been deprived of alcohol for 16 months, I have no wish to return to heavy drinking again. Apart from a rare glass of wine imbibed every now and again in social circles, I have to all intents and purposes become abstinent. Similarly, while my loss of weight was enforced by prison life, I do feel fitter and healthier for it, and there is no wish to return to my former weight since I feel so much better as I am now.

Prison life did leave some physical scars though. For months after my discharge, I suffered serious skin problems on my face, my body and especially on my head. My hair condition was so bad that I did not only suffer from excessive dandruff, but my head was actually full of cradle caps. The condition was eventually diagnosed as the possible result of nutritional inadequacies. I attributed this to the prison administration's denial of access to the health supplements that I had grown accustomed to for more than a decade. It took four months before a renowned dermatologist cured me through a combination of various treatments. People of my age cannot withstand harsh conditions that young men could. Prison authorities should be mindful of this.

The effect of a conviction is more than the mere serving of a prison term. It impacts on many areas of a person's life. The record deprives one from serving on any listed boards. It disqualifies one from practice in most professional capacities. It creates problems on immigration into certain countries and it generally puts a spanner in the works on many pursuits in which one might otherwise be able to be gainfully engaged.

I am no longer a member in most of the clubs, including the Hong Kong Cricket Club which I had served as president for 11 years. I remain a member only of the Foreign Correspondents' Club, where some of the nicest and the most genuine people are found. I am grateful and proud that they continue to have me in their membership ranks.

Life is not all misery. I am delighted that I am back with Gail and the family. I have learnt the warmth of the family gives me the strength to surmount difficulties and if I take the correct mental approach, I can continue to look optimistically to the future. After all, the majority of people manage to live without being members of clubs. In any event, by my own calculation, I probably save at least HK$20,000 in club bills each month. Perfectly acceptable alternatives are there. There are interesting historical places to visit in the New Territories which I never had the inclination to explore before. Instead of golfing at the Hong Kong Golf Club or Shek O Golf Club, it is still possible to play golf in China or elsewhere. While my interest in horse racing has to a large extent been lost in Hong Kong, I remain keen on the sport outside Hong Kong where I can continue to participate and enjoy the wonders of the equine world.

In April, Natasha married Ben in Hong Kong. They decided to have the wedding ceremony on board a 'Star' Ferry, an icon of Hong Kong and a company that I had managed during my time with Wharf. It was a windy day, but the happiness of the occasion consumed the interest of the guests to the extent that most did not even notice the rocking of the boat caused by the swell. The banquet that followed at the Watermark Restaurant benefited from the magnificent ambience resulting from the creative genius of the decorator Ramon Pastor from the Philippines. The bride and the entire entourage of bridesmaids and flower girls looked beautiful in their couture dresses. All the overseas visitors including Ben's parents and friends from Des Moines, Iowa, had a great time as did as the local hosts. The young couple kicked off the first dance with a scintillating display to the music of "Dirty Dancing" much to the enjoyment of all. The revelry ran into the wee small hours. With this marriage, my five fillies have finally all been sold. All that remained with Gail and I was our young colt Sean!

Sean returned to his university in Wellington after the wedding and has less than two years before he graduates. It is our intention that he should be given the same opportunity as his sisters by sending him to a post-graduate university course in China to study Mandarin Chinese. In the meantime, Sean continues to delve deep into his love of basketball. Despite it not being cricket or golf, I will support him in this highly skilful and athletic game so long as he is so committed to it.

In the past months, my final round of appeal to the CFA came to an abrupt end when the three judges denied me leave of appeal to the CFA. That was a massive disappointment and surprise to my team of lawyers. Personally, however, I took it surprisingly well. Of course there was disappointment, but this sentiment was perhaps softened by my own low expectations since every step along the legal route had met with obstacles. I was curiously relieved in a strange way as I was tired of what seemed an endless legal process. I was also grateful that I would have no further legal costs to bear.

My bus had reached the terminus. I just had to live with it.

I have gone the full distance and now find myself in an all-out effort to claw my way back. To me, the important lessons to remember are firstly, *avoid living on past glory,* and secondly, *accept that people of our generation do not retire. We just keep going.*

I am a believer in the power of the universe, and that self-belief generates the energy necessary to bring success and happiness. *I have a strong belief that good things are on their way!*